UNLOCKING THE CHURCH

UNLOCKING THE CHURCH

The lost secrets of Victorian sacred space

WILLIAM WHYTE

OXFORD
UNIVERSITY PRESS

OXFORD
UNIVERSITY PRESS

Great Clarendon Street, Oxford, OX2 6DP,
United Kingdom

Oxford University Press is a department of the University of Oxford.
It furthers the University's objective of excellence in research, scholarship,
and education by publishing worldwide. Oxford is a registered trade mark of
Oxford University Press in the UK and in certain other countries

Published in the United States of America by Oxford University Press
198 Madison Avenue, New York, NY 10016, United States of America

British Library Cataloguing in Publication Data
Data available

Library of Congress Control Number: 2017932100

ISBN 978-0-19-879615-2

Printed in Great Britain by
Clays Ltd, St Ives plc

Links to third party websites are provided by Oxford in good faith and
for information only. Oxford disclaims any responsibility for the materials
contained in any third party website referenced in this work.

For E. J. G. and J. M. C
With heartfelt thanks

PREFACE

All Victorian collections of sermons—and I have read hundreds, if not thousands of Victorian sermons in the writing of this book—begin with a conventional apology, with the author declaring 'I had no intention of publishing' what follows. Sometimes this was probably true; quite often one closes the volume assuming that it really can only have been in response to the entreaties of well-meaning friends that the author's unremarkable reflections found themselves in print. But when a writer like F. W. Farrar, who is listed as the author of no fewer than 298 publications in the British Library catalogue, observes at the opening of his collection of sermons that 'in allowing them to appear in this form I yield to considerable pressure', the reader might be forgiven for wondering what pressure he was actually under.[1]

The pressure to publish for a modern academic is a very real one. And it's not just kindly friends who urge you on. It would be simply dishonest to pretend that I was inveigled into producing what follows. But, just like my Victorian forbears, I do owe a real debt to those who have encouraged me. At the heart of this book is a revised version of the Hensley Henson Lectures which I gave in the closing months of 2014. I am enormously grateful to the Henson electors for inviting me to give them, and thankful to those who attended the series.

Many of these ideas have also been tried out in response to other invitations. I must thank Robin Griffith-Jones and David Park for asking me to speak at their conference on the Temple Church at the Courtauld Institute in 2008; Peter Jan Margry and Jan de Maeyer for inviting me to participate in their workshop on 'Material Reform' at the University of Leuven in 2012; Alex Bremner and Jonathan Conlin for asking me to speak at their conference on E. A. Freeman at St Deniol's Library in 2012; Peter Scott for inviting me to lecture at his conference at the Lincoln Theological Institute in Manchester in 2013; Matthew Walker for inviting me to present a paper at his symposium on the afterlife of Wren in 2014; Jill Campbell, Mark Gardiner, and Liz Thomas for asking me to give the opening address at their 'Buildings in Society International' conference in Belfast in 2014; and Edward Gillin and Horatio Joyce for doing the same at their conference on 'Architecture and Experience in the Nineteenth Century', held in Oxford in 2016. I am grateful, too, to the Oxfordshire Historic Churches Trust, who asked me to give their Blenheim lecture in 2014 and the Berkshire Historic Churches Trust, for whom I gave the Englefield Lecture in 2016. Just as I was putting the finishing touches to the text, Stephen Wildman invited me to give the Mikimoko Memorial Ruskin Lecture at Lancaster and I most sincerely thank him for such a marvellous opportunity to explore these ideas still further.

Along the way, I have also given papers on these subjects at seminars in Cambridge, Edinburgh, Lewes, London, Oxford, and elsewhere. I have had the opportunity to try out some early thoughts in a number of books, including Joe Sterrett and Peter Thomas, eds, *Sacred Text–Sacred Space: architectural, literary, and spiritual convergences in England and Wales* (2011) and two forthcoming volumes: the *Oxford Handbook of Nineteenth-Century Christian Thought* and the *Oxford Handbook of Victorian Medievalism*. I am grateful to George Clarke and the team from Channel 4's *Restoration Man* who have taken me with them to explore churches and chapels from Plockton to Little Braxted. I must likewise thank Rachel Boulding and Sally Fraser for letting me try out some of this in the pages of the *Church Times*. The real starting point for all this work was my involvement in *Redefining Christian Britain: post-1945 perspectives* (2007), and I should like to express my gratitude to my co-editors and contributors for that wonderful experience.

In addition to all the many people who have commented on this work at lectures, seminars, workshops, and in print, I should like to thank the anonymous readers whose wise advice and stern counsel proved immeasurably helpful. I am also grateful to two historians of very different periods and somewhat different interests—George Bernard and Otto Saumarez Smith—who read the whole of my draft and offered telling advice. My editor Matthew Cotton was enormously encouraging from the first and helped me transform the text from my initial lectures. Luciana O'Flaherty then very kindly took me on. I am terrifically grateful to Gayathri Manoharan, Dawn Preston, Kizzy Taylor-Richlieu and Donald Watt, who have miraculously turned my text into a book, and I must also express my thanks to those who shared their work with me, especially Philip Aspin, James Bettley, Simon Bradley, Kate Giles, Edward Gillin, Matthew McDade, Otto Saumarez Smith, Ruth Slatter, Geoffrey Tyack, and Martin Wellings. All errors, of course, remain entirely my own. For permission to reproduce images, I thank the Bodleian Library, Jane Garnett, the Historic England Archive, Historic Environment Scotland, the Dean and Chapter of Lichfield Cathedral, the Manchester Climbing Centre, the North

Devon Athenaeum, and John Whitworth. John Betjeman's 'A Lincolnshire Church' is reproduced with permission from John Murray Press.

This project could not have been undertaken, much less completed, without the support of the Oxford History Faculty and of St John's College, who very generously granted me a year's research leave. Together with the Faculty of Theology and Religion, St John's also underwrote the cost of image reproduction and I am deeply sensible of this generosity. I am grateful to successive Theology Chairs—Sarah Foot and Johannes Zachhuber—for all their support before, during, and after the Henson Lectures, and am especially thankful to my historical colleagues at college—Antonia Fitzpatrick, Dan Hicks (an honorary historian for the occasion), Kit Kowol, Elizabeth Macfarlane, Hannah Skoda, Alan Strathern, and Mark Whittow. Joshua Bennett was particularly heroic in taking on my teaching. The library staff at St John's, Worcester College, and the Bodleian were immeasurably helpful throughout. And I am most grateful to the parishioners of Kidlington with Hampton Poyle who have put up with much of this in sermon form over the last ten years (without, it should be said, ever insisting I publish any of it).

Above all, I must thank my family: my parents, Bill and Marian Whyte; my parents-in-law, Denis and Carole Waxman; my brother Al and his family. I'm hugely grateful to Zoë Waxman, who has read it all, and Nahum and Jacob Whyte, who have not. All three have helped improve it in their rather different ways. Without them, nothing would be worth doing, and without their support and forbearance nothing would ever get done. I am particularly grateful to Zoë, who is my inspiration as well as my best critic. Small wonder I love her beyond measure.

. This book is dedicated to my two doctoral supervisors, Jane Garnett and Joe Mordaunt Crook. Together, they, more than anyone, helped make me a historian. They have not read the manuscript and don't need to read the book. Everything I write, in a sense, is written with them in mind, and many of the ideas it contains are probably theirs, or at any rate were generated in response to their work. But I hope they will be pleased to know just how thankful I am for all their support, encouragement, and criticism.

CONTENTS

LIST OF ILLUSTRATIONS

Introduction

England,...let it be thankfully said,...is again a Church-Building Country.

J. H. Markland, *Remarks on English Churches*
(Oxford, 1842), p. viii.

What that sight was to her, only those who have shared in the joys of Church building can know.

Charlotte M. Yonge, *Abbeychurch, or Self-Control and Self-Conceit* (London, 1844), p. 20.

If you live in England, or Scotland, Wales, Ireland—or indeed much of Europe, North America, Australia, or New Zealand, the chances are that you live near a nineteenth-century church. Indeed, you may even live inside one, such is the number that have been converted into accommodation in recent years. And even if your local church is older, it will almost certainly have been restored—which often meant rebuilt—by the Victorians. Their influence is inescapable. In the hundred years between 1800 and 1900, tens of thousands of churches were built and still more altered in England alone. By the 1860s, indeed, a brand-new Anglican church was consecrated every four or five days, whilst the number of Nonconformist chapels increased at an even more dizzying pace. In a sense, every church built since is a

Victorian church, because even those erected or reordered after the nineteenth century have to respond to the extraordinary efflorescence of ecclesiastical architecture produced in that time.

I could start with any number of striking London churches: the jewel-like **All Saints Margaret Street,** perhaps, or the solid, stolid, and substantial Union Chapel in Islington. Or, then there are the great northern minsters: **Leeds Parish Church**; All Saints, Haley Hill, in Halifax; the Church of the Holy Angels, Hoar Cross, in Staffordshire; and beyond. There are small churches and chapels in every village; large churches and cathedrals in almost every town. An enormous, lavishly illustrated, exhaustively researched, and deservedly prizewinning recent book by the historian Alex Bremner, which traces church building across the globe between 1840 and 1870, shows us just how far we might go: from the rough-and-ready St Thomas, Tamaki, in New Zealand, to the imposing and richly ornamented St Andrew's cathedral in Sydney; from the part-Venetian, part-Indian, part-Romanesque All Souls, Kanpur, in India, to the robust and rugged St Barnabas on Norfolk Island, Melanesia.[1]

Given such an impossible choice, I will start close to home, or at any rate close to where I work, in Oxford. Instead of the delights of London, Leeds, Tamaki, or Kanpur, let's begin in Littlemore. Now a suburb of the city, in the nineteenth century it was, in Matthew Arnold's description, 'a dreary village by the London road'. 'It presents nothing charming in its aspect or situation', observed another contemporary in 1840; 'it exhibits no delightful villas, nor agreeable woods and meadows, but one unvaried uniform appearance, rather dull than pleasant'.[2] Don't be put off, however: in the midst of all this there still stands a small—but important—church. Described accurately, but scarcely

Fig. 1. Littlemore Church

enthusiastically, in Jenifer Sherwood and Nikolas Pevsner's *Buildings of England* volume for Oxfordshire as 'chaste and severe, with... neither chancel nor aisles', this little church at Littlemore is worth looking at again—and not just because I can cycle to it in less than half an hour.[3] In truth, as the well-placed, wealthy, and highly influential Victorian layman, Alexander Beresford Hope, observed in 1875, this 'mere oblong shell' was 'the undoubtedly visible germ of the revived worship of the English Church'.[4]

Littlemore church was built on the cusp of the Victorian age by the architect Henry Underwood, a man whose career, as the historian Howard Colvin deliberately, if somewhat tastelessly, puts it, was later 'cut short' by a nervous breakdown which led him to slit his own throat.[5] Underwood in the 1830s, however, was very much the coming man. London-trained, but living in Oxford, he had recently built a church in the smart suburb of Summertown and was concurrently building what would eventually become the city's choicest hostelry—the church of St Paul in Walton Street, now better known to Oxford students as a rather smart cocktail bar. Underwood's client was a still more up-and-coming individual, John Henry Newman, later a Roman Catholic convert and now halfway towards becoming a saint, but still at that point an Anglican, still a fellow of Oriel College, and still vicar of the University Church of St Mary the Virgin, within whose parish Littlemore fell. Newman began building at Littlemore as he wrote the latest in the series of Tracts which had made him and his collaborators famous as the Tractarians.[6] He was riding high on the Tractarian wave, the country's most famous member of the Oxford Movement, a figure everyone knew.

Small wonder, then, that Newman's enemies—his very many enemies—seized on this ostensibly 'chaste and severe' structure. Small wonder that they came in their dozens to explore the church that Newman built. Small wonder, too, that they were appalled by what they saw. Visiting Littlemore just after its consecration, the chaplain of New College—who was also chaplain of All Souls—professed himself disgusted at what he found. Publishing his experiences as *The Popery of Oxford Confronted, Disavowed, and Repudiated*—a text which did exactly what it promised to do—Peter Maurice described his visit to Littlemore in terms taken from a Gothic novel. Looking at the east window, he wrote, 'my offended eye detected one pane of glass, like a drop of blood, polluting the whole'. Worse still,

4

I felt an indescribable horror stealing over me, as I carried my eye towards the eastern wall of the building, and beheld a plain naked cross, either of stone or a good imitation of it, rising up and projecting out of the wall, from the centre of the table of communion.

Nor was it just the architecture that Maurice objected to. Nearby he saw 'the hassock, upon which, not long before, a minister of the Reformed and Protestant Church of England had been kneeling...May my natural eye never fall upon such a degrading spectacle.'[7] From the windows to the walls to the hassocks: the whole church sickened Peter Maurice.

Now it must be admitted that Maurice was to make a career out of being similarly shocked by other people's churches. From his fastness first in New College and then as vicar of the nearby village of Yarnton, he poured forth a stream of architectural philippics for the next four decades.[8] He decried the growth of vestries 'constructed after the popish models, with a door on the outside for the purpose of allowing them to go round the Church, and re-enter in processional array'. He condemned the choral services at the newly founded north Oxford church of St Philip and St James, on the grounds that 'there is no other class of persons more given to gaiety and non-serious habits than those in whom the musical talent is strongly developed' (an observation which presumably owed much to his experiences with New College choir). His tours of the area also took in St Barnabas in the north Oxford suburb of Jericho, which he described as an attempt at 'the development of the Christian Paganism of the Greek or Eastern Apostasy'; the church in the village of Radley, which he portrayed as a 'mongrel adaptation to the interior of an Italian mass-house'; and the parish of Freeland, where, Maurice claimed:

Such was the effect produced upon the nervous temperament of one clergyman when he looked up at the Image of the Crucifix (above the

Cross on the Altar Table) that he was noticed to turn deadly pale, as if filled with horror at the hideous spectacle; for there is something so peculiar about it, and so like a reality, that it is impossible to gaze on it without a shudder.[9]

The church at Littlemore, in that sense, was just the start of a very long journey for the man who would go on to become disgusted of Yarnton.

Nevertheless, it would be wrong to think that for all his monomania, Peter Maurice was either absurd or atypical in taking church buildings seriously. He was not even exceptional in his volubility. As we shall see, there were numerous other authors who shared his fears and his habit of publishing them. Nor was this debate confined to the obscure but disputatious clerics of Oxford who found themselves moved to fury or disgust by church architecture. At the same time, more major controversialists like Francis Close, perpetual curate of Cheltenham, were reaching for their pens and drawing similar conclusions.

Close was a really big name. Indeed his dominance of his own parish led Tennyson to dub him Pope of Cheltenham. Such was his appeal to his parishioners, that over his three decades of dominance—what one contemporary termed the 'Close Season' in Cheltenham—he was the recipient of no fewer than 1,500 pairs of slippers embroidered by grateful members of his church.[10] His truly national significance was made manifest when he was appointed dean of Carlisle Cathedral.

So, if Maurice can be seen as a merely local irritant, then it matters that Close too was drawn into this debate. And it matters that he expressed similar ideas—and in equally emotive language. The 'Restoration of Churches', he argued in an eponymous pamphlet of 1845, Is the Restoration of Popery.[11] This was not the first, nor would it be the last of his eruptions. Over several decades Close would publish a steady stream of articles, sermons, and books, all of which reiterated the objections laid out in an earlier broadside, where he complained that:

> The pointed arch—and the fretted roof—and the gloomy crypt and the secret stairs—and stone altars—and elevated chancels, credence tables, and painted windows, the reredos, the trypticks [sic], the reliquaries…are emblems of a gloomy, false idolatrous worship, from which we were mercifully delivered at the Reformation.

And he went on:

> With what feelings…of humiliation and sorrow should we contemplate a Christian sanctuary! We may decorate it with splendid masonry—lavish vast sums on its shrines, create 'a dim religious light', by means of costly painted windows;—and after we have done all, as we traverse the aisles—and muse on the solemn scene around us—well may we exclaim—'What is all this?' It is sin! Sin has raised this vast pile, it is a house of refuge for the guilty! What is this temple but a lazaretto for infected souls![12]

For Francis Close, then, buildings were theologically and emotionally troubling—and buildings like the church at Littlemore were, in his words, little more than festering sores, evoking feelings of disgust.

It's worth remarking, too, that similar emotions prompted parliamentary debates, and legislation, and acrimonious court cases. They likewise evoked visceral, violent responses from crowds who rioted against ritualism, and from earnest Evangelical parsons who protested against the introduction of new architecture or ornamentation into old churches. By the late 1880s, even St Paul's Cathedral was subject to attack, with a new reredos behind the high altar the focus for complaint, a 'puritan demonstration' during public worship,[13] and a series of intractable legal actions from those who found this highly ornamented megalith, in the words of one *Times* report, little less than 'a thing of terror'.[14]

More importantly still, it is clear that these attacks were not wholly misplaced. Returning to Littlemore, there is evidence that Newman and his allies were every bit as emotionally invested in the building as his critics claimed and feared. Fellow Tractarians were moved by it, with Henry Wilberforce—later to follow Newman over to Rome—observing in 1839 that 'the whole interior...is really something beyond description—so solemn and Catholic'. The High Church Fredric Rogers, with Newman a fellow of Oriel College, expressed his agreement, writing that the church 'is certainly one of the most perfect things for its size I ever saw. The altar is beautiful and the rest is so well kept under that when you come in you seem to see nothing but the altar.' The hard-to-please Cambridge journal the *Ecclesiologist* agreed, praising 'its solid walls and lofty roof, its honoured altar, its quiet half-light, and religious services', whilst the Oxford Architectural Society would suggest that Littlemore should be the model for all new churches.[15] To that end, it published not one, but two books, providing first, in 1840, *Views and Details of Littlemore Church*, and then, still more helpfully, in 1845, a pattern book of *Elevations, Sections, and Details*.[16] Certainly, it was influential in some Tractarian parishes, and there are suggestions that it helped shape the great Gothic architect Augustus Pugin's first church, St James in Reading.[17]

But even more significantly, it is evident that Newman himself invested this building with emotional significance. It meant something to him—and was intended to mean something to others. His sisters embroidered the altar cloths; his mother, who died in

Fig. 2. The Jemima Newman memorial at Littlemore Church

1836, would be memorialized there with a relief that suggested to one of his friends not a funerary tablet but an annunciation. More strikingly still, she is depicted in front of the as yet unfinished church, shrouded, as it was, in scaffolding. In the original, unpainted memorial, she held a plan of the building in her hand.[18]

It is scarcely surprising, then, that Newman took enormous care with the place. Indeed, his friend and future curate John Rouse Bloxam recalled that their first encounter was in the church two days before its consecration. 'Seeing the chapel door open,' he wrote, '[I] entered. You were alone placing the stone cross over the Altar. Turning around and seeing a stranger, you asked me, if I thought it threw a sufficient shadow.'[19] Together, Newman and Bloxam would fill Littlemore with coloured glass and candlesticks and all the things that Peter Maurice and his allies so abhorred. And it was in this church, of course, on the seventh anniversary of its consecration, that Newman preached his final sermon as an Anglican—'On the Parting of Friends'—to a weeping group of his allies. On the day of his conversion to Roman Catholicism, his fellow convert Frederick Oakeley recalled not Newman, but his church, remembering the rain coming down in torrents:

> The bell which swung visibly in the turret of the little gothic church at Littlemore gave that day the usual notice of morning and afternoon prayers; but it came to the ear in that buoyant bouncing tone which is usual in a high wind, and sounded like a knell rather than a summons.[20]

Here was a building that did not just stand in for Newman metaphorically, but which seemed to speak to its visitors—for good or for ill.

Now, such an intensity of focus, such an apparently exaggerated response to architecture and church furnishings raises many questions. How could such a 'chaste and severe' structure—a building, which, as one contemporary noted, was 'so plain throughout as hardly to satisfy the builder or glazier'—how could this come to evoke such powerful emotions, be they of reverence or revulsion?[21] Why was Peter Maurice moved to 'indescribable horror', whilst Henry Wilberforce was rendered speechless with delight? Historians used to know the answers to these questions—and they were relatively simple ones. Indeed, Francis Close himself gave us a much quoted explanation: 'As Romanism is taught *Analytically* at Oxford,' he wrote, 'it is taught *Artistically* at Cambridge...that it is inculcated theoretically, in tracts, at one University, and it is *Sculptured, painted*, and *graven* at the other.'[22] In other words—it's long been argued—these architectural and ornamental developments were the outgrowth of two distinct, parallel, but comparable movements: on the one hand, the Oxford Tractarians; on the other, the Cambridge Ecclesiologists.

It's worth saying that there is much to commend this analysis. The Oxford Movement and the Cambridge Movement—the Tractarians and the Ecclesiologists—can seem like mirror images of each other: the first interested in the doctrine of the Church as a whole; the other interested in the architecture of the parish church more particularly. The Tractarians, who emerged as a force in the 1830s and argued for a revival of Catholic doctrine within the Church of England; the Ecclesiologists, coming together only a few years later, to agitate for the revival of Anglican Catholicism through architecture, art, music, and liturgical reform. By rebuilding the churches of medieval Christendom, they hoped, the faith of medieval Christendom would be revived.

Comments made by the key figures in each movement can suggest that such a distinction is worth maintaining. It was the Anglican priest, scholar, and hymn writer John Mason Neale, a leading light amongst the Ecclesiologists, who reproved his co-agitator Benjamin Webb in 1844 with the words: 'I hope and trust you are not going to Oxonianize. It is clear to me that the Tract writers missed one great principle, namely that of

Aesthetics, and it is unworthy of them to blind themselves to it.'[23] In Oxford, it was the great Tractarian Edward Bouverie Pusey himself who warned against excessive emphasis on the externals of worship and who once, rather magnificently, turned to a companion whilst dining at Christ Church to enquire, 'Do tell me what a cope is.'[24] As Pusey's importance within the Oxford Movement was such that its members were also known as Pusey-ites, this apparent disengagement from questions of aesthetics can seem very telling. After all, the cope—a long cloak worn by clergy when participating in the liturgy—was one of the few ecclesiastical vestments to have survived the Reformation in several cathedrals. His ignorance—feigned or otherwise—is intriguing.

Many historians have tended to stress the differences between these twin developments, arguing that the Ecclesiologists and Tractarians were separated not just by their different places of origin but also by their differing inspirations. Writers like George Herring, for instance, have proved keen to establish that the Tract-arians were 'deeply suspicious' of the Ecclesiologists in particular, and had significant 'reservations about aesthetics' in general.[25] Even when Tractarians built, he argues, their decisions were dictated 'as much for practical as doctrinal or antiquarian reasons'.[26] Or, as Owen Chadwick put it, in his magisterial two-volume history of the *Victorian Church*: 'The Tractarians were concerned first for truth and then for the issue in worship.' The Ecclesiologists, by contrast, he thought preoccupied by 'decoration, ritual, the structure and seating of churches, because these affect the way in which men worship'.[27]

It would, however, be a mistake to draw too sharp a distin-ction between these two movements; between Oxford and

Cambridge, the Tractarians and the Ecclesiologists. It was New-man, after all, who urged on his friend Henry Manning in 1839 with the words: 'Give us more services, more vestments, and decorations in worship.'[28] And the notion that the invisible church should be made manifest in the visible church was in fact central to Pusey's own theology.[29] Asked by one enquirer 'What is Puseyism?', he replied, 'Regard for the visible part of devotion, such as the decoration of the house of God, which acts insensibly on the mind.'[30] The Ecclesiologists, too, were not just interested in architecture and the externals of worship. Just like the Tractarians, they were serious theologians.[31] John Mason Neale, for instance, wrote about buildings, but also about the Bible, Eastern Orthodoxy, and the religious life.[32] There was considerable common cause between these two movements.

Still more importantly, the extent to which both Oxford and Cambridge movements were part of a bigger change and were anticipated by earlier developments is becoming much clearer. The Ecclesiologists, in particular, now seem part of a much deeper-rooted and wider-spread enthusiasm for a revival of Gothic church buildings: an enthusiasm they spoke to, rather than engendered. They were just one of many similar organizations founded in the 1830s and 1840s—including an Oxford equivalent, and local societies in most English dioceses. That the Ecclesiologists were the most voluble does not necessarily make them the most immediately influential.

Moreover, it is now evident that all these societies drew on a resurgent interest in medieval architecture which predated their foundation and prefigured their injunctions. At the Temple Church, for example, in 1840 a massive restoration project was begun, ripping out Wren's fittings and replacing them with a fantastic, multicoloured, medieval revival scheme at enormous expense. It has been described by one historian as the moment at which 'ecclesiology engulfed antiquarianism', as the theological ideas propounded by the Ecclesiologists became dominant.[33] Yet it has been seen by another, more recent writer as an essentially 'secular, historical' project, in which Ecclesiology played very little part.[34] Contemporaries were equally ambiguous. This was, proclaimed the leading proponent of the church's restoration, an 'Anglo-Catholic' project; but it was one that the Ecclesiologists themselves condemned because they thought it too antiquarian. This was a historical project; but some of those who had argued for it initially were appalled by the theological implications of what was eventually done, fearing that a wholesale reintroduction of neo-medievalism—even a neo-medievalism that the Ecclesiologists sneered at—was somehow, in some way synonymous with Roman Catholicism.[35] The result was something *sui generis*, but also something which reflects hundreds of projects undertaken before the Ecclesiologists got started or the Tractarians publicly expressed any opinions on architecture. In that sense, any account of architecture or theology that simplistically attributes change to the influence of either the Tractarians or the Ecclesiologists on their own simply does not work.

Littlemore Church is another, even better illustration of all of these themes: built by a Tractarian, and conceived in advance of the Ecclesiologists' campaigning publications, it drew its inspiration from an eclectic range of sources. Just as would be done at the Temple Church, the suspiciously antiquarian and far from earnestly Ecclesiological Thomas Willement was employed to produce stained glass. Its furnishings and ornaments similarly owed their inspirations to ideas which long predated the 1830s. Imitating practices which had been introduced in Magdalen College chapel in the 1780s, two candlesticks were set up on the altar and two on the floor. An 'offertory basin'—or plate for collecting alms—was placed at the centre of the altar, again in imitation of the old collegiate practice rather than in an effort to recreate medieval, much less Roman Catholic models.[36] This was, it's clear, meant to be meaningful—but its meaning, and its place in history, are far from clear, and certainly can't be reduced to simple party labels, much less a clear distinction between the Oxford and Cambridge movements.

And there is, of course, an additional twist in our tale. For these developments, which would shape buildings in parishes influenced by the High Church revival all across Britain—indeed, as I've hinted, all across the empire—also came to shape the architecture of Evangelicalism and, more surprisingly still, the architecture of Nonconformity. A renewed interest in the buildings of the Nonconformists in recent years has shown just how much they too were influenced by this turn towards medievalism—and much the same can be said for the Presbyterian Church of Scotland.[37]

Contemporaries recognized this transformation too. As the journalist and writer J. Ewing Ritchie observed in his survey of *The Religious Life of London* in 1870, Dissenting chapels were now 'built like churches—they cling to their steeple, which the stern old Puritans considered an abomination'. 'The meeting house', he concluded, 'has ceased to exist.'[38] 'All over the land,' complained the Protestant polemicist Walter Walsh at the end of the century,

> We find new churches built, and old ones restored in a style which can only delight the hearts of the Romanisers, although those Churches are frequently in Evangelical and Protestant hands. Why should Protestant clergymen permit their Churches to be so arranged as to make them ready for a Roman Catholic priest to say Mass in?...And what do *they* want with Communion Tables erected on high, like Roman Catholic Altars? And why do they permit Chancel gates and screens to be erected?[39]

These are all very good questions—and it is a puzzle; one made all the more intriguing by the fact that many of even the greatest critics of the Ecclesiologists and the Tractarians ended up being seduced by the approach they articulated. After all, Francis Close himself also embraced these ideas, constructing a series of Gothic churches in Cheltenham and Carlisle. An early example—Christ Church, Cheltenham—was built in 1838, just after Newman's Littlemore project, and a year before the Ecclesiologists established their society. Another of his churches even had a stone altar—just like the one that so horrified Peter Maurice on his visit to Littlemore. As Close's critics exulted, "'The restoration of churches is the restoration of Popery' is the oracular declaration of one who, nevertheless preaches at the consecration of churches, and that, too, of churches on which much skill and art have been deployed."[40]

So how do we explain this? How can we account for such a profound change in church architecture and church furnishings: a change which swept across the British Empire and beyond, which had multiple sources and manifold influences, which shaped the High Church, the Low Church, and those outside the Church of England? How can we explain the enthusiasm which it engendered—and the horror, the anger, and the disgust which it provoked? The temptation when presented with a kaleidoscope of themes is to

Fig. 3. Christ Church Cheltenham

conclude that it was all very complicated and leave it at that. But, of course, in history, *everything* is always very complicated—and neither variety nor ambiguity should lead us to ignore what was a dramatic and consequential change in British history.

Nor would it be right simply to attribute this change—as some scholars have—to a range of factors outside the church, seeing the adoption of Gothic styles chiefly as the outcome of a fleeting architectural fashion, for example. True enough, the turn towards medievalism owed much to the growing professionalism of architects, who used their technical knowledge of the Gothic to establish their distinctive place within the building world of the age.[41] It's also true that the demand of their clients for neo-medievalism owed much to wider shifts in taste and thought—not least a broad, pan-European Romanticism which prefigured and shaped many of these debates: from Chateaubriand's celebration of medieval faith in his *Génie du Christianisme* (1802) to Goethe's celebration of Strasbourg Cathedral in 1812 to Schinckel's embodiment of German national identity in his great oil paintings of fantastic and fabulous Gothic cathedrals throughout the 1810s.

But even these more capacious explanations will not do for our purposes. They are not precise enough. They don't help explain why so many people who were *not* architects or intellectuals were engaged in this debate. Moreover, such arguments tend to assume rather glibly that what happens in the church is simply the outcome of forces acting on it from outside. This will no longer do. As Sarah Foot, Oxford's Regius Professor of Ecclesiastical History, has recently argued, we need to think *religiously* about the history of religion. We need to accept that religion is dynamic, not static; active, and not simply the outcome of other, wider, social and intellectual changes.[42] We need, in other words, to acknowledge that religion is causal; that it makes things happen.

What, then, should we do instead? How do we uncover what the Victorians believed about their churches? How do we take them, their beliefs, and their feelings seriously? In her wonderful book of 1998, *The Craft of Thought*, the medievalist Mary Carruthers observed that church buildings are never just empty spaces in which worship happens; they have a force, a power of their own. 'A church building', she writes, 'has, as it were, moving parts. It works as an engine of prayer, not simply its edifice.'[43] Yet, as she goes on to remark, this is not because sacred architecture has some intrinsic power of its own. 'There is nothing inherent in the physical shapes themselves...that has meaning wholly independent of the communities which produced and used them.' In other words, each community—each era—understands and experiences sacred space differently. To solve our problem, to address the question of how the Victorians actually experienced their churches, we need to think about what it was that made their experience particular and distinctive.

It's important to stress the distinctiveness of the Victorian church, because it would be all too easy—though fundamentally quite wrong—to think of these debates as little more than the backwash of the Reformation. Fights over church buildings, church fittings, and ecclesiastical art were, indeed, far from confined to the nineteenth century. The iconoclasm of the sixteenth and seventeenth centuries, the attempts to defend the 'beauty of holiness' which characterized many writers in the Stuart church: these do indeed reflect the ongoing importance of aesthetics to religion, and they would be reference points throughout our period. But to focus only on continuity, to see no difference between the debates undertaken by the Victorians and those pursued by the Tudors (say), is hardly historical. It smacks of the pious sermon—of 'the 1,000 years of prayer' that so often get mentioned in guidebooks, keen to insist on unbroken tradition instead of showing an awareness of change, disruption, even breaks with the past.

The Victorian church was different from what had been built—and experienced—before. Its builders were acutely conscious of living in unpredictable and ever-changing times. The French Revolution and the Industrial Revolution both undermined old certainties and created new, sometimes alarming possibilities. The political and religious crisis of the 1820s and 1830s saw the failure of what has been called the 'New Reformation' in all four of the nations which made up the United Kingdom.[44] The established Churches of England, Ireland, and Scotland proved incapable of countering the threat from Nonconformists and Catholics. The old establishment made way for a new pluralism.

This meant that the environment in which all the Churches operated had changed. It also meant that what was at stake in theological debate and confessional contestation had been profoundly altered. As the link between the established Church and the State was weakened, it meant that new sources of authority needed to be found for both. As religion increasingly came to resemble a market, it meant that all denominations were in some way in competition. Traditional notions of 'the Church' (singular) could not be sustained in a world with multitudes of different Churches (plural).

Even self-confessed conservatives found themselves unable to resist innovation—indeed, they came to embrace it. 'In the years around 1830,' writes David Bebbington, the leading authority on the subject, 'there was a change of direction in Evangelicalism.'[45] Although they claimed to be standing for never-changing truth, in fact they were every bit as shaped by their environment as the liberals they opposed. The Tractarians, too, were products of this new and modern world, however much they argued for an unflinching, unyielding, apostolic tradition. As Peter Nockles has shown, in his definitive work on the Oxford Movement, although the Tractarians drew on older traditions, they nonetheless represented an undeniable break with the recent past, with 1833—the year the movement was publicly proclaimed—a 'genuine watershed' in Church history.[46] So, too, Nigel Yates argued in his path-breaking account of the subject, 'the ritualism that developed from the late-1830s was a radical departure from traditional Anglican beliefs and practices'.[47]

New arguments were generated by these changes, while old arguments were reanimated. Questions of belief were loudly and bitterly contested and issues about practice were no less subject to debate. How to worship, where to worship, what to wear at worship: all these became increasingly important subjects. As we shall see, even the question of whether flowers could be displayed in church suddenly developed a significance it had not possessed for centuries. A renewed focus on the sacraments—especially the Eucharist and baptism—redirected the attention of both High Churchmen and, perhaps surprisingly, Evangelicals towards the liturgy and the places in which the sacraments were celebrated.[48]

It is this aspect of Victorian religious life that we will explore. The central claim of this book is that these wide-ranging changes had architectural consequences: not just because more churches were built, and built in new and different styles, but because the Victorian Church came to understand architecture differently in this period. The result was a sharp break with the past—especially the recent past—which reshaped buildings and how buildings were experienced. The Church of England was, in many respects, the forum in which this change was debated. But the argument that Anglicans helped develop proved so compelling that it reshaped ideas about architecture in almost every other denomination. It is that dramatic and comprehensive change this book will seek to explain.

This is a big project—and, it was once thought, an impossible one. Basil Clarke, in his still illuminating *Church Builders of the Nineteenth Century*, began with the commonplace statement: 'we cannot see things as the Victorians did'.[49] Yet, what I'm proposing is absolutely that: to try to see things, to feel things, to understand things just as the Victorians did—to understand the fears and excitements, the horror and enthusiasm for Victorian church buildings that the Victorians felt themselves. The result will be, I hope, a new way of understanding both Victorian architecture and Victorian faith, and a new realization of why both became so tightly intertwined in this period.

To do so, I'm going to draw—above all—on the words and on the buildings of the Victorian era. I'm going to look at what architects and clerics wrote and built; at what many ordinary people—those who sat in the pews, visited, or worshipped in churches—said and did. Over the next two hundred pages or so, I will quote terrible hymns and dreadful novels and excruciating poetry. I will introduce—or, more likely, reintroduce—you to scores of different buildings: new churches and old; rebuilt, restored, and constructed from scratch. I will also explore the wider world beyond the church building—looking at schoolhouses and parsonages, churchyards and cemeteries; considering the religion of the streets, squares, roads, and lanes of Britain. Much of this evidence, it's true, was produced by preachers, teachers, writers, and social leaders. But by paying attention to what ordinary people did as well as what elites said, and by surveying the rich range of reminiscence and memoir which was left behind, we can gain some insight into the wider implications of architectural and religious change.

I will also draw on some of the latest and—it seems to me—the most fertile and interesting insights from the works of historians and anthropologists of religion, from scholars of the senses and of the emotions. Within the last decade—indeed, within the last five or six years—whole new fields of investigation have developed which can illuminate the Victorians' particular experience of their churches, shedding light on what they saw and felt, on what their churches meant, what they did, and what they were expected to do.[50] This work encourages us to think about how people saw and heard the churches of the past; how they sensed, how they were moved by them. These approaches help us to think about the interplay of sight and sound, emotion and reason, considered thought and sudden impulse. This is a very different way of thinking about churches from that usually adopted by either architectural historians or writers on the history of religion.

Although I have learnt much from them,[51] architectural historians have, on the whole, been preoccupied with architects rather than architecture.[52] When they have examined buildings, they have tended to remain so obsessed with their formal qualities that they fail to think about their function or their effect: they have studied *style* instead of *experience*.[53] This has yielded enormous insights into the architectural world of the nineteenth century, into the thinking of architects and—increasingly—of other designers. There has even been some interest in the architects' clients. But this focus on form, this emphasis on style, and this exclusive preoccupation with the production rather than the interpretation, use, and experience of architecture has led scholars to ignore other, equally important questions. This has been problematic for architectural history, which has, as a result, either tended to exist in its own academic cul-de-sac, seemingly unable to communicate to those outside it or has proved to be parasitic on the work of other scholars, employing their insights in studying the built environment but contributing little in return.[54] By focusing on the experience of architecture, we can use the study of buildings to shape our understanding of the world beyond them. Architecture is meant to *do* things. It doesn't just represent or reflect them.

A focus on architecture will also help us, I hope, to redefine what it is that historians mean by 'religion' in nineteenth-century Britain. Conventionally, religion—especially Christianity—has been equated with belief, with a set of rather abstract mental processes.[55] Religious history has therefore focused on what people thought rather than what they did, much less what they felt. Such an approach has created real problems for those who wish to make sense of Victorian religion. It has produced, for instance, the artificial dichotomy between Tractarians and Ecclesiologists that has prevented historians from reaching any sort of consensus on their role. Distinguishing between 'appearance and reality'—between the ostensible 'reality' of ideas and the supposedly superficial 'appearance' of aesthetics—historians have inadvertently narrowed the definition of religion and prevented a genuine engagement with the past.[56] To assume that Christianity can be reduced merely to a mental process is surely to impoverish our understanding of a religion that is—and is essentially—embodied. 'Beliefs', argues one recent and important study, 'are what people do, how they do it, where and when. Not just why.'[57]

This book is thus not just the familiar story of Gothic Revival, Ecclesiological triumph, and Tractarian reform (although these will be important elements of the tale I have to tell). Nor is it the story of the slow but steady triumph of ritualism—whose history has already been told so masterfully elsewhere.[58] It is not a textbook, setting out to offer a comprehensive account of everything; nor, like the many very good studies that have appeared in the last few decades, is it a precise delineation of one particular place, denomination, architect, or style. No: it's an argument; an argument about how to study church buildings and how to understand the ways in which our ancestors hoped they and we would experience them. To make that argument, we need to transcend the sorts of boundaries that have constrained previous studies: looking for similarities between different theologies, different denominations, and different social groups; looking for resemblances between buildings that outwardly, at a first or even a second glance, appear quite unlike each other.

There is a loss in this, of course: perhaps a loss of nuance; certainly a loss of the sorts of precise and subtle distinctions that some sorts of scholars love so much. But there is also a gain, as we look beyond superficial differences and find some common themes: a shared way of understanding church buildings. It is something hinted at by Church historians like David Bebbington, who points out the way in which 'the new Evangelical mood' of the 1820s and 1830s 'shared a great deal in common with the Oxford Movement'. Yet this sense is barely acknowledged by architectural historians, who have continued to emphasize doctrinal difference and party principle whilst overlooking aesthetic and material similarity.[59] This book seeks to right that imbalance.

At the heart of Chapter 1—Seeing—is the rather controversial claim that the Ecclesiologists and the Tractarians, and the great polemicists of both Gothic and neoclassical revivals, were all engaged in a debate not just about the *style* of churches, but also—indeed, chiefly—about the very *nature* of church architecture itself. Indeed, in this wider debate the so-called battle of the styles—Greek versus Gothic, Ecclesiology opposed to iconoclasm—was a second-order issue. In the 1830s and 1840s, there was a bigger, more fundamental shift in how church architecture was understood and how churches were seen. It's an argument that challenges most of what historians have said about those crucial decades of the nineteenth century—and it's one that has, I think, rather important implications for both architectural and ecclesiastical history. Perhaps above all what it suggests is that architecture itself—how it was understood and thus how it was valued and experienced—was utterly transformed by the Victorians; and it was transformed above all by a debate over churches. In that sense, far from seeing ecclesiastical architecture as an outcome of wider shifts in thought, I will argue that it was the Church that reshaped other forms of architecture in its own image.

But, of course, the Victorians did not merely look at churches, or indeed just debate them. In Chapter 2—Feeling—we go beyond the question of what church buildings looked like, to consider what it was they were meant to *do*. This involves thinking more about sight but also about the other senses—especially hearing, smell, and touch; it involves thinking about people's emotional responses to architecture: the fury, enthusiasm, devotion, and disgust that churches variously evoked in the nineteenth century. It also involves more practical and pragmatic questions, as we explore where people sat and how they were supposed to sit; the ways in which churches were heated and lit; and how the church building was transformed by the advent of new technologies. The church building itself became understood as a technology: a device for achieving certain effects. Such a development helps at least partly to account for the Victorians' huge enthusiasm for church building; for the scores of restorations and the thousands of new churches and chapels; for what one historian has termed a nineteenth-century church-building boom in which 'the Victorian notion of sacred progress [was] measured in ecclesiastical bricks and mortar'.[60]

Chapter 3—Visiting—looks at the implications of these two changes. In regarding churches as more than just passive receptacles for worship—in arguing that they were meant to communicate and to move—the Victorians placed a premium on the power of architecture. The implication was that church buildings should be open and available; that they should be built not merely as the practical solution to population growth but, as the bishop of Oxford, Samuel Wilberforce put it in 1847, amongst the 'foremost means...which God is pleased to use for the communication of Himself to men'.[61] These assumptions also extended to the surroundings of the church, with graveyards given a renewed importance, and with schools and parsonage houses becoming sacred symbols too. The growth of religious processions and new liturgical formulations; the rediscovery— and sometimes the invention—of church dedications; the development of parish histories and even parish magazines: all this extended the reach of the church building beyond itself. The result was an attempt to 'resacralize' the landscape—and, perhaps especially—the townscape of Victorian Britain. In an age of anxiety about faith, in 'a society of strangers', as it has recently been characterized, architecture and topography were called in to bolster the claims, the effects, and the experience of religion.[62]

Other sorts of church visitor are examined in Chapter 4, which is entitled Analysing. None of the changes I'm exploring could have taken place without the work of archaeologists, antiquaries, architects, and other enthusiasts. From the first, they helped to redefine the nature of church buildings, and their records give us a sense of precisely how informed opinion—and opinion formers—engaged with church architecture. As more churches were built and still more restored, as the campaign to keep churches open grew in strength, and, as interest in church architecture was stimulated by the debates about it, so increasing numbers of other people became church visitors. Yet this development was problematic. A growing emphasis on the power, importance, and attractiveness of the church building itself—rather than the activities that took place within it—led some to value the church building's form more than its function, seeking to preserve churches for their own sake, not because they had any religious significance. Chief amongst these people were dedicated, animated, idealistic figures like William Morris, whose campaign to end restoration and freeze churches in time was to prove—in the long run—both highly successful and hugely problematic for religious communities. It presented them with a dilemma, a dilemma that continues to haunt the Churches. Should these buildings be valued for their art-historical importance or their religious effectiveness? Should they adapt to changing times or seek to preserve the patterns of the past? What could and should change? What should stay the same—and why?

This history, though, is not just a matter of the past. It is also a matter of current concern and future importance—especially, but not exclusively, for the Church of England. Responsible for 16,000 church buildings, a quarter of which are grade I listed, and almost all of which were either built, restored, or refitted by the Victorians, the Church of England is still wrestling with the problems and some of the assumptions bequeathed to it by the nineteenth century. In Chapter 5—Revisiting—we explore what the arguments in this book imply for churches in the twenty-first century. If I'm right, then we have misunderstood what our Victorian forbears were doing and we are, as a consequence, continuing to misunderstand those buildings that resulted—to misunderstand them, and to mistreat them. Our current frustrations with their echoey churches; their fixed and uncomfortable pews; their formal plans and neo-medieval fittings: all these grow out of our incomprehension. In this book—and especially in Chapter 5—I hope to explain why things are as they are, and why that may even prove useful to the contemporary Church as it seeks to explain itself to a society which often seems hostile, indifferent, or merely uninformed.

To recapture past experience is far from simple. Experience, after all, is an intensely subjective business. Any group will have very many different experiences in a single place. Even an individual may have strikingly dissimilar experiences over time. Think of John Everett Millais's two portraits of 1863–4: 'My First Sermon' and 'My Second Sermon'. Both depict the same sitter— the artist's daughter, Effie. Both show her in church, sat on a pew, with a bright red cloak and fur muff. But her attitude is very different in each. In 'My First Sermon', the young girl is serious, attentive, sitting upright with a solemn look on her face; in 'My Second Sermon', she is asleep. A whole spectrum of experiences in just two images.

The book seeks to recapture something of this spectrum by looking at buildings and at what people said about buildings; what they built, why they built, and how they used it. The churches and chapels of Britain are still witnesses to the story I will outline; so are the novels, the pamphlets and ephemeral magazines, the memoirs, the very many sermons, the schools, the churchyards, and much more besides. As we will see, perhaps the greatest evidence for this transformation can be found in our own attitudes—for we have inherited the understanding of the church that the Victorians first conceived. 'The innovations of the nine-teenth century', observes one historian, were so decisive that we 'still conceive of a "proper" church building' in the terms devised by the Victorians themselves.[63] This, perhaps more than anything else, helps to suggest that the radical rethinking about ecclesiastical architecture which began in the early nineteenth century became a widespread and popular phenomenon. It was certainly a powerful and dynamic one, for its effects can be discerned today.

There will, of course, always be other experiences and in the Afterword, I invite you to experience the Victorian church for yourself. In a series of short studies, we will look at specific buildings—some very well known, all very easily accessible, and each shown in **bold** when it appears in our text—which provide an entrée into the world and the way of thinking this whole book is designed to uncover. Equipped with an understanding of the experiences that the Victorians hoped their churches would engender, we too may come to experience—and understand—them anew.

1

Seeing

We are on our way to recover the true theory and practice of Divine worship, and to recognise the symbolical order of our Churches and the emphatic meaning of architecture, and the relation of all that is costly, beautiful, and majestic in forms and harmonies, with the Worship of Almighty God.

> Henry Manning, *A Charge Delivered at the Ordinary Visitation of the Archdeaconry of Chichester in July, 1842* (London, 1842), p. 10

Puseyites have endeavoured to make religion as much a mere pageant—a mere show—as they possibly could. Jesus Christ is no longer the one thing needful; for equally if no more indispensable are Altar Crosses and Crucifixes, Long Coats and Waistcoats which conceal the shirt front; Processions and Processional Crosses and Banners.

> 'Adam Bede' (William Horsell), *The Natural History of Puseyism: with a Short Account of the Sunday Opera at St Paul's Brighton* (Brighton and London, 1859), p. 15

L et's return to Littlemore—and, more particularly, to the small church of St Mary and St Nicholas, built there between 1835 and 1836 by the architect Henry Underwood and his client, John Henry Newman. As we have already seen, it was a building that provoked a widely diverging range of responses: the horror experienced by the Evangelical Peter Maurice when confronted by a building he thought idolatrous; and the huge attraction it presented to members of the Oxford Movement, who saw in this small, suburban chapel, first, some glimpses of a brighter, more Catholic future, and then a terrible symbol of the 'Parting of Friends'. We also noted Newman's own commitment to the church: the way in which he drew his family into its construction and furnishing, the way in which he preoccupied himself with the details of its ornamentation. It is clear that Newman also saw this place as significant, as meaningful, as moving.

What I could not do, however, is anything more than sketch in the theological meaning of this building: its role as a work of theology in its own right. That will be the subject of this chapter,

Fig. 4. Littlemore Church

in which we will explore the ways that the Victorians came to understand buildings as theological texts. It's a central question for anyone seeking to explore the issue of how they experienced church architecture and it's one that Newman directly addressed in a sermon delivered only a few weeks after the building was consecrated. Here Newman spelt out precisely how it was that he wanted his parishioners to see their new spiritual home. He wanted them to see it not so much as a building, but as a sort of tract, not unlike the Tracts he was writing at the time. 'What I shall say', he preached, 'will (as it were) turn this Church into a book, a holy book, which you may look at and read, and which will suggest to you many good thoughts of God and heaven.'

This was radical stuff.[1] It was also very new. I have spent months looking for similar sermons and weeks ploughing through the addresses given at church consecrations over the previous forty years. None comes anywhere close to this. Not one offers anything like it. Indeed, most consecration sermons before this barely mention the building at all, let alone seek to use it as theological text in its own right. Typical of even the most High Church argument was the sermon preached by the impeccably orthodox Charles Daubeney at the consecration of the remarkable and now redundant church of Christ Church, Rode, in Somerset, in 1825. Modelled loosely—insecurely, frankly laxly—after King's College chapel in Cambridge, it was an inescapably striking edifice. Yet Daubeney was clear: although it was a 'fair and goodly fabric', 'we are not so absurd as to attribute any inherent holiness to this building itself'.[2] Almost two decades before, in 1797, the equally proper Jelinger Symons had made the point still more clearly at the consecration of St John-at-Hackney, built by a prominent High Church group known as the Hackney Phalanx. Although fully committed to the idea of consecration—something that was suspicious for many more Evangelical clergy, Symons wasted no time in describing the building, cutting off all discussion by observing it was built for solely 'spiritual worship to which external forms must always be subservient'.[3] Newman's focus on the structure and on its meaning was consequently most unusual and highly innovative.

In his sermon, Newman took his listeners on a virtual tour of the tiny building, pointing out the three windows over the altar, which—as with the three aisles at St Mary's, the University Church in Oxford—he took to typify the Trinity. The cross over the altar—the cross that his friend Bloxam found him affixing at their first meeting—this Newman took to typify Christ:

> Thus, I say, at first sight on a person's entering the Church, and again, when he takes his place and looks straight before him, he is reminded of the two great doctrines of the Gospel, the Trinity and the Incarnation—the three windows intimating the Trinity, and the Cross still more plainly Christ's Incarnation, on becoming flesh and dying for us.

Newman didn't stop there. The three windows, he went on, also typified the three sacraments of baptism, confirmation, and Holy Communion; and the three virtues of faith, hope, and charity. The seven arches under the windows—just like the seven niches over the altar at the University Church—he took to typify the seven days of creation and the 164th verse of the 119th Psalm: 'Seven times a-day do I praise thee.' As for the door—and the fact that there was only one entrance—this, too, typified Christ, the only door to salvation. Seen properly, Newman suggested, every aspect of the building was designed to communicate a message.[4]

Newman's sermon—just like his church—offers us a new and instructive way of understanding how the Victorians saw ecclesiastical architecture. They saw it not just as bricks and mortar, nor merely as a necessary if expensive means of housing worshipping communities. Rather, they came to see church buildings as a mode of communication. They denatured architecture, in other words—just as Newman did—turning buildings into books. What we might call a 'textual turn' in architecture, this was a revolutionary, transformative doctrine, although it has been almost completely overlooked by previous writers.[5] It radically changed attitudes towards churches—and also helped to redefine architectural debate more generally throughout the nineteenth century. In that way, it was perhaps the most important—and, oddly, the most neglected—contribution ecclesiastical architecture made to the wider world of building and thinking about building.

It was also, as I suggested in the Introduction, a hugely controversial development. After all, amongst the most objectionable aspects of Newman's church for Peter Maurice—the powerful Protestant polemicist who found Littlemore so horrifying—was precisely the symbolism he found there. Indeed, he was very specifically horrified to learn that Newman had preached on the symbolic significance of the architecture.[6] Later, he was to observe:

> The people have learned to their sorrow, that these symbols are no shadows; or if shadows, that they are only too true an indication of the near approach of the most grievous burdens...If they see buildings rising up, beautiful in symmetry to the eye of nature, but debased with the peculiar garniture of the old superstitions of Antichrist Papal and Pagan, they will sicken as they gaze upon them, and turn away with loathing and horror.[7]

Maurice was, as I've said, a monomaniac—a man incapable of even enjoying the Great Exhibition, for example, for fear that the Crystal Palace somehow signified the approach of the Apocalypse.[8] But he was not a fool, nor, for that matter, an extremist—indeed, he was to befriend Newman after the latter's conversion to Roman Catholicism. More importantly, Maurice was right to take symbolism seriously.

He was right because it mattered to people like Newman and he was right because it soon came to matter to many others too. For the understanding of architecture which Newman offered in his sermon at Littlemore quite quickly became the dominant mode of experiencing church buildings for many of those who very profoundly disagreed with much of the rest of Newman's theology. The assumption that buildings could be reduced to texts, that churches could be read rather as one might read a book, represented a revolution in architectural understanding that affected almost every denomination. Even those Nonconformists who specifically rejected Newman, Anglicanism, Ecclesiology, and the Gothic Revival found themselves seduced by the concept of the church as a means of communication in its own right. It is this change, more than anything, that helps to explain the puzzle with which we began this book. Why was it, asked the Protestant controversialist Walter Walsh, in words I have already quoted, that:

> all over the land we find new churches built, and old ones restored in a style which can only delight the hearts of the Romanisers, although those Churches are frequently in Evangelical and Protestant hands. Why should Protestant clergymen permit their Churches to be so arranged as to make them ready for a Roman Catholic priest to say Mass in?...And what do *they* want with Communion Tables erected

on high, like Roman Catholic Altars? And why do they permit Chancel gates and screens to be erected?[9]

They did so, I will suggest, because they had come to believe—just as Newman believed—that unless they did this, what they built weren't actually churches after all. It was an assumption that rested almost completely on the conclusion that churches could and should communicate and that they communicated in very particular ways.

My argument also helps to solve a puzzle about Newman himself. Despite his involvement in the church at Littlemore; indeed, despite his role in the building of the nearby St Clement's Church and in the restoration of the Oxford University Church; despite his evocations of Oxford architecture in his books: despite all this, it has often been argued that Newman's architectural interests were somehow ephemeral or essentially less serious than his theological preoccupations. However involved he became in architecture, writes James Patrick in an otherwise marvellous article on Newman, Pugin, and Gothic, Newman's interest was only 'moderate' and 'not central to his theology'.[10] In his biography Ian Ker equally seeks to distinguish the serious, cerebral Catholic Newman from the silly, inconsequential Anglicans with all their interest in buildings and the like. 'Personally,' he claims, 'Newman remarked he had never sympathized...with the antiquarianism of the [Ecclesiologists] which struck him as "unreal".'[11] And, indeed, it must be said that Newman was not a *parti pris* Gothic Revivalist: he admired classical architecture too, and would, as a Roman Catholic priest, come to embrace the baroque of the Post-Tridentine Church.

But it is surely a mistake to confuse commitment to a particular architectural style with an interest in architecture more generally, much less to assume that architecture is not serious, whereas theology obviously is: with buildings basely material and words more suitably spiritual. In reality, recent research of a rather different sort has suggested just how seriously Newman took the built environment. The architecture and antiquities of ancient Rome were, for instance, critical in shaping Newman's theology and his own understanding of faith.[12] His literary works—especially his *roman-à-clef, Loss and Gain: the story of a conversion* (1848)—are saturated with imagery and filled with an emphasis on the 'reality' of the material world compared to the 'unreality' of so much Victorian spirituality.[13] It's worth remembering, too, that amongst the greatest pains occasioned by Newman's conversion were aesthetic, as he left behind Littlemore for the Roman Catholic Chapel in Oxford. 'Nor is it a slight trial', he wrote, 'to go to what to outward appearance is a meeting house.'[14] It was because architecture communicated—and because it was not simply reducible to style or to taste; because a church should look like a church and should operate, as Newman put it, like 'a book, a holy book' which taught its viewers spiritual truths: it was because of all this that architecture mattered to him. And, in this case, Newman was just one of many, part of a wider movement. What was true for him also became true for the Victorians as a whole.

It needs stressing, of course, that the analogy between buildings and books, the assumption that architecture had a communicative function was not one confined to the Victorian period. As the Victorians themselves would enthusiastically remark, medieval writers had similarly stressed the symbolic significance of buildings—especially churches. The poetry of George Herbert—especially his work *The Temple*—drew on similar themes, and would be equally influential, not least on Tractarian poets like Isaac Williams, Newman's curate in Oxford and a major benefactor of the church at Littlemore.[15] Even more practical and self-consciously Protestant figures had acknowledged the capacity of churches to bear meaning. Nicholas Hawksmoor's early eighteenth-century churches, for instance, can be seen as elaborate, majestic attempts to express key theological insights—not least an assertion of the Church of England's continuity with primitive Christianity.[16]

But it must be said that the later eighteenth century had taken a rather different view of architecture—especially the architecture of its churches. This was not, of course, because there was no church building going on, much less because no one cared. Recent research has demolished the idea that the Georgian church witnessed a wholesale collapse in ecclesiastical building work.[17] The Victorians may have wanted to write off their forefathers, condemning them for negligence and neglect. They may have delighted in tales of churches whose doors were left open, whose roofs were rotten, whose naves were used to shelter cattle.[18] It was easy to find examples of places like the little parish church of Caddington, in Bedfordshire, where the graveyard was soiled by sheep and inside, 'Under the words—"This do in remembrance of me," was stretched a bench, turned upside down.'[19] In truth, however, the second half of the eighteenth century saw numerous building projects, large-scale schemes of restoration, and considerable sums of money lavished on ecclesiastical architecture.[20] As with so much of the eighteenth-century church, the pattern was particularist, with each parish having a rather different history and some places tolerating real abuses whilst others engaged in very impressive building campaigns.[21] Nonetheless, the general picture of church architecture throughout Britain after about 1750 was not bad—rather, it was different. It reveals a very different understanding of the church as a building from that which was to follow. It was this, above all, that the Victorians objected to.

A good example of this can be found in a church that Newman would have known, and many of his allies knew very well indeed: Dorchester Abbey, a little way out of Oxford. It is—and was—a magnificent building, an antiquarian's dream. But its treatment from the 1740s onwards showed a very different set of priorities from the Victorians'. The vast Gothic space was compartmental-ized, with 'modern lath and plaster' walls dividing up the church.[22] One part of the place was used to store the village fire engine; much was left empty; the rest was filled with comfortably fur-nished box pews: those private, often locked, and usually high-walled compartments within which worshippers sat, shielded from cold draughts and from the prying eyes of others. The windows were reduced in size, blocked up with bricks to stop the draughts. The medieval roof was lost behind a flat plaster ceiling that cut across the top of the east window, obliterating some of the fine fourteenth-century tracery. The remaining stained glass was removed, relocated, and 'tastefully arranged' in the chan-cel, to the despair of later scholars who would struggle to recreate the complex iconography of the original schemes.[23] A simple classical altarpiece was installed and a pulpit with sounding board above and reading desk below became the chief focus of the church. It was, as the historian Nicholas Doggett points out, an 'auditory layout', designed to facilitate preaching.[24] It couldn't have been further removed from Newman's Littlemore—and, sure enough, this arrangement would be swept away from the 1840s onwards, as the old dispensation at Dorchester was replaced by something closer to the vision of architecture Newman had for his church.[25]

The treatment of Dorchester was typical. It was just one 'auditory church' amongst many. This is a well-observed phenomenon, first noted as long ago as 1948.[26] But it is not well or fully understood, at least not by British historians. Our American counterparts, however, have pushed further and deeper.[27] In particular, Louis Nelson's work on the churches of South Carolina reveals a transatlantic movement which reshaped church buildings in the second half of the eighteenth century. There was, he shows, a rejection of explicit symbolism in Anglican churches. What Nelson terms 'the spiritually animated view' of architecture, in which the plan, elevation, and ornamentation were all meant to express some theological principle, was at a discount. Instead of a high-vaulted ceiling, a church garlanded with images of angels and larded with biblical quotations, a building panelled with sweet-smelling wood, came a space which owed its inspiration to pattern books and the trends in contemporary country houses: 'Later-eighteenth-century builders replaced barrel-vaulted ceilings with more fashionable ceilings; cherubs disappeared...texts were relegated to prescribed panels in the chancel; cedar was supplanted by mahogany.' Even the way in which churches were described began to change, with the highest praise being saved for those features which were seen as 'convenient'. As Nelson observes, by the early nineteenth century, this no longer meant 'spacious or commodious'; it now just meant comfortable.[28]

Signs of this can be seen in many of the new churches of late eighteenth-century Britain. In Lancashire, for example, the scene of a Georgian 'church-building boom', the *Manchester Guide* of 1804 reserved its greatest praise for the latest example of the type.[29] James Wyatt's neo-Palladian St Peter's (1788–94) was a plain Doric monument to fashion: symmetrical and rectangular, with a massive pulpit to the west and a communion table opposite, in the east.[30] 'The inside of the church', observed the guidebook, 'is a model of elegance and taste. The subscribers had the good sense to reject old rules which had not utility for their object, and dared to introduce comfort, convenience, and propriety, into the temple of God.' Function even dictated the furnishings, with acoustic effect uppermost: 'The floor is boarded, and covered with matting, so that all noise, apparent hurry and confusion, too visible, on the entrance of some congregations, is avoided; and the highly esteemed minister is heard equally well by every individual within the walls.'[31] Here was the auditory church incarnate; and it was just one of many. In 1819, the architect W. F. Pocock produced the first ever English pattern book for churches, a volume which would be reprinted— unaltered—again in 1823 and 1835. He was clear about the design principles which informed his work, concluding that 'the principal point for consideration is, *the most convenient method of seating the greatest number of persons to hear distinctly the voice of the reader and preacher*'.[32]

This was all a long way away from George Herbert or even Nicholas Hawksmoor. It was, however, an entirely rational approach—and it explains many of the things that the Victorians were to find so objectionable about their predecessors. If everyone had to hear, then the pulpit needed to be large and high, and surmounted with a sounding board. It was best, too, to pack as many people in as close as possible to it. Hence the ever increasing number of galleries; hence the disregard for the chancel; hence, too, the box pews—for if listening was more important than seeing, then it really didn't matter which way you were facing, so long as you could hear the sermon. In many churches, these private compartments were located behind the pulpit. In still more, these locked boxes had seats with their backs to the preacher. The result can be seen today in places like **St Mary's Whitby,** which began building galleries in the seventeenth century and never really stopped, even erecting one across the chancel arch, cutting off the church from the communion table. The Victorians regarded this as utterly objectionable—and it makes little liturgical sense to us now. But for the people of the eighteenth and very early nineteenth centuries, the arrangement made perfect sense: here was, as it were, a machine for listening in.

This practical, rational architecture found its fulfilment in the churches erected in the 1820s by the engineer Thomas Telford, churches like the one in the small fishing village of **Plockton.** Built with government money for the Church of

Fig. 5. St Mary's Whitby

Scotland, they were intensely functional, with the only ecclesiastical symbolism confined to their slightly pointed windows, intended as a reminiscence—a sort of subliminal evocation—of the fenestration in older churches. They were galleried and T-shaped, with a central two-decker pulpit and a space in front for an annual celebration of communion. Appropriately enough for a Calvinist establishment, there was no further religious embellishment. This was a church that came into being when it was full of its congregation. The building itself was meant to be meaningless.

Now, the Church of Scotland was—self-evidently—not the Church of England. But it is noteworthy that these T-plan churches mirrored developments south of the border. Still more remarkably, they echoed the example of earlier Roman Catholic Churches. Late eighteenth-century Ireland saw a scattering

Fig. 6. Plockton Church

of similarly shaped structures, the best preserved of which, **St John the Baptist, Drumcree** (1783), can still be seen at the Ulster Folk Museum, whence it was moved, lock, stock, and barrel organ, in 1995. It remained notably 'plain' even after extensive refitting in 1831.[33] These churches, and the many other rectangular and even L-plan buildings erected at the same time, tended to maximize accommodation and minimize symbolism, eschewing cruciform plans and installing galleries, sometimes on three sides. This—just like the Roman Catholic Chapel in Oxford that Newman found so off-puttingly plain—was not simply a response to residual anti-Catholicism; it was the product of a particular and rather widely accepted approach to religious architecture.

For it was not only in impoverished Ireland or solely in response to persecution that late eighteenth-century Roman Catholics erected these boxy buildings, characterized by what the Georgian Jesuit and aesthete, John Thorpe, described as 'an elegant Plainness'. Writing to Lord Arundell in 1771 to advise him on the fitting up of Wardour Castle Chapel, Thorpe cautioned against 'much ornament'. 'Angels holding candle sticks or crucifix may look pretty in a drawing,' he went on, 'yet if executed on an altar will perhaps have too much of the Puppet show in England.'[34] The structure which resulted, by the fashionable architect James Paine, fully illustrated this point; as did another even more remarkable edifice of the 1780s: John Tasker's Lulworth Castle Chapel. Both of these ambitious, aristocratic Catholic churches were centrally planned, circular, and surprisingly unostentatious. Even after it was redecorated by the Victorians, Lulworth would be described as more like a mosque than a church.[35] As this suggests, both chapels would be fitted up with more elaborate furnishings in the nineteenth century, with

Lulworth, for instance, reimagined 'in a style suitable as possible to the glories of medieval England'.[36] The same would prove true for the many Catholic churches erected at the same time, which proved to be too 'plain' and too preoccupied by pure function rather than expressive form for the Victorians.

For the late eighteenth and early nineteenth centuries witnessed a remarkable range of experimental churches and chapels. This was especially true for Nonconformist congregations, of course, with their rejection of 'superstitious' symbolism and enthusiasm for the sermon leading to some truly wonderful buildings—like the octagonal Wesleyan Chapel at Heptonstall (built in 1764 and extended in 1802) or the elliptical Rosemary Street Presbyterian Church in Belfast (built in 1793). In 1770, indeed, the Methodist Conference specified that octagonal chapels should be preferred, not least because they were 'best for the voice, and on many accounts more commodious than any other'.[37] But Anglicans joined in too, for as Nigel Yates puts it in his standard work on the subject, 'Doctrinal differences were not always reflected in architectural ones.'[38] There were octagonal churches like the one at Stoney Middleton in Derbyshire (1758–9); elliptical ones like All Saints Newcastle upon Tyne (1789) and St Chad's, Shrewsbury (1790–2); and a semicircular one at St Mary in the Castle, Hastings (1818). In his *Familiar Architecture* (published in 1768; reprinted in 1789 and again in 1795) Thomas Rawlins offered an 'octangular church...for a person of quality' as well as an 'octangular Church or Chapel'.[39] A few classical details aside, there was no Christian symbolism here, no real sense that different denominations might have different requirements, nor any real belief that buildings could—or should—communicate theological ideas.

Fig. 7. An Octangular Church, from Thomas Rawlins, *Familiar Architecture* (1795). Note the pews focused on a pulpit to the north

Surprisingly enough, even a turn towards Gothic architecture did little to change the basic assumptions which underlay these remarkable, functional buildings. Indeed, when the hugely influential Incorporated Church Building Society resolved to advocate medieval styles in the 1820s, it argued for neo-Gothic primarily on the grounds of cost, believing that the unsymmetrical, crudely carved, and easily adaptable style would prove cheaper than massive, monumental, rule-based neoclassicism.[40] From the late eighteenth century onwards, other people had chosen Gothic for a range of other reasons: antiquarianism; the influence of picturesque theory;[41] above all—as the architectural historian Simon Bradley has shown—the desire of many members of the Church of England, High and Low alike, to assert its place as the national church, with an unbroken history dating back to St Augustine. This was an impulse so strong that it influenced Evangelicals as much as High Churchmen, and it also began to influence Roman Catholic church design—as at places like St Mary's, Wigan, of 1818–19.[42]

But these neo-Gothic churches were still basically preaching boxes—and I say that not as a condemnation, as the Victorians did, but instead as a statement of fact. They did not represent a major shift in architectural form or understanding. Although they often applied medieval details and decoration; although they sometimes used pointed- or round-headed arches; although the most adventurous sometimes employed plans which owed something to medieval precedent: the truth was that these buildings differed little in structure or function from neoclassical churches erected at the same time. Whether 'Gothic' or not, pre-Victorian churches were designed for convenience rather than their communicative function. They lacked the intense focus on architecture as a sort of text which would characterize the next generation's experiments in church building. The advent of Gothic was not the key development in and of itself. The critical change came in the 1830s and 1840s—and it transformed the basic conceptualization of architecture itself.

It is impossible to discuss this development without also discussing the Cambridge Camden Society, a group which would become known—and would become notorious—as the Ecclesiologists. This is not because they were the only important figures who helped effect a revolution in church architecture. They were not. As we will see, they were part of a much bigger process: speaking to, and for, and with, a wider movement which incorporated Anglicans and non-Anglicans, and which transformed how churches were built, how they were seen, and how they were intended to be seen. This was the 'wholly new theory about the planning and arrangement of churches' which Addleshaw and Etchells point to, but do not elucidate, in the still standard work on *The Architectural Setting of Anglican Worship*, published as long ago as 1948.[43] It was a change so substantial that it could scarcely be the product of a single society's work—even one that was run by aggressive, energetic, and single-minded Cambridge undergraduates. But the Ecclesiologists were, nonetheless, important; they were voluble and left behind masses of documentation; above all, they have been widely studied—and, it seems to me, often misunderstood. So I shall start with them.

The Cambridge Camden Society was founded in 1839. It was just one of many such societies. An Oxford equivalent was also established in that year, and the 1840s would see a slew of similar organizations set up: Exeter in 1841, Lichfield, Down and Connor and Dromore in 1842, Lincolnshire in 1844, and many more besides. Initially, the Ecclesiologists looked like a simple antiquarian society of the sort that had been established all across Britain. They also looked much like the diocesan building societies which reforming bishops had been starting since the mid-1820s, with the hope of raising money for ever more church extension.[44] Quickly, however, it became clear that the Camdenians were not like these other groups: they were assertive, aggressive, polemical.

What made them so important, so high-profile, and so controversial? In some respects, it's easier to say why they were controversial and high-profile than why they were important. Their leaders, who included the indefatigable Benjamin Webb and John Mason Neale, had a seemingly endless appetite for a fight. They were also hugely prolific: writing poetry, novels, and hymns; producing pamphlets and letters, and above all editing a fierce and opinionated journal, *The Ecclesiologist*, from which they derived their soubriquet: the Ecclesiologists. With its lists of architects 'approved' and architects 'condemned', with its slating reviews of churches and its serious surveys of ecclesiastical art old and new, it was almost impossible for anyone at all interested in the subject to ignore it—and, indeed, *The Ecclesiologist* proved not just an instant hit, but also a serious provocation. The society would shed members, split, and then reform over the journal's aggressive and polemical writing.

So much for why the Ecclesiologists got noticed; what about why they mattered? They mattered not because the ideas they were articulating were particularly novel or, for that matter, especially well put. *The Ecclesiologist* was so unpleasant so often that it deterred more readers than it attracted, whilst no one who has read John Mason Neale's novels surely ever chooses to read them again. The hours of my life spent reading his *Ayton Priory* are hours I will never get back. A novel of 1843, it was intended 'to set forth the advantages and all but necessity, of the re-introduction of monasticism'. This is a rather tricky subject for a novelization, you might have thought; and you would be right.[45]

No, what made the Ecclesiologists matter—both to us and to their contemporaries—is the fact that they were articulating some pretty widespread ideas, two of which were especially pervasive.

In the first place, of course, the Ecclesiologists were standard bearers for the re-Gothicization of the Church of England. Everything they wrote, everything they campaigned for, tended towards this end. And in arguing this, they were pushing—rhetorically speaking—at an open door. As early as 1770, *The Builder's Magazine* had observed that 'The Grecian taste certainly best suits...publick buildings...but for religious structures, Gothic, undoubtedly, ought to be preferred.'[46] The argument was a typological one and also a psychological one; one that assumed that each type of building should have its own distinct style and that the forms of Gothic architecture were most conducive for religious experience. This was an old idea: one articulated in Milton's much-quoted passage evoking the impact of the 'dimm [sic] religious light' of an ancient church.[47] But it was an idea given still greater salience by a growing interest in antiquarianism and the increasing desire of Anglicans to assert their continuity with the past by employing medieval architecture.[48] That many believed Gothic to be cheaper than neoclassicism only added to the appeal.[49] To advocate neo-medieval architecture for churches in the 1830s or 1840s, therefore, was scarcely to stand out. The Ecclesiologists were useful because—like the other societies founded at the same time—they provided guidance on exactly what form this should take.[50]

In the second place—and much more importantly still—the Ecclesiologists were amongst those who helped to articulate a new reason for adopting Gothic. Instead of favouring neo-medieval styles on typological, psychological, historical, or simply economic grounds, they urged the adoption of Gothic architecture because they saw it as the embodiment and the expression of faith. As the *Ecclesiologist* put it in 1846: 'Pointed Architecture seems to be so true a correlative of Christian doctrine, that we cannot suppose...that any future style will be discovered, in which the Pointed Style shall not predominate.'[51] What this meant was that the Ecclesiologists saw in the Gothic—or 'Pointed'—style an architecture uniquely capable of bearing and articulating theological meaning.

This was a theme that ran throughout Ecclesiological writing—from Neale's breathless descriptions of church buildings in his fiction, to the remarkable passage in the analysis of medieval architecture which he co-wrote with his coadjutor, Benjamin Webb. Describing a visit to a cathedral, they declared:

Far away, and long ere we catch our front view of the city itself, the three spires of the Cathedral, rising high above its din and turmoil, preach to us of the most Holy and Undivided Trinity. As we approach, the Transepts, striking out cross-wise, tell us of the Atonement: the Communion of Saints is set forth by the chapels clustering round Choir and Nave: the mystical weathercock bids us watch and pray and endure hardness: the hideous forms that seem hurrying from the eaves speak of those who are cast out of the church: spire, pinnacle and finial, the upward curl of the sculptured foliage, the upward spring of the flying buttresses, the sharp rise of the window-arch, the high-thrown pitch of the roof, all these, over-powering the horizontal tendency of string course and parapet, teach us that vanquishing earthly desires, we also should ascend in heart and mind. Lessons of holy wisdom are written in the delicate tracery of the windows: the unity of many members is shadowed forth by the multiplex arcade: the duty of letting our light shine before men, by the pierced and flowered parapet that crowns the whole.[52]

Their rediscovery and retranslation of the *Rationale Divinorum Officiorum* of William Durandus, written in the thirteenth century, and presenting a highly allegorical interpretation of ecclesiastical architecture, only seemed to confirm this analysis. The Ecclesiologists claimed this discovery for their own, and sought to systematize it. This was, they claimed, not a subjective account or a merely antiquarian one. This was *fact*. Indeed, it was a new science—a science they termed sacramentality. Ecclesiology—at least as Neale and Webb understood it—was the study of this new science.

In reality, even this move was not all that distinctive. Indeed, one of the reasons that the Ecclesiologists were so keen to claim historic validation and scientific bona fides for their approach was precisely that they were far from alone in articulating this notion. It was a point, after all, that the German poet, philosopher, and philologist Friedrich Schlegel had articulated forty years before in his *Lectures on the History of Literature*.[53] Tellingly, indeed, these lectures would be translated into English in 1841 and Schlegel's assertion that 'All architecture is symbolical; but none so much so as the christian [*sic*] architecture of the middle age' approvingly quoted.[54] This was an idea which had clearly found its time.

In Oxford, too, the Oxford Society for Promoting Gothic Architecture—later renamed the Oxford Architectural Society— was engaged in exactly the same debate at exactly the same time. A key moment came in 1845, when Basil Jones, later bishop of St David's, spoke on symbolism in architecture. There were, he argued, two ways of analysing architecture symbolically. One— the way he associated with the Ecclesiologists—rested on what he called 'the symbolism of certain facts'. Instead, influenced by Plato's *Phaedo*, and also by Samuel Taylor Coleridge's *Literary Remains* (1836), he argued for another; something he called 'proto-symbolism': the notion that Gothic was not best approached as an architecture which represented certain facts, but as a style that embodied a particular—and particularly Platonic—idea.[55] It was, in other words, not just an aesthetic but an ethos. Jones's notion of protosymbolism was one that his friend, the Oxford historian Edward Freeman, took up immediately. In a paper given to the Oxford Society only a few months after Jones first set out the concept, Freeman developed it yet further, arguing that 'a work of Architecture . . . will be and must be the material expression of some predominant idea in the individual or his age'. This, he went on, was, 'the real symbolism of Architecture, proto-symbolism . . . a true and philsophick view applicable to all art in all ages'.[56]

But even this alternative view did not exhaust the range of writings on the symbolic analysis of architecture. In Exeter, for example, in 1842, the dean, Thomas Hill Lowe—a poet and much-published preacher, but scarcely a figure of exaggerated Ecclesiological fervour—similarly spoke to the local diocesan architectural society about the hidden meanings of church buildings. 'In a rightly-ordered Church,' he claimed, 'spiritual truths are embodied under sensible images, and impressed on the minds of those who are taught their meaning with the utmost force and perspicacity.' Until recently, he concluded, this truth had been ignored. Ecclesiastical buildings had shown, he went on, 'but small pretence of the character of Churches. They are, rather, preaching-houses and nothing more.'[57] As I've suggested, he was quite right. He was also right in thinking things had changed.

Moreover, writers did not have to be exclusively committed to Gothic architecture to reach this conclusion. Writing in 1837, the architect William Bardwell, for example, was keen to defend the idea of church buildings as a 'witness to the truth of the invisible world, of which they are, in every part, the *symbol* and the *type!*' Every church tower 'that rises between the trees', he asserted, 'is a hieroglyphic of the word "GOD"'. This was, Bardwell went on, a truth most realized in medieval architectural forms—with their 'cruciform plan—the constantly recurring idea of the Trinity, presented in the triple aisles, windows, ornaments, &c.' Quoting the Coleridgian Joseph Henry Green, he observed that a medieval cathedral is 'the *architectural* word for the *omnipresence of God*'. But style was not the key point for him. Rather, he concluded, all ages used 'appropriate forms and appropriate sculpture to awaken in the minds of the people, and to impress upon them the peculiar tenets or doctrines, such forms were made to represent'. Thus it was that he felt able to praise Wren and Palladio as well as the Goths, so long as each building clearly asserted 'it *is a Church*, not an unmeaning public room, with pews and a pulpit'.[58]

So widespread was this new view of architecture that it transcended Oxford and Cambridge, the Tractarians and the Ecclesiologists, the High, Low, and Broad Church traditions. That it predated the Ecclesiologists and was enthusiastically embraced by the Tractarians can be seen not just in Newman's church at Littlemore, but also in the church built by the great inspiration for the movement—John Keble, poet and priest, whose sermon of 1833 is often seen as the great rallying cry of the Tractarians. His poems, written in the 1820s, were quoted favourably by enthusiasts for a symbolic interpretation of architecture and condemned by their opponents.[59] More intriguingly still, when in 1847 he himself came to build, Keble created a church at Hursley in Hampshire which was saturated in symbolism. From the texts on the tiles to the sculpture on the walls, everything was designed to be read. Images of St Peter and St Paul 'as exponents of the inner mysteries' were carved either side of the chancel; those of St Athanasius and St Augustine 'as champions of the faith' were carved by the east window; the windows themselves, as Keble's sister recorded, were 'meant to be a course of instruction in Sacred History from Adam to the last day'. It was, as the novelist Charlotte M. Yonge observed, as though one of his verses had been turned into a building—and, of course, that was precisely the intention.[60]

That this notion was attractive to a wide variety of thinkers can also be seen in the south-coast diocese of Chichester. Here in the early 1840s, two very different men with very different views nonetheless concurred about buildings—and, as the two arch-deacons of the area, were in a position to enforce their analysis on the parishes they oversaw. One was the liberal, rationalizing Broad Church Julius Hare; the other was the reactionary Trac-tarian Henry Manning—later to become a Roman Catholic Car-dinal Archbishop. Manning's views were quoted at the start of the chapter: 'We are on our way', he declared to the clergy of Chichester in 1842, 'to recover the true theory and practice of Divine worship, and to recognise the symbolical order of our Churches.'[61] Here is Hare two years before in 1840, and again to a conference of clergymen and church wardens: 'The great primary idea of a church is, that it should be a house of prayer and to this end, the whole arrangement of the building was in old times subordinate: this was typified by the rising columns and spires.'

By contrast, he went on, modern churches were nothing more than 'a house of preaching', places which denied a deeper spiritual meaning and overemphasized the importance of the sermon. 'This thrusting forward of the pulpit', he went on, 'has indeed a symbolical meaning, showing how the intellect, which ought to guide and open the way to Christ, will often bar us out from him.'[62]

These few examples could be multiplied again and again.[63] What they show is that, from the 1830s onwards, the idea that buildings were somehow reducible to their symbolic meaning, somehow equivalent to text, had become a commonplace. For the clergyman G. A. Poole, 'Ecclesiastical architecture' was, in fact, nothing more (and nothing less) than 'a language'.[64] For G. F. Bodley, who trained as an architect at this time, architectural style was 'after all, only language'.[65] Still more strikingly, in his *Palace of Architecture*, published in 1840, the architect George Wightwick described a visit to a cathedral in extraordinarily literary terms: 'a Cathedral is an epic poem', he wrote:

> It has its ruling theme, and subservient machinery—its progressive conduct and climax. What an opening passage is its *Front*! Then onward toward its *Nave*, flows the current of its fable with the collateral accompaniments of its *Aisles*, till it expands in the comprehensive triple tide of *Transepts* and *Tower*, and concludes in all the condensed magnificence of its *Choir*![66]

And it was not just peripheral figures like Wightwick or Poole, even High Church architects like Bodley, who spoke in similar terms. This notion was central to the pre-eminent art critic of the age, John Ruskin. Now, Ruskin loathed the Ecclesiologists, but he nonetheless also argued for an architecture which would leave the viewers 'reading a building as we would read Milton or Dante, and getting the same kind of delight out of the stones as out of the stanzas'.[67] Indeed, as the critic Robert Kerr put it, Ruskin was 'Neither more nor less than the High Priest of a faith which directly identifies Architecture with Poetry; and this for the first time in artistic history.'[68] It was for this reason, after all, that Ruskin wrote of St Mark's in Venice 'less as a temple wherein to pray, than as itself a Book of Common Prayer'.[69]

Such a far-reaching and radical change inevitably inspired comment and criticism. There were those, like the architect and theorist James Fergusson, who utterly denied the capacity of buildings to convey any meaning whatsoever.[70] Later in the century, too, the architect J. T. Micklethwaite would condemn 'a certain vague nothing, called *symbolism*', in church buildings, arguing that any symbolic content was always *ex post facto*.[71] But the very fact they needed to respond to the new view about symbolism is telling—as is the response of Joseph Gwilt, author of the most popular *Encyclopaedia of Architecture* published in the mid-nineteenth century. The first edition, produced in 1842, said nothing about the subject. A revised version of 1851 included an appendix on Gothic architecture, one that observed, 'we hold symbolism in churches to be an idle conceit'. Yet the very same section now devoted pages to the subject of symbolism and appended a list of Christian symbols.[72] Small wonder, for, as the Harvard historian Neil Levine has shown, the assumption that architecture bore meaning was becoming hard to resist. Indeed, it was becoming the dominant understanding of the subject in this period—and not just in Britain.[73] And, in any event, for our purposes, it was another, rather louder, rather more important group of critics who matter more: the very many Evangelical Anglicans and Nonconformists who were horrified by the argument that architecture was symbolic, and shocked to think that buildings could be a medium for spiritual communication.

It was this, of course, that led to Peter Maurice's attack on Newman's church at Littlemore, for here, as he pointed out, was a structure not only filled with symbolism but also interpreted symbolically. It was this too that led another figure we have already encountered—Francis Close, the dean of Carlisle—to criticize the Tractarians for their baleful architectural influence, blaming the Oxford Movement for encouraging 'many idealists and symbolists' to content 'themselves with architectural and pictorial Popery'.[74]

And the criticisms were even more various than this. For the distinguished classical architect C. R. Cockerell, the symbolism of medieval churches was simply further proof that, in Gothic architecture, 'solidity is sacrificed to superstition'.[75] For the proudly puritanical J. A. Tabor, an Essex Congregationalist, symbolism was a self-evident sign of idolatry. 'Christianity', he claimed, 'has nothing in common with the development and display of the arts or sciences.' Christians, as a result, should feel ashamed to participate in the 'vain-glorious erection, for the worship of God, of highly architectural and gorgeous edifices, with lofty and defiant towers'.[76]

Yet, as Tabor's own language revealed, the problem with this argument was that admitting the potential for symbolism—admitting that symbolism equated, in his terms, to a 'highly architectural' edifice—effectively conceded the claims of those who advocated a symbolic understanding of church buildings. Indeed, he simply, literally inverted the argument made by people like Neale and Newman, arguing that in a Gothic church, 'The towering and ambitious spire, in a spiritual sense, points *downward.*[77] The same was true of passionate opponents of Gothic architecture more generally. So it was, for example, that when the great Scots Presbyterian architect, Alexander 'Greek' Thomson, attempted to prove the 'Unsuitableness of Gothic Architecture to Modern Circumstances', he boldly stated that it was classicism which conveyed the higher spiritual truth, whilst the architecture of the 'Romish church' merely sought to impress with unmeaning spectacle.[78]

An analogous argument, which rested still more heavily on a linguistic analogy, was made by the great Baptist preacher C. H. Spurgeon, whose massive, 6,000-seater Metropolitan Tabernacle in South London seems at one level far removed from the arguments of the Ecclesiologists and Tractarians. Predictably enough, Spurgeon explicitly rejected the Gothic Revival and all its associations, which he thought were dangerously popish. But even he could not avoid the idea of buildings as text and architecture as language. The Tabernacle, Spurgeon affirmed, had to be 'a Grecian place of worship'. This was not because of the beauty or even practicality of Greek art, but because 'It seemed to me, that there are two sacred languages in the world: there was the Hebrew of old; there is one other sacred language, the Greek, which is very dear to every Christian heart. Every Baptist place should be Grecian, never Gothic.'[79] As this example again illustrates, once the notion of architecture as text was put forward, it proved very hard—perhaps impossible—to escape.

In that way a divergent and apparently discordant group of commentators came, in the end, to sing a somewhat similar tune. Even if used only metaphorically, this new idea nonetheless had the power to transform discourse, experience, and buildings alike. Tellingly, even those Nonconformists who rejected the suspicious associations of Gothic nonetheless came to read their buildings, interpreting their symbolism in new and striking ways. In Wales, for instance, three-light windows became known as Trinity windows.[80] And those Nonconformists, like the Congregationalist architect James Cubitt, who did come to embrace the Gothic did so, as he made clear, precisely because he believed that in neo-medievalism 'every stone ... tells in a universal language' of the idea for which it was built.[81]

What we might term a 'textual turn' in architecture drew on a wider revival of interest in symbolism more generally, something exemplified by Coleridge's influential writings—from 'The Destiny of Nations' (1797) to his *Lay Sermons* (especially the first of 1816)—on the need for Christian truth to be transmitted in symbolic form.[82] A revival of typological analysis in biblical studies, in art, and in literature similarly encouraged a new sort of architectural analysis.[83] Just as a Pre-Raphaelite painting or a Pre-Raphaelite poem was intended to be read—almost in a way decoded—for its deeper meaning, so church buildings came be seen as vehicles for holy writ. 'Things seen are types of things unseen,' observed one author, defending *The Symbolism of Churches and Their Ornaments*, in a book of the same name in 1857. 'Things on earth are copies of things in heaven.'[84] In asserting this, he drew on the writings of John Keble and John Ruskin as well as Coleridge. He might equally well have quoted the Tractarian poet Isaac Williams. For, as the literary scholar Kirstie Blair has shown, the writings of both Ruskin and Williams share a similar assumption: both, she writes, 'fundamentally uphold the view that poetry is architectural just as architecture is poetical'.[85] In this they spoke for a whole generation—for the generation of the 1830s and 1840s, who came to redefine the nature of church architecture, to equate buildings with texts, and to build or rebuild their churches as a result.

Moreover, the effects were not confined to architecture alone. A wider search for symbolism, and a growing sense of the communicative power of the material world, also encouraged changes to church furnishings and to the whole environment of church life. Hence the fact that churches began to acquire candles, vestments, frescoes, embroidery, and much more besides.[86] 'There is not a single article of Church furniture', wrote one enthusiast, 'which does not teach its special lesson; which is not a sign of some deep, full, abiding truth;—which is not a "messenger".'[87] 'One of the great beauties of ancient embroidery', wrote the architect Augustus Pugin, 'was its appropriate design; each flower, each leaf, each device had a significant meaning.'[88]

Just like the battles over buildings, this was, naturally enough, a highly contested issue. There were attacks on the vicar of St Peter's in Plymouth just because he introduced cloth purses for the collection of the offertory which were considered danger-ously popish.[89] Even the introduction of flowers into churches—a development of the 1840s and 1850s—was not uncontroversial, for their symbolism, especially when they were arranged into a cruciform shape, was definitely suspect.[90] But slowly, even this innovation—just like the changes in architecture and a growing enthusiasm for vestments and fancy furnishings—came to be embraced by many Evangelicals. 'Some of the most "orthodox" churches, which never knew a floral device or blazoned a cross on their walls, had this year caught the contagion,' wrote the Rev. C. Maurice Davies in 1875:

> I saw one such,—a proprietary chapel near Grosvenor square—
> where a dear Conservative old parish clerk was moaning and groan-
> ing like Mrs Gummidge herself because a young lady brought the
> sacred emblem wrought in green and camellias by her fairy fingers,
> and the minister was putting it up with his own reverend hands.
> To his bewildered mind it was a closing-in of a dispensation.

'Whether we like it or not,' concluded Davies, 'there is a decided movement in favour of aestheticism and symbolism.'[91] The effect continued to appal a diminishing minority. It's hard, too, not to wonder whether it was always entirely successful. I for one would have liked to have been present at St Paul's Hammersmith on Christmas Day 1874, which was marked—Davies tells us—by a cross of white feathers on the pulpit and texts on the windows made out of tapioca.[92] But the truth was that for all denomin-ations and almost every church the old ways of building and the old assumptions about buildings had been overturned in favour of a new dispensation.[93]

In that way, the Ecclesiologists and the Gothic Revival they hoped to effect were both symptoms rather than the cause of changing ideas about architecture. It was because people sought symbolism that that they chose a style—whether Gothic or classical—that was believed, for a variety of different reasons, to be symbolic. Far from creating this attitude, the Ecclesiologists, the Tractarians, and the others were simply very successful—and vociferous—in articulating it. Naturally enough, not everyone agreed. But even those who rejected such claims were forced to frame their arguments within the terms of the textual turn. In a generation, then, the old auditory church had been replaced by a visual church: a place not designed solely for preaching, not characterized by 'plainness', but also intended to communicate in and of itself; to be seen and to be read just like a text.

Churches were, in other words, no longer the passive receptacles of worship; they had become both the medium and the message in their own right. Opponents of this transformation, who included the Evangelical Anglican William Peace, expressed horror that 'the eye, as well as the ear' was becoming an organ of faith.[94] The Methodist preacher James Caughey agreed, fearing a future 'when the *eye* will be more consulted than the *ear*, when *pulpit effectiveness* must give way to *architectural appearances*'. 'The time may come,' he warned, 'when *vagaries* in church architecture will be neither few nor far between' and *'the twenty-five minutes' sermon'* would replace the good hour or more of exhortation he was used to.[95] Writing in 1853, he was already too late. The revolution in church architecture had already begun—and, as we shall see in Chapter 2, it did not just stop with an emphasis on the eye. Churches in the nineteenth century were indeed intended to be seen in different ways, but they were not only intended to be seen. They were now meant to reshape the whole body and soul of the worshipper.

2

Feeling

He has reflected little on his own constitution who does not know that, as the mind affects the body, so the body affects the mind.

Charles Harbin, *The Grounds and Duty of Praise: a sermon* (Salisbury, 1834), p. 18

If it has been ordained that the senses shall be the channels of a large part of our perceptions, why should we not make them monitors of heavenly truth, instead of leaving them avenues to be occupied exclusively by things mischievous, things secular, or things indifferent.

W. E. Gladstone, *Church Principles Considered in Their Results* (London, 1840), p. 337

On 22 July 1845 the clergyman and controversialist William Gresley preached a sermon at the consecration of St Mark's church in Great Wyrley, south Staffordshire. Small, unostentatious, designed by a little-known local architect—Thomas Johnson of Lichfield—St Mark's rates only four short sentences in Nikolaus Pevsner's guide to the architecture of the county.[1] The parish website is no more forthcoming, with the section on the church building simply observing that 'St. Mark's is a Victorian church with a sound system and induction loop. Toilets are available in the adjacent Church Hall.'[2] Yet for Gresley, this small structure embodied something very important. 'What was

Fig. 8. St Mark's Great Wyrley (1859)

yesterday but a heap of stones', he preached, 'is now God's House—separated from common uses—hallowed—consecrated to Him for ever.' More than this, for Gresley, it exemplified the four key principles of ecclesiastical architecture.

One of these was the point outlined in Chapter 1: everything about the building, he argued, was intended to teach; the church, in this sense, had become a sort of text. 'Inscribed on the walls', Gresley observed, 'is God's handwriting ... Thus the very walls speak the language of inspiration.' The windows, too, were intended to instruct, with the triple lancets speaking of Trinity and Unity. The altar, he went on, 'brings to our mind the mystical Union with Christ and with each other'. This dissolution of building into text; this assumption that architecture was both

Fig. 9. St Mark's Great Wyrley (1859)

medium and message: this was, as we've seen, one of the biggest
changes to people's understanding of church buildings in the
early nineteenth century.

But Gresley did not stop at that; there were three other
themes that he developed. He argued—secondly—that as God
is eternal, 'His House should bear some impress of *durability*.' He
also argued—thirdly—that 'the very structure of God's house
should be *genuine and real*—nothing should appear what it is not'.
Both of these were also important points—and echoed the sorts
of arguments made by the Ecclesiologists and Tractarians, by
Pugin and Ruskin, and by advocates for the Gothic Revival more
generally. Both these themes have been explored very fully by
other studies of this subject; and we will return to them later in
this book.

The current chapter, however, will concentrate on William Gresley's fourth point, which he made, I'm afraid, rather lengthily: 'The House of God,' he declared:

> ought to be a building *distinct in character* from all others—distinct from our private dwelling houses—and our buildings of public resort—our school-rooms, our theatres, our lecture-rooms. It should at once convey the impression to him who enters it that he is on holy ground. His conscience should be impressed with reverence—an involuntary awe should fall upon his mind. He should feel that worldly, frivolous, or wicked thoughts are altogether inconsistent with the place.[3]

Gresley was famously prolix, publishing furiously throughout his long and disputatious life. But the point he made here is important—and worth exploring a little further. For Gresley, it's clear, a church was not just any old building, nor just a building that taught the mind, or sought to convey complex theology. It was a particular sort of building, one that shaped the emotions, addressed the senses; one that had a particular sort of effect. It was meant to move as well as to teach.

This is an important insight—and it's important that it was William Gresley who captured it at the consecration of this otherwise rather unimportant building. Gresley was a Tractarian—so again, we see the importance of buildings beyond the circle of the Cambridge Camden Society. Indeed, he became a member of the Ecclesiological Society only in 1846—a year *after* he preached this sermon.[4] More interesting still, as the historian Simon Skinner points out, although Gresley was a 'pugnacious champion of the Tractarian movement', he 'never belonged to its extreme wing. He remained unsympathetic to Roman Catholicism as well as to later ritualist developments.'[5] In other words, what Gresley offered here was not the analysis of an extremist or the views of just another Ecclesiologist. In fact, his insight—that a church was a sort of machine for moulding people's emotions—became ubiquitous and enormously significant to the Victorians as a whole.

In Chapter 1 we explored the ways in which the 1830s and 1840s witnessed a textual turn in architecture, one that transformed church buildings into a medium of theology. But this was not the only change that occurred in that crucial, early Victorian generation. In this chapter, we will uncover another—perhaps even more important—development that happened at the same time, and was intimately and intricately bound up with this textual turn. We will see that the first few decades of Victoria's reign also saw the evolution of a new idea of affective architecture: architecture that shaped the emotions by touching the senses. To do that, we will tease out the set of assumptions that undergirded Gresley's words—and which helped to shape the church he spoke in. We will look at the technologies that made this possible and which helped to remake the Victorian church, turning it into a thoroughly modern engine of emotions, intended to touch the heart and soul as well as inform the mind. And I will suggest some ways in which I think these changes helped to shape people's experience of churchgoing.

It goes without saying, of course, that this change—like the others we have explored—was controversial. William Gresley may not have been an extremist or a ritualist or have been tempted to dabble in Roman Catholicism. He may, as Skinner puts it, have offered little more than 'standard restatements of the Anglican *via media*', the 'middle way' between Catholic Rome and Calvinist Geneva. But he was considered highly suspect by more Evangelical members of the Church of England—and would later draw the ire of the vociferous, disputatious, and energetic Brighton Protestant Defence Committee (every bit as much fun as they sound), who feared that he was just one of many 'going out of the light of Protestant Truth into the darkness of Papal falsehood'.[6]

In particular, the notion that churches should move worshippers, that buildings should themselves shape spiritual experience, marked a radical departure from the Protestant architecture of the recent past. As we have already seen, the late eighteenth-century Church—Anglican, Nonconformist, and even Roman Catholic—had radically rejected the idea of religious symbolism in church design. One of the key changes of the 1830s was the rediscovery—and then the overwhelming triumph—of architecture's communicative function. As we have also noted, this was deeply troubling for many Nonconformists and Anglican Evangelicals, who saw the rise of architectural symbolism—the textual turn in church building—as recrudescence of popery.

The architecture of affect proposed by people like Gresley was, if anything, still more alarming to many pious Protestants. The point was this, that for them architecture was potentially a snare and a delusion—a distraction from the worship and the Word of God. The whitewashed walls, the plain, uncoloured glass in the windows, the absence of ornament: this was not because architecture was unimportant to eighteenth-century Protestants; rather, it was because they feared it could become all too important. Old ideas about idolatry and superstition dating back to the Reformation, if not before, were deep-rooted and readily reanimated. More than this, as John Harvey has shown in his study of eighteenth-century Welsh chapels, this deliberately spare, unsymbolic, aniconic approach to church design emphasized two other principles of Protestant worship.

In the first place, it drew attention to the gathered community of worshippers. 'Against the backdrop of the meeting-room's naked simplicity,' Harvey observes, 'the congregation assumed a visual prominence greater than its Roman Catholic counterparts, lost amid the embellishments and grandeur of a church. The unobtrusiveness of chapel "architecture" in this way realized the new covenant's high views of the worshipping community.'

Secondly, as Harvey goes on to observe, this approach was in some respects an attempt to convey a particular idea of the Divinity: a God that was spirit; an invisible, unrepresentable deity. The interior of a late eighteenth-century chapel, he concludes, 'drew no attention to itself, comprising furnishings, forms and materials that were only too familiar to the worshippers' everyday experience and ordinary habit. In this respect, the context of worship was effectively transparent.' An invisible God was seen, if he was seen at all, in the faces of the worshippers, or in the world outside—visible through clear glass, rather than being shut out by stained glass or painted windows.[7]

This was a notion revived by opponents of the change we're exploring: people like William Peace, an outraged Protestant who wrote in 1859 to argue that architectural embellishment was in fact a literally satanic ploy. Sounding as much like a seventeenth-century iconoclast as a resident of Victorian Bognor Regis, he played off traditional Puritan fears. 'It has been, and is', he expostulated in a letter to the Bishop of Oxford:

> the most mischievous engine of which the arch-enemy of truth has made use; the pretext of placing before the worshippers allurements, or aids to devotion, is but a snare to entrap the unwary, and to draw

him from spiritual devotion to sensuous adoration. The preacher may preach pure religion, but the idol will teach idolatry. Artistic, ceremonial, musical performances, objective instruction, are very obnoxious to that pure religion which is the fruit of the Spirit.[8]

Against devil-made materialism, Peace offered a God-given Spirit; against idolatry, the Word of God; against colour and music and 'sensuous adoration', he offered a transparent, spiritual worship.

As the anthropologist David Morgan has argued, this attitude—this attempt to make the church transparent—also had a practical, even liturgical function, with church builders seeking to downplay architecture in order to play up the importance of words—and, especially, of both the Bible and biblically inspired preaching. This was a process not of just iconoclasm, or philistinism, but also—perhaps chiefly—of what Morgan calls 'sublation': the deliberate downplaying of one sense (in this case, sight), in order to emphasize another (in this case, hearing), thus allowing worshippers to 'park their bodies and heighten hearing, to make ears of the whole body as it were'.[9]

Such a process of sublation was not unique to the late eighteenth century, of course. As Victoria George has argued in *Whitewash and the New Aesthetic of the Protestant Reformation*—a book so impressive that it manages to make whitewash interesting—this was a legacy of the Reformation itself, and of the attempts of Reformers to purify churches. It also rested on a sharp analytical distinction drawn by Protestants themselves between a reformed religion—a religion of the word—and the excesses of Roman Catholic worship.[10] As Christopher Wren put it in 1708: 'The Romanists, indeed, may build larger Churches, it is enough if they hear the Murmur of the Mass, and see the Elevation of the Host, but ours are to be fitted for Auditories.'[11] Over a hundred years later, on a visit to Italy, the young Thomas Babington Macaulay—the liberal son of an Evangelical father—made exactly the same point, expressing horror at the Mass, and a 'religion which furnishes its votaries with a great deal to see and great deal to smell but nothing intelligible to hear'. He was, he said, astounded to find 'so many reasonable beings come together to see a man bow, drink, bow again, wipe a cup, wrap up a napkin, spread his arms and gesticulate with his hands; and to hear a low muttering which they could not understand interrupted by the occasional jingling of a bell'.[12] This predominantly visual liturgy—in which the only sounds were 'muttering' or the 'jingling of a bell'—was everything against which Protestants traditionally defined themselves. Their churches, as a result, were to privilege hearing over seeing; the sermon over any formal liturgy; whitewashed walls and clear-glazed windows over ornament, colour, and—as we saw in Chapter 1—all this over any form of sacred symbolism.

It was a set of such deeply ingrained assumptions they retained a degree of power throughout the century—at least for some.[13] Certainly, the response of a vocal minority of Unitarians to the gorgeous stained-glass windows in Manchester College chapel in Oxford as late as the 1890s suggests the continuation of this long-standing tradition. The pseudonymous 'Jerubbaal', taking the name given to Gideon after his destruction of Baal's altar,[14] for instance, was so horrified at the introduction of stained glass that he not only wrote to the Unitarian journal, *The Inquirer*, but then published his lengthy letter as a pamphlet. He condemned coloured glass on principle, writing, 'I, for one, cannot see why we should have the light of heaven shut out by the devices of the colourist.' He also disliked the representation of non-biblical figures: 'idle women shuffling along with fantastic robes and gaudy wraps of impossible feathers, doing nothing but make eyes at those who court them'.[15] The combination of a quite strikingly gendered critique and the belief that stained glass shut out the light of heaven or of reason was trotted out repeatedly throughout the Victorian era.

This long-standing tradition also provides the context for the great debates of the 1830s and 1840s that came to reshape the very nature of the Victorian church, and especially the emotional and sensory experience of the church. Once again, our old friend Francis Close—curate of Cheltenham and then dean of Carlisle—provides a good entrée into the thought of mainstream Evangelical Anglicans. He was not a Calvinist, nor an iconoclast, but rather had come under the sway of the hugely influential Evangelical thinker Charles Simeon whilst a student in Cambridge. Nor was Close immune to the appeal of church architecture—and its effect on worshippers. Indeed, that was precisely the point of his interventions.

In a marvellously haughty address of 1839—a *Sermon, Addressed to the Chartists of Cheltenham* (a sermon, it must be said, only equalled for its condescension by its twin, *A Sermon, Addressed to the Female Chartists of Cheltenham*)[16]—Close made plain his belief that a church building was a holy place. 'I entreat you to pause before you pollute the sanctuary of the Lord of Hosts, and convert the church of God into a political engine,' he exhorted the visiting radicals. But the church was holy for Close because of what happened in it—and especially what was heard in it—and not because of what it was, much less because of how it was built or what it looked like. 'I trust', he concluded, 'that the sweet sounds of divine service, perhaps new to the ears of some of them, may have sunk into their hearts, and that they have found a beauty in the worship of the sanctuary, which they have not thought of before.'[17]

This was a familiar call—one repeated in sermons at the opening of new Evangelical churches from the eighteenth century onwards—and one that reflected the fact that like most other Evangelical and even some Broad Church Anglicans, Close was all too aware of both the appeal and hence the dangers of more elaborate church buildings. In his *The 'Restoration of Churches' Is the Restoration of Popery*—a sermon delivered on the significant date of 5 November, a day hallowed for Protestants by memories of both the Gunpowder Plot of 1605 and the Glorious Revolution of 1688—we can see the culmination of this particular view of church buildings. Indeed, his attack on medieval and neo-medieval church architecture can stand in for dozens—scores—of other, similar self-consciously Protestant criticisms:

> What were these...churches built for? The orgies of superstition! For long processions of priests repeating dirges and the de profundis, and Stabat Maters...for the solemnization of masses, and elevations of the Host: where blind priests might perform superstitious idolatrous services to and for the dead in an unknown tongue; such Churches are palpably unfit for all the circumstances of modern worship. We want light physical and spiritual—we want to see to read—and that the people may hear the Gospel—in a word, we want Protestant Churches, not Popish Mass-houses![18]

Here again, then, we see a conflation of Roman Catholicism with a religion not just of idolatry, but also—more specifically—of darkness, aural unintelligibility, unreason, and an absence of God's Word. Protestantism—and the architecture of Protestantism—is, by contrast, characterized by light, by true perception, by aural acuity, by reading, and by preaching.

So far, so familiar. But Close's other point is also worth noting: for his objection to these 'orgies of superstition' was not simply on denominational grounds. Just like the Welsh Nonconformists that John Harvey studied, there was a profound theological and a deep emotional content to this comment. Close—and his co-religionists—feared the emotional appeal and the sensuousness of a religion that did not privilege hearing over the other senses. They feared what Close called 'a religion of sensation' and they feared it because, in Close's words: 'A religion of sensation is essentially idolatrous, and remote from the true worship of that God who is a Spirit, and will be worshipped in spirit and in truth.'[19]

It was precisely this fear of sensation that Tractarians like William Gresley and Ecclesiologists like John Mason Neale hoped to overturn. And, indeed, it wasn't just those who were obviously *parti pris* who began to make this argument in the 1830s and 1840s. Take William Christmas, for instance, editor of the old High Church journals the *Churchman* and the *Church of England Quarterly Review*, and a notoriously disastrous librarian of London's Sion College, where he was condemned for wasting money on 'very expensive foreign works on numismatics' and on 'some questionable specimens of French novels'.[20] Christmas was never a member of the Cambridge Camden Society nor associated with the Oxford Movement. Yet, here he is in 1845 complaining about the churches of the Church of England: 'All that makes worship sensuous without making it sensual, has disappeared; the link that bound, as it were, the soul and body in one act of devotion is snapped, and an attempt made to establish a purely spiritual worship.'[21] And he was, of course, in good company in making this assertion. It was not only the Evangelicals of the late eighteenth century—with their religion of the heart and ecstatic conversion experiences—who had rediscovered the importance of emotion and of sensation in Christian life. Nor just High Churchmen who saw the importance of an architecture of affect. After all, that far from orthodox writer John Ruskin voiced similar ideas in his essay on the *Poetry of Architecture*. 'Architecture', he wrote, 'is, or ought to be, a science of feeling more than of rule, a ministry to the mind more than the eye.'[22]

Moreover, as the historian John Toews has recently noted, there was a broader, pan-European movement of religious thinkers who similarly sought to articulate the need for a more vital, emotional, sensual sort of religion. It was an ideal found in the German theologian Friedrich Schleiermacher's definition of religion as the unmediated 'intuition and feeling' of the 'infinite nature of totality,' a 'childlike' encounter with the absolute. It was a notion rather differently articulated by the French philosopher François-René de Chateaubriand, who—in Toews's words— 'rediscovered the power of the doctrines, rituals, institutions, and language of Christianity in the context of the emotional, aesthetic and cognitive needs of a finite, temporally and naturally individuated, human subject'.[23]

Analogous—though, it must be said, somewhat less sophisticated— views can also be found in the numerous novels written by Tractarians and Ecclesiologists in the 1840s; and they are worth attending to, because, as their sternest critic, the perennially disgruntled Evangelical vicar of Yarnton, Peter Maurice, put it, 'nothing in the whole movement... tended so much to the poisoning of the minds of the young' as its novels—especially those of Francis Paget, a Tractarian clergyman and for many years chaplain to the bishop of Bath and Wells.[24] So what did Paget say? And what of the others?

What of John Mason Neale, for example, who combined his work as a leading Ecclesiologist and hymnodist with the occasional burst of novel writing?

The critical point to make is that these novels were often as much about buildings as they were about people or, for that matter, about plots. Neale's *Ayton Priory, or the Restored Monastery* was preoccupied with architecture. Paget's publications included *Milford Malvoisin: or pews and pewholders* and *St Antholin's; or churches old and new.*[25] Indeed, this latter book is a particularly remarkable testament to just how important buildings were because of their emotional effect. Paget's point was clear: look properly at a medieval church, he wrote, and:

> Something there will be in the fretted roof above; some name on the pavement beneath his feet ... some form of an arch, or aisle, or screen, or canopy ... some circumstance connected with font or altar ... some effect of light and shade; some feature of beauty or desolation, which will take the thoughtful Christian back to better times, transport him from the visible to the invisible world, and bring him, as it were, into closer communion with those whom we are continually tempted to forget.[26]

John Mason Neale's evocation of the emotional impact of ecclesiastical art is even more remarkable, perhaps especially because it shines out of a novel that few can ever have read with pleasure. As the author of fiction, Neale lacked much: he lacked pace, plot, style, or any real interest in plausible characterization. But his love for buildings—for the richness of their art and architecture, for their affective appeal—can, nevertheless, at times, very suddenly make his rotten novels into a romance; a love story between a man and a church:

> Colonel Abberley seemed lost in astonishment, and could hardly find words to express his admiration ... There were the eastern window of

five lights, and the three side windows of three, all glowing in stained glass that would not have disgraced an earlier age; there was a plain altar-slab, supported on three simple shafts; the ascent to the altar, seeming to defend itself from profane feet by its own majesty, and standing in no need of rails; the floor of the chancel was laid down with encaustick tiles, inscribed with flower work, hereldick [sic] devices, badges, and foliated circles; those beyond the altar steps were richer and represented the Holy Lamb, the Thirsty Hart, the instruments of Crucifixion, and the like. Before the steps stood an oaken praying-desk, flanked with two poppy heads, and lined with red velvet, on which the letters IHS [Jesus] were worked in gold thread. The roof was an imitation of those magnificent specimens of woodwork which have made Suffolk famous.[27]

Small wonder that Colonel Abberley is so moved by this scene—a scene, as Neale puts it, 'both morally and physically, beautiful'—that he gives his lands to found a new monastery in their place.[28]

This belief that the emotional, sensory—indeed, sensual—qualities of the church had an important role to play in shaping people's religious lives, in forming them as Christians, can also be found in the future prime minister William Gladstone's early writings, quoted at the start of the chapter. 'The natural entry of grace into the soul of man is through the affections,' he wrote in 1840; 'it is rationalistic to trust exclusively to teaching as an instrument of faith.' 'We cannot fail to see the religious importance of having some avenues to the affections otherwise than through argumentative methods,' he concluded.[29] Such a sensibility can be found, too, in the writings of campaigning parish priests like Thomas Chamberlain, who asserted in 1856 that God has always used 'beauty of colour and form to ravish the eye' and thus convert the soul.[30]

This view also plays a neglected part in the writings of the influential architect Augustus Pugin, for his defence of the Gothic

Fig. 10. Leeds Parish Church

was not, as some have suggested, purely functionalist or simply
stylistic. It was also, very clearly, emotive. 'In the modern world,'
Pugin wrote in his essay on the *Present State of Ecclesiastical
Architecture* in 1843, 'where almost every spot...is poisoned with
heresy, infidelity, and licentiousness!...The only recourse left...
is to create an ecclesiastical atmosphere, a green spot in the
desert, where both the architecture and fittings of the edifice
breathe the revered spirit of the ancient days.'[31]

And this notion that the church building should inspire a
particular economy of emotion—should be set apart from the
emotional landscape of the outside world—was likewise not
confined to Tractarians, Ecclesiologists, or polemicists like
Pugin, who influenced both. It can also be found, for example
(and there are lots of examples), in the official guide to the newly
built **Leeds Parish Church**, consecrated in 1841—that is, just
before the *Ecclesiologist* was first published:

On entering the church, through the deeply recessed North doorway...its inner porch forming a rich canopied arch, terminated with an old statue of St Peter, and having the angels buttressed and pinnacled...its lofty and, in part, groined roof, supported on an arcade of eight pillars and arches on each side, the former beautifully clustered, the latter elegantly pointed...its ample dimensions in length and breadth, combining solidity and strength with the most airy lightness; above all, its developement [sic], amid the solemn light transmitted through its many and richly coloured windows, of the great mysteries of our faith...are well calculated to impress the mind with that reverential awe which should ever accompany sinful man as he enters the Temple of the Omnipotent and Holy God.[32]

Written by William Henry Teale, a traditional High Church clergyman and translator of Luther's Augsburg Confession (a book hardly likely to appeal to either Ecclesiologists or Tractarians), this description shows just how widespread the emphasis on the emotional effect of a church actually was.

Teale's words are worth exploring a little further, for they contain within them a synopsis or distillation of almost all the themes we've been exploring so far. There's something here about history—the 'Old statue of St Peter', the Gothic vaults, and so on. We will explore that a little further in Chapter 4. There's much here, too, about the emotion—the feelings of reverence and awe—that a church should inspire. But above, all, it's worth emphasizing the sensory overload that he described: the pillars and arches; the vaults and pinnacles; the 'many and richly coloured windows'. This is not just the binary opposite of the plain, whitewashed, clear-glazed, auditory church of the eighteenth century; it's a completely different experience—and intended to be so. The church, in this understanding, forces the worshipper to encounter the divine not by removing distractions, but by overwhelming every sense.

Hence the extravagant ornamentation of Leeds Parish Church. Hence the stained-glass windows; not intended, as critics suggested, to shut out light—indeed, Victorian architects were always clear that stained glass was infinitely preferable to painted precisely because the stained glass was translucent and the painted glass opaque—but, rather, meant to transform light, to make it jewel-like, colourful, and iridescent: to change how the church was seen, how it was experienced. Hence all the new materials and all the colours that came to fill the churches of Victorian Britain. 'Architects, Gothic, Italian, "Victorian"—sacred and profane,' wrote the great High Church patron and critic, Alexander Beresford Hope a few years later, 'are all vying with each other who can produce most red brick, and yellow brick, and black brick, most granite, serpentine, and encaustic tiles all over their buildings.'[33] He should know—for he commissioned **All Saints Margaret Street** in London: a building that exemplifies all these trends; an overwhelming sensory experience, even without the ritualism with which it became synonymous. Hence, too, another building by All Saints' architect William Butterfield: Keble College chapel in Oxford; an edifice in which the outside world is effectively shut out, and the worshipper or visitor confronted by a dizzying array of colours, materials, patterns, pictures, themes; 'a Te Deum, strictly ordered but manifestly triumphant'.[34]

It was not just in new churches and chapels that this change was made manifest. All across the country, church 'restoration' involved the removal of the old sensory dispensation and its replacement by the new. Box pews and galleries were removed; whitewash and plaster scraped away. The archdeacons of Chichester—the Broad Church Julius Hare and the Tractarian

Henry Manning—were each equally clear and both spoke for many in arguing for this change. 'Pews'. declared Manning, 'are a strong abuse, a triumphant usurpation.'[35] Whitewash, observed Hare, was 'a white shroud in which the limbs of our churches have been wrapped up'; a 'white sheet in which they have been constrained to do penance'.[36] It was such a comprehensive process that scarcely a church escaped. By 1870 a third of all churches had been effectively rebuilt.[37] As the architectural historian Matthew Hyde put it a couple of years ago, 'Now that the whitewash has gone, we can only imagine the way these churches shone like beacons in the landscape.'[38] Instead of an architecture of sublation, here was a vivid, colourful architecture of affect.

When such profound change proved impossible, many churches filled the gap with flowers and embroidery and other colourful material. In the mid-1860s, the architect E. W. Godwin wrote of his hope that the 'dull cold walls of our churches may...be warmed into life and loveliness again by pictured cloths of tapestry or appliqué work, panels painted with the effigies of patron saints and angels, and banners and pennons all ablaze with the heraldry of Christian life'.[39] In many churches, in many places, it is clear, congregations and clergy did just that; as, for example, in the Norfolk village of East Dereham. Here the diaries of the vicar, Benjamin Armstrong, show how a four decade-long process of gradual accumulation and almost sedimentary change transformed his church in the years after 1850. First with flags and banners, then with a surpliced choir, then with a cross, flowers, and candlesticks on the altar, and finally in 1885 with a wholesale restoration: 'the galleries having been removed and the substitution of a wagon roof for the old ceiling makes it look a different building', he recorded with gratitude in December 1885.[40] It was just one of many.

This change was obviously of deep visual significance. Indeed, it reflected the new emphasis on the eye as an organ of faith, and followed the turn against the purely auditory church. 'Evidence of the eye is superior to that of the ear,' asserted the chemist George Field in 1841, and churches seem to have followed this direction.[41] Certainly, recent arguments that 'a conscious shifting' of emphasis 'from teaching by ear to teaching by eye' dated from the 1860s do not make much sense of developments which in fact can be traced back at least thirty years before.[42]

It was a change emphasized by the other ways in which the church fabric was being reformed. The removal of box pews, for instance, made a major contribution to this, turning all eyes to the east; as did the removal of galleries.[43] Writing to the churchwardens of St Lawrence in Reading in 1846, the bishop of Oxford, Samuel Wilberforce, articulated this view quite clearly. 'No architect ought at the present time to have given in a plan turning so large a proportion of the sittings westwards,' he observed. The pews were too high and too wide, he went on, and the proposal for galleries 'unworthy' of a church. The whole, he concluded, was 'quite at variance with ecclesiastical architecture'.[44] Architects like E. B. Lamb struggled hard to produce modified neo-medieval plans, in which the roof structure minimized the need for obstructive columns, so that in churches like St Margaret's Leiston in Suffolk (1853–4) nearly 98 per cent of the seats had a clear view of the east end.[45] When one compares this—say—with Francis Close's parish church of Cheltenham, in which many pews were actually situated *behind* the preacher, the change is revolutionary—and the fact that Lamb predominantly worked for Low Church and Evangelical clients also hints at how wide-spread this move towards a more visual religious culture proved to be.[46]

But these changes were not confined to the realm of sight. There were acoustic effects too. Removing layers of whitewash and—especially—removing plaster; removing the galleries and removing the comfortable box pews, with all their cushions, curtains, and other fabrics; exposing stone walls and installing brick, and mar-ble, and encaustic tiles: all this profoundly altered the soundscape of the Victorian church. The eighteenth-century auditory church had been perfectly designed for preaching. As Richard Cullen Rath has shown, the hard, low, often barrel-shaped plaster ceil-ings bounced any sound straight back. The high pulpit with its sounding board also 'fattened' the preacher's voice by reflecting it back outwards. The galleries and the pews muffled resonance, ensuring that every sound was distinct. By stripping all this away, the Victorians created an echoing, reverberant space, what the twentieth-century writer Hope Bagnell would come to call 'the acoustics of the cave'.[47]

This may not have been the intention. There were those, like the architect William Bardwell, who argued for a stripping back to stone on auditory as well as aesthetic grounds, claiming 'that linings of every description are injurious to sound'.[48] But, in truth, the study of architectural acoustics was so undeveloped until the twentieth century that few understood what they were doing and still fewer had any conception of how they might do it differ-ently.[49] This reverberant acoustic was also wildly different from the soundscape of the medieval Church for, as historians have noted, the great minsters of the Middle Ages were not echoey spaces, but rather an environment in which 'the choir was insulated with tapestries, drapes, banners, and rugs, all of which softened the reverberations'.[50] Instead, this general move meant an adventitious return to the association between echoing space and religious feeling that stretched all the way back to the temple of Zeus in Olympia, constructed around 460 BC.[51]

More important than this aural atavism was the fact that the resurgence of reverberance also radically altered what was now acoustically possible and aurally effective within a church. It could make preaching more difficult. Certainly, the preacher would have to cope with a rather less helpful environment for his (and it was always his) voice. The great Methodist preacher James Caughey was clear: the changes being made to Wesleyan chapels as they became more like churches were ruinous. 'Whatever advantages they might afford to *oratories*, they are the bane of oratory.' High ceilings, Gothic architecture, 'sloped, or concave, or arched ceilings': all this served to 'weaken', 'dishearten', and 'tax' a preacher.[52]

Musically, too, these highly reverberant spaces were deeply problematic. Again, as experts on acoustics have observed, 'most forms of music and vocalization do not work effectively in spaces with so much reverberation'. Within the Western musical tradition, the sole exception they identify is Gregorian chant, which was perfectly acclimatized to such echoey edifices. It may only be a coincidence, but it is noteworthy nevertheless that amongst the sidelights of both Tractarian and Ecclesiological church reform was the revival of precisely that: the close harmonies of monastic chanting. Indeed, by 1875, it was observed that one in five London parishes were using Gregorian chant at Sunday service.[53] Inadvertently or not, by reshaping the acoustic conditions of the church, they had created the ideal environment for this. They had also produced a soundscape in which the old

Western gallery tradition of mixed singers and instrumentalists could not shine; instead, a new breed of hymns and hymnbooks—most notably *Hymns Ancient and Modern*; a new sort of uniformed choir, placed in the east end, at the acoustic heart of this reverberant church; and new sort of organ with the 'brasher, more strident style of voicing' identified by the historian Nicholas Thistlethwaite: all this came to dominate church music.[54]

These visual and aural changes were accompanied and reinforced by what we can only call other reforms of the congregation's bodily discipline. These echoey spaces coped poorly with noise—whether that be people talking, walking, or whispering. The reverberations threatened to pick it all up. Churchmen had always complained about poor behaviour—muttering, giggling, yawning—but this new environment placed a still greater premium on silence.[55] As Mark M. Smith has noted in his aural history of antebellum America, this period was characterized by a new attentiveness to 'quietude' in church. 'The gentleman at Church', reported New York's *Colored American* in 1838:

> comes in good season, so as neither to interrupt the pastor or the congregation by a late arrival...Opens and shuts the door gently, and walks lightly...and gets his seat quietly...Does not whisper or laugh...does not rush out of the church like a trampling horse, the moment the benediction is pronounced, but retires slowly, in a noiseless, quiet manner.[56]

The removal of box pews and galleries contributed to this process. The banging of pew doors could be, as one campaigner observed, 'a constant source of noise'.[57] More significantly still, open benches helped police behaviour by exposing the noisy, naughty, and refractory to the rest of the church community.[58] In the novelist Charlotte M. Yonge's words, 'When all sat on forms without the shade of pews, example taught a lesson of reverent attitude to the congregation, who felt obliged to lay aside any bad habits which might have grown up out of sight.'[59] No longer, too, would galleries exist to be 'the refuge of the petty aristocracy in towns, and of the disorderly in villages'.[60] As the wonderfully terrible High Church magazine, the *Old Church Porch*, put it in 1854, the result could be transformative. Where there 'used to be sad scenes of irreverence, jesting and laughing—if not something worse, there is now a solemn and beautiful silence'.[61]

As this suggests, the effect of these changes was not intended to produce an unconstrained emotional response. 'The object of building a church', declared James Skinner, vicar of that ritualist icon, St Barnabas Pimlico, was 'the encouragement of religious earnestness.'[62] Emotions were to be controlled and disciplined— just like the bodies of the congregation. As William Gresley observed at the consecration of St Mark's, Great Wyrley, there was nothing worse than 'to see men sitting in irreverent postures when they ought to kneel—gazing listlessly around, when their whole souls ought to be intent on God's worship'. The building— its sights and sounds, its furniture and its ornamentation—was intended to enforce the message that 'It is a very solemn thing to enter God's House...you should leave behind you all worldly, frivolous, and carnal thoughts, you should subdue the feelings of your soul to reverence and holy awe, and let your every look and gesture be composed accordingly.'[63] Indeed—in stark contrast to the attitudes of the eighteenth century, or for that matter today—a certain degree of discomfort in church was considered spiritually appropriate.[64] What the architect G. E. Street wrote off as 'The mere comfort of the worshipper' was now at most a second-order issue.[65]

This solid, silent, powerful architecture was also, naturally, gendered; as was the emotion it was intended to evoke. This was a masculine space, with a manly faith in its product. To argue this is, of course, to challenge two common assumptions of nineteenth-century church history: firstly, as the historian Callum Brown has argued, that religion was feminized in this period; secondly, as Gordon Westwood and others have suggested, that the High Church and ritualist traditions were often associated with an ambiguous, unmanly, esoteric sexuality. And it is worth noting that some contemporaries, too, made these accusations, with the ever-offensive dean of Chichester J. W. Burgon preaching against 'the solemn foppery, the effeminate passion for finery, the pitiful *millinery*' of High Churchmen in 1873.[66] Burgon, it is worth remembering, had form for this sort of thing. He was also author of the sermon, '*Inferior to us* God made *you*: and our inferiors to the end of time *you* will remain: an address to the women of Oxford.'[67]

What's more notable than this, however, is the language used by the proponents of architectural change within the Church. Take the Tractarian novelist Francis Paget, for example. In his novel of 1841, *St Antholin's*, it is the old, eighteenth-century understanding of church building and furnishing that is feminine. On his visitation to Tadbrook St Antholin, the archdeacon is horrified to see the private pew of the squire's wife, Mrs Clutterbuck. '"Pew!", exclaimed Dr Sharpe, "I thought it was her *bed*. Why it is all curtains and pillows... Churches are houses of prayer... not bedchambers.' But Mrs Clutterbuck's bad taste does not end there. Her essentially feminine and fundamentally unspiritual nature is revealed in her response to a design for a new church—a preaching house, not a house of prayer, prepared by the Nonconformist jobbing builder Mr Compo. 'This sounds a very delightful plan,' she observes, 'warm comfortable church ... snug easy pews ... really there will be every temptation to people to attend, if it be only for the luxury of the thing.' Her every word—warm, snug, easy, temptation, luxury, comfort—condemns her and condemns her church in Paget's mind.[68]

This gendering distinguished ecclesiastical from domestic space; indeed, the vulgarity of the feminine home contrasted with the purity and nobility of the church—even the ravaged nobility of a decaying church—is a tiresome trope in many a Tractarian novel.[69] The box pew was a particular target of this attitude—for it was a literally private space: bought and sold in many churches; the exclusive property of the pew holder.[70] At Ludlow, in 1860, a place could be rented for as much as £1 or as little as 5 shillings a year.[71] At smarter churches, like St Philip's Regent Street, a forty-four year lease cost £55 in 1875.[72] At Close's Christ Church Cheltenham, tickets were sold each Sunday, leading one critic to demand a seat in 'the dress circle' rather than the gallery.[73] The furnishings of these pews—with their cushions, curtains, water bottles, and the like—further established them as secular space, and space, moreover, that, like the home, was the province of female control.[74] 'My dear wife yesterday sent cushions and hassocks to Area Pew 63,' recorded one diarist in 1854, 'and today [we] felt more installed than previously.'[75]

There was no room for this in the increasingly public, increasingly masculine environment of the reformed Victorian church. And as the home became ever more understood as the domain of the private and feminine, so it became still more vital to define the church as distinctive and different and masculine. Whitewash, jeered the journalist James Martin in 1847, threatened to reduce 'chancel and nave into the same condition as a common par-lour'.[76] The use of plaster, he observed five years later, could produce a church 'ceiled like a drawing room'.[77] 'A seat,' he mocked two years after that, 'said to be the property of the chief owner of the land, is fitted up in the true parlour style; a suite of chairs such as would adorn an opera box, or a lady's boudoir.'[78] Quoting another frequent author on the subject—Rev. G. A. Poole—Martin concluded that 'It is impossible to see without regret "the splendour, the carpeting, and tapestry, the gilding and painting of the drawing-room brought into God's house".'[79] In that sense, then, far from witnessing a feminization of religion, architecturally speaking we see quite the reverse.

Moreover, this desire for architectural distinction—for a church to be and to feel definitely unlike other buildings, and especially unlike the secular, private, feminized home—had even more far-reaching effects. It prompted a campaign to separate the sexes, with an aisle dividing men from women.[80] At Hursley in Hampshire, for instance, John Keble not only insisted on open benches which were designed to facilitate and encourage prayer, but also distinguished them—with the men's pews, to the south, equipped with iron rods for holding their hats.[81] It led to liturgical change, too, with choirs started both to improve the service and to attract male singers. Although the bishop of Oxford, Samuel Wilberforce, worried that choirs could be vexatious, he nonetheless welcomed them because they were such 'a great help in getting hold of young men'.[82] As this suggests, Callum Brown is absolutely right to identify a contemporary fear that religion was being feminized in the nineteenth century. He is, however, quite wrong to assume that the threat of feminization went unremarked; indeed, it was strongly—and, in some places, successfully—resisted.

The Victorians very deliberately sought to combat any suggestion that religion was fit only for females. They used architecture to counteract any feminization. Their work was meant to make churches safe—and welcoming—for men.

These new ideas helped to transform church architecture more generally in the Victorian era. As I have already suggested, the argument that a church building should move the emotions, should transmit some sort of spirituality, should help to inculcate some experience of the divine, was highly controversial at the start of our period. It went against centuries of Protestant teaching and the more recent experience of the Church in the eighteenth century. Yet this new 'architecture of affect' nonetheless became the dominant understanding of church buildings for many Evangelical Anglicans and even for some Nonconformists in the Victorian era. What this reflected was precisely the transformation of ideas about architecture that we've explored in this chapter.

In the first place, the notion that architecture was emotive—and was meant to be emotive—gained almost universal acceptance. In the second place, the belief that the church was a distinctively different sort of building—and one that evoked emotions differently—this too gained a purchase that opponents found almost impossible to shake off.

> Have we not all of us at times experienced a solemn, holy sensation of devotion to a Being unseen, when entering a noble cathedral, from the street full of noise and hubbub? A voice whispers, 'This is the House of God!'—feelings that have slumbered for years awaken for a moment, tears almost stand in our eyes.[83]

Thus a self-styled 'Layman' in a pamphlet of 1858. That he could assume this as a universal experience showed how far and how fast the debate had come.

But was he right? In the last two chapters, I've suggested that the experience of churches was profoundly changed by two interrelated developments in the 1830s and 1840s: first a textual turn that reduced buildings to the status of a message; second the rise of an architecture of affect, which assumed that churches were—quite properly—engines of emotion. What about those who visited them? What about the place of church building within the landscape and—especially—the townscape? What about those who only saw the outside of a church and had no interest in its symbolic meaning or emotional effect? Those questions will be the subject of Chapter 3.

3

Visiting

In all parts of the land it is a goodly sight to see the house of God rising above the habitations of men, reminding us, even by its form, that we have higher and nobler aims set before us than any supplied by the cares and interest of this world.

Julius Hare, 'The Temple of God', in Henry Michell Wagner and Henry Samuel King, eds, *A Course of Sermons Preached in St Paul's Church, Brighton, during the Week of Its Consecration, on the Feast of St Luke, 1849* (Brighton, 1849), pp. 55–88, p. 62

And let us not only feed those who shall come and sit at our feet for instruction, but also go out into the highways of our parishes...playing the part not only of a Presbyter in the Church, but of an Evangelist or Missionary throughout the Parish.

William Walkinger, *A Sermon Preached at the Consecration of St John's Church, Lewes, 3rd June, 1840* (Lewes, 1840), p. 21

On 16 June 1889 the controversial Anglican priest Herbert Hensley Henson—a past Oxford don and a future bishop of Durham—presided over a temperance meeting in the grounds of his vicarage. It was Trinity Sunday; it was very hot; but he wore both his cassock and surplice nonetheless. Later on, when Henson had become a firm opponent of temperance reform, he would look back on this with some embarrassment. Even at the time, he recorded that 'The speakers uttered the most astonishing drivel: but it is better that they should utter it under my sanction than against me.' He estimated that 1,500 people had filled his garden and was sufficiently carried away by the event to promise that he too would not drink alcohol—except on doctor's orders—so long as he remained vicar of Barking. He left Barking a few years later.[1]

This temperance meeting on Trinity Sunday 1889 is, in many respects, an eminently forgettable affair: an unimportant incident in what Henson in his memoirs self-consciously called *An Unimportant Life*.[2] But, in truth, the details of this warm summer's afternoon are wonderfully revealing of Victorian religion. They emphasize the importance of moral crusades like temperance reform. They show established and Nonconformist churches working together in rather unexpected ways—for Henson estimated that the majority of his visitors that day were Dissenters. Henson's choice of clothing is equally telling, for the cassock and surplice were still controversial, the signs—for some—of a potentially extreme High Churchmanship. His own father, after all, was driven from the Church of England in part by parsons who insisted on wearing them; and there had been riots occasioned by their introduction into churches in other parts of London. Above all, though, it's worth focusing on *where* this meeting happened—for it matters, and it matters more than you might think, that it was in Henson's vicarage garden.

This chapter is about vicarages, and about gardens, churchyards, and graveyards, and about schools. It will consider what it was that clergymen like Henson thought these places were for, and it will seek to show, too, what laypeople—people like the 1,500 who processed through his garden—also thought about them. It will link this exploration of the material culture of parish life with the insights that we've been uncovering about ecclesiastical architecture. Over the last few chapters, we've seen that the beginning of the Victorian era was characterized by a profound change in how church buildings were understood and experienced. We have seen that a 'textual turn' helped to transform churches into vehicles of communication, turning buildings into books. We have gone on to observe that an interlinked process helped to transform churches into an 'architecture of affect', deliberately designed to move the emotions. Now, it's time to examine what the implications of these changes were for church visitors, for passers-by, and for the other buildings, places, and spaces associated with religious life in Victorian Britain.

In this chapter, therefore, we will see that this new emphasis on the didactic and emotive power of architecture changed parish life in multiple ways. It placed a new premium on the church building itself—and on the need to get people to engage with it, to come into it, to understand it, and to be moved by it. But this new understanding of architecture also shaped the treatment of other buildings—and other places. The result was a revolution in religious life, in liturgy, and in the everyday practice of faith. It was a change which sought to resacralize a landscape and—especially—a townscape, which many Victorians believed had become not just secular, but positively hostile to belief.

In his important study of what he calls *Religion in the Age of Decline*, the historian Simon Green has noted that 'church building became a means—perhaps indeed the most important means—through which organised religion responded to the physical movement of the population'.[3] He's quite right, of course; indeed, this whole book rests on the assumption that he's right. He's right, too, in his argument that religion in this period 'became something of a religion of the building'. But, as this chapter will go on to show, it was not just the church that was intended to combat the challenges of urbanization and wider social change. Other sorts of buildings were also erected and reconceived in similar ways. Moreover, precisely because churches had become reimagined as active messengers—as missionaries, in a sense, in their own right—their use as well as their construction became an important issue for clergy and committed laypeople alike.

Indeed, it is hardly an exaggeration to say that the Victorians were obsessed with how their churches were used: an obsession marked by recurrent campaigns against ritualism; an obsession that yielded parliamentary debates, royal commissions, and legislation intended to limit the liturgical excesses of Anglican incumbents.[4] Perhaps above all, it was an obsession that produced an extraordinarily rich and detailed range of data from all denominations as they compulsively enumerated the number of churches, schools, and mission halls erected; the number of people that each could seat; and the number of people who were actually sat within them.[5] That the nineteenth century saw churches counting buildings and people more extensively and intensively than ever before was, it's true, partly the product of wider social trends: the curious strength of positivism within British thought; the example of an ever more quantitative state apparatus, for example. But it also reflected the churches' own, home-grown anxieties about their ability to respond to a rising population living in increasingly urban environments. They counted because they cared: they feared that they did not have enough buildings; that their buildings were not good enough;

that they were not being used well enough; that they were not full enough.

Filling the church was a particular cause of concern. It was the fear that there simply weren't enough seats for an expanding population which initially provoked the extraordinary burst of church building which characterized the period. In the pamphlet of 1815 which inspired the Church of England's first nationwide campaign to erect new churches, the clergyman Richard Yates estimated that there were within eight miles of London alone approaching a million more people than the churches could accommodate.[6] The religious census of 1851 still more alarmingly suggested that no fewer than five and a quarter million people were failing to attend church, and were—in the words of one contemporary—'as utter strangers to religious ordinances as the people of a heathen country'.[7] This induced yet more building. Denominational competition also found expression in bricks and mortar: 'let us erect two churches for every meeting house', proclaimed the Anglican journal the *Church Builder* in 1862.[8] Eight years later, in 1870, J. Ewing Ritchie observed that one of the forces pushing Nonconformists into ostentatious architecture was the fear of losing eligible members of the congregation: 'Dissenters tell us', he wrote, 'that they have modified their customs in order to retain a hold upon the young of the wealthy classes.'[9]

But the churches did not just want to build more; they wanted to do more with what they built. Hence the growing number of churches was accompanied by a rise in the number of services held within them. The old pattern for the Church of England, in particular, had been a rather minimalist one. Daily worship in most churches died out in the late eighteenth century.[10] Sunday worship was characteristically confined to one, or at most two services: the first in the morning, and the other in the early afternoon.[11] In the 1820s, only one church in the whole of Oxford held an evening service on Sundays.[12] The Victorians—drawing on the pioneering work of previous Evangelical reformers— sought to expand the number and the variety of these events by adding a third, evening service on Sundays.[13] True enough, this was sometimes intended as a challenge to other denominations. Certainly, it marked an end to the old pattern in which church and chapel worshipped at different times, enabling parishioners to attend both.[14] A third service was also, in some places, an opportunity to try out new liturgies or hymns; indeed, it was actually opposed by some critics on the grounds that it provided a back door to liturgical irregularity.[15] There were also those who worried about the consequences of this crepuscular innovation on other grounds, noting darkly that 'We believe it to be a fact that, where evening services abound, there illegitimate births have increased.'[16] Nonetheless, opening the church in the evening became increasingly popular. By the mid-1850s it could be assumed that three services were 'usual in most town churches'.[17]

These new evening services needed to be lit, and indeed the very act of illuminating churches was believed to be a means of attracting a congregation. Writing in 1839, one reforming Berkshire rector observed that the candlelight of his new Wednesday evening services made 'such a charming effect that anybody who sees it must be irresistibly tempted to walk in'.[18] The introduction of gas lighting made an even greater impression and, as the social investigator Charles Booth observed at the turn of the twentieth century, people were indeed drawn to the 'bright lights shining through painted glass, and ... the attractive force of the sound of hymns'.[19] Clergymen were, if anything, still more impressed by this new dispensation. Surveying his church in Norfolk, newly lit for a third Sunday service, the vicar, Benjamin Armstrong, was delighted. 'It is very beautiful and Catholic in appearance. The chancel is a flood of light... and the tout ensemble more resembles some grand effect in a cathedral abroad than the ordinary appearance of an Anglican church.'[20]

It was not just Sunday services that increased in number. Throughout the nineteenth century, there were successive campaigns to reintroduce daily prayer—and, in the highest of High churches, even Holy Communion every day. One enthusiast in 1856 called for a huge increase in services—'say seven or eight on Sundays, and fifteen or twenty through the week', and although few can have matched this, there was movement in that direction.[21] The rising tide of religion—or, at any rate, of public worship—can be measured in successive editions of church guidebooks published at the time, which show almost all churches, and especially those in large towns, offering an ever larger number of daily opportunities for worship. In 1854 daily service was held in only 650 churches in the whole of England; by 1919 both matins and evensong were celebrated each day in no fewer than 5,427 churches. The number of churches offering a daily communion service had likewise risen: from only three in 1854 to 1,215 six decades later.[22] Small wonder that clergymen, including Trollope's Reverend Harding, felt they were working harder than their predecessors; nor that High Churchmen should celebrate the fact that actuaries were now required to rethink the assumptions on which they calculated clerical life insurance.[23] Formerly, wrote one reformer, clergymen were expected to lead lives of a more than average length; but now— 'consequent on the revival of the missionary spirit in the

Church'—they were expected to die, exhausted from overexertion, well before their time.[24]

The Church of England also turned its attention to what were called the occasional services—baptism, burial, confirmation, marriage, and the like. Here again, Victorian clergy sought to escape the pattern they had inherited from the eighteenth century: a pattern of generally private and often domestic baptism, for example; a situation that had enabled Nonconformists to have their children christened without the need to name godparents,[25] and which had also suited rather grander members of the parish who wished to avoid the *hoi polloi* observing their family affairs. Marriages, too, as one contemporary recalled, had also often been domestic: 'a hasty recitation of the service duly mutilated...over a drawing-room table by special license'.[26] Instead, as the historian Frances Knight has shown, clergymen—against much resistance—began to enforce public baptism, almost always in church, and generally on a Sunday. They sought, too, to encourage the public churching of women after childbirth and the celebration of marriage in church.[27] Indeed, in a wonderful illustration of the ways in which the past truly is a foreign country, there were complaints that when couples married in church, they didn't make enough fuss or employ sufficient floristry. In 1860 the reverend Edward Cutts bemoaned the fact that churches were often ornamented with black for funerals, but nothing, he mournfully observed, was ever done to decorate churches at a wedding. Increasingly, as we now know to our cost, his prayers would be answered. Increasingly, too, the occasional services would take place within a church rather than elsewhere. In the last two decades of the nineteenth century, for instance, the number of church baptisms grew and the number of marriages solemnized in church soared by 80 per cent.[28]

All these extra services were not just about using the church; they were also about using it properly. This rise in the number and range of services reflected denominationalism—and, in particular, the growing sense of the Church of England as just one denomination amongst many. They also reflected the change in the role and authority of parish clergy, who attempted to bolster their position vis-à-vis lay patrons, their congregation, and other religious leaders by asserting control of the parish church itself. But, from our perspective, these are all somewhat second-order questions, for they do not engage with the primary issue of why the church building should matter at all, much less why it should be the focus for such intense contests for control. The answer to that question can be found in the wider argument this book has attempted to articulate. In other words, this battle for control, this new emphasis on the need for more and better services in church, was a consequence of the broader cultural, intellectual—that is, theological and architectural—change we've identified. The new sense of sacred space that we've been exploring—that sense of church buildings as places set apart, as a means of inculcating spiritual truths, as active participants in worship and not just the passive receptacles for it—it was this that made it imperative not only that the church should be used more but that it should be used appropriately.

It's this that helps to explain, for instance, the increasing concern of many Victorians to ensure not just that there were more events held in church, but that those events were appropriate and fitting: something expressed in the growing distaste many clergy felt about holding vestry meetings within churches, for example.

Vestries were the basic units of parochial government as well as the bodies that oversaw the church itself. In modern terms, they were both parish council and parochial church council. This twin responsibility caused problems, not least because the voters for the vestries included Nonconformists, Roman Catholics, and those of no formal religion at all, as well as active and committed members of the local parish church. Amidst the denominational controversies of the nineteenth century, this meant that even the location of vestry meetings was problematic. Writing in 1868, for instance, Benjamin Armstrong expressed himself most satisfied that the East Dereham vestry meeting 'took place in the Assembly Room, and so saved our beautiful chancel from the profanation of puritans and freethinkers with their hats on'.[29]

It was not just these theologically, politically charged events that came to be seen as a sort of sacrilege. Even concerts were potentially suspect, with Bishop Kaye of Lincoln writing of his 'horror' that musical entertainments might mean people 'sitting upon the seats of a Church as upon the Boxes of a Theatre'.[30] There was always, cautioned John Baron, vicar of Upton Scudamore in Wiltshire, and a pioneer in the development of the modern organ, a need to distinguish between 'musical performances and musical worship'.[31] It should come as little surprise to find that the Tractarian novelist Francis Paget also waded into the debate, attacking the performance of music in churches as an abomination in his now wholly and justly neglected work, *The Curate of Cumberworth and the Vicar of Roost*, published in 1859.[32]

The new sense of the church as an embodiment of faith—a text that could be read, a space that could give rise to the most profound emotions, a place that should be used more and in different ways—is rather wonderfully captured in Edward Stuart's sermon of 1851 on 'the chief hindrance to the church's work in towns'. Eton- and Oxford-educated, Stuart was a well-born, well-connected, and wealthy man, someone who could trace his descent back to the kings of Scotland. He was a church builder as well as a clergyman, and founded the ritualist slum church of St Mary Magdalene Munster Square in London. Ostensibly in a sermon attacking 'the Pew System', at tremendous length, he actually set out the details of the project we're uncovering. Selected highlights will give a sense of just how wide-ranging the programme of reform was intended to be. 'Is the parish Church in any parish decayed and ruinous?' Stuart asked:

> Then rebuild it. 'Has the font been set aside?'—then replace it. 'Has the altar been suffered to fall into shameful neglect?'—then restore, and know, and wait upon it. 'Have the private pews of the rich, consciously or unconsciously, thrust aside CHRIST's poor into the worst places or altogether driven them out of Church?'—then throw open freely to all the house of HIM who died freely for all ... 'Has prayer declined?'—there is daily service, and there is a building which is meant to be open daily for those whose homes give them but little opportunity of quiet and retirement.[33]

Amidst the lengthy list of changes he advocated—and it is such a lengthy list that it could take up much of this chapter—it's worthwhile pausing to note Stuart's last point. It draws attention to an all but forgotten movement within the Victorian Church of England: the campaign to open churches every day; not just for worship, but also for private prayer, something that was evidently a key part of the reform of the Church he and others advocated.

This, again, could be understood in a multitude of ways. But it makes most sense only if we accept that the desire to open churches to visitors reflected above all the belief that an open church had a religious meaning and religious message and—it was hoped—a religious consequence. The late eighteenth century had, again, bequeathed a different understanding. Conceiving of church buildings in predominantly functional terms—simply the containers for worshipping communities—most Georgians hadn't seen the need to open the church between services. Yet the new understanding of church architecture we've been exploring represented this approach as not simply inexplicable, but also immoral. In a pamphlet of 1858, one supporter imagined 'an uncivilized heathen...or even a foreigner' being struck by the locked churches he observed. 'What singular-looking prisons these English build! he thinks: had it not been for the dreary and desolate appearance it bears, and for the fast-closed doors, I should have imagined it to be a church!' Encountering a Low

Fig. 11. 'Churches as they are now' and 'Churches...as they will be', in Paget's *Milford Malvoisin* (1842)

Church parson, the 'uncivilized heathen' enquires at this strange state of affairs. It is the English way, observes the vicar, going on to note that should one wish to enter the church, the parish clerk would open it for a fee and show all the antiquarian sights.[34] For supporters of the Open Church campaign, which was backed by societies in many major cities, and found its national mouthpiece in the Free and Open Church Association, established in 1866, this represented everything that was wrong with the old understanding of the church building.[35] An open church, observed one campaigner, 'becomes useful as well as ornamental'.[36] It became useful because it was assumed that architecture had consequences: that it had an effect.

The effect of the 'free and open' church was believed to be multiple. Abolishing pew rents enabled poor people to sit rather than stand. Opening the church during the day permitted passersby to pray. 'The very impression produced on the mind on entering an unappropriated Church, by the character of the arrangement which strikes the eye, is itself most valuable,' wrote one enthusiastic advocate of the cause. 'It forces sight itself to serve to the purpose of faith, it gives a kind of visible evidence of things not seen, and substantial reality to things hoped for.'[37] In the Manchester *Church of the People* (published 1858–77), in the London *Free and Open Church Advocate* (1872–1900), in novels like W. P. Mann's *Reminiscences of a Pew* (in which 'a Pew records its gradual conversion to belief in the Free and Open system'), and a thousand other publications, the utility, the symbolism, the effect, and the affect of open churches was hammered home again and again.[38]

Importantly, this new understanding did not just affect churches alone. A renewed emphasis on architecture meant a renewed interest in parsonages, schools, and also in their surroundings and the sites of worship more generally.

Take graveyards, for example. Until comparatively recently, these spaces were essentially ignored by historians. But recent work is beginning to help us understand just how important graveyards were in the religious world of the nineteenth century—not least, though not only—as the focus for denominational struggle.[39] And it's true that Anglican clergy were certainly alarmed at any threat to their control of the churchyard, fearing— as one put it—that allowing Nonconformists to officiate at funerals there was 'of course, only a prelude to their officiating in our Churches'.[40] Bishop Wilberforce of Oxford agreed, observing in 1856 that 'I have the strongest conviction that the real and deepest struggle in which the Church is engaged is for the ultimate possession of the Fabrics of the Churches.'[41] Graveyards were just a part of this. Yet, the truth was that most churchyards remained associated with the parish church and, in many cases, under the effective control of the vicar and churchwardens throughout the century.[42] Moreover, and more importantly, these sites had a more than merely denominational importance: they were consecrated ground—'God's house in the open air', as the bishop of Beverly put it in 1902—and they had a special part to play within the new understanding of sacred space that we have been exploring.[43]

Just as the church came to be seen as a set of signs and symbols communicating a deeper spiritual truth, so the churchyard was reimagined by the Victorians. The Georgians had viewed the land surrounding the church as a private resource: somewhere that should be fenced and locked; something that could be rented out as pasture. In his tour of Bedfordshire churches in the 1840s and early 1850s, the indefatigable antiquary John Martin frequently bemoaned the condition in which he found their churchyards, where cattle and sheep were allowed to graze and worshippers only admitted for a Sunday service. Even the absence of yew trees—something he regarded as an essential sign of ecclesiastical life—betokened neglect, for, of course, yews were poisonous to ruminants and therefore prevented the churchyards' use for pasturage.[44] In that way, the reintroduction of yew trees was symbolically significant: revealing churchyards which had been resacralized. 'Planted with appropriate shrubs and flowers, it might indeed be rendered a scene of cheerful contemplation and instruction to all ages,' he noted on a visit to St James, Biddenhall, in 1847, 'but with rare exceptions churchyards are in a great neglect; graves trodden down by cattle and access prevented by locks and keys.'[45]

What was it that the churchyard was intended to teach—and how was it meant to do it? The answer was given by numerous writers. 'The churchyard', observed the Tractarian poet Isaac Williams in 1841, was a spot of ground 'lying between two worlds ... the living and the dead'. It was in this sense, he went on, that the churchyard was a sort of text—a 'type', as Williams put it, of the church building more generally, which similarly brought together the witness of those present and those who had departed.[46] The emotional effect of the churchyard was also captured by many writers, not least Augustus Pugin, who observed in *The Present State of Ecclesiastical Architecture in England* that 'nothing can be more calculated to awaken solemn and devout feelings, than passing through the resting-place of the faithful departed'.[47] Indeed, improving the state of the churchyard was analogous in many writers' minds with restoring the fabric of the church and the faith of the people. For Francis Paget, for instance, both the 'rickety pews...whitewashed walls...close, fusty smell of rotting hassocks' of the church and a surrounding churchyard which was 'in part...used as a playground for the village children; in part...a tangled maze of nettles, rank grass and headstones' were each equally alarming signs of religion's decline.[48]

The Victorian era consequently witnessed many attempts to improve—as well as extend—churchyards: something that can be seen in the yews planted, the gravestones erected, and the ancillary buildings constructed throughout this period in almost every parish. A forest of lychgates was built—indeed the lychgate, the covered entrance defining the way into the churchyard, marking it off as separate and sacred—became a desideratum for many churchmen, inspiring poetry, pictures, and even a terrible serial in the High Church magazine, the Old Church Porch.[49] At John Keble's Hursley, a lychgate, built—like the church—in 1848, was seen as the embodiment of lines in his verse Lyra Innocentium: 'This is the portal of the dead...the holy resting place,/Where coffins and where mourners wait,/Till the stoled priest hath time to pace/His path towards this eastern gate.'[50]

And it was not just these bigger, architectural interventions that changed. In the same way that churches were increasingly filled with flowers and symbolic floristry, so clergy sought to turn decorations on graves into something more meaningful, something distinctively Christian.[51] They sought, in other words, 'the substitution of graceful and symbolical accompaniments for puritanical dryness'.[52] Thus the diarist Francis Kilvert tried to train his parishioners to arrange their flowers 'instead of sticking sprigs into the turf aimlessly'. 'I am glad', he wrote—deadpan as ever—in April 1870, 'to see that our primrose crosses seem to be having some effect.'[53] On high holy days, too, clergy sought to use decorations and especially flowers in the churchyard—and on the inevitable lychgate—just as they hoped to use the church building itself as a means of attracting congregants. 'The entrance to the Church, and the precincts of the Church,' observed the clergyman Edward Cutts in 1860, 'should give premonitory indications of the festive adornments within the temple.'[54] Church and churchyard were in that sense reimagined as aspects of the same emotional and spiritual experience.

Nor was it just the immediate surroundings of the church that were transformed by this new sense of sacred architecture. As George Neale Barrow poetically put it when preaching at the consecration of Christ Church Hanham, Gloucestershire, in 1842: 'The consecrated church almost casts its hallowed shade upon the house of the pastor, and even upon the parish school.'[55] And it's true that both parsonages and parish schools were extensively built and rebuilt in this period, with several thousand of each constructed across the nineteenth century. They were also, more importantly, reimagined in light of the wider changes that had reshaped church architecture.

Parsonage building was, of course, a necessity if the Church was to be able to achieve its stated goal of an incumbent living in every parish. But the efforts made to create an appropriate architectural effect in many parsonages suggest that there was a strong symbolic as well as a purely practical impetus underpinning these projects. 'Next in importance to the erection of the church itself', wrote Pugin, 'is that of a suitable edifice for the habitation of those ecclesiastics who are appointed to serve its altars.' It was vital, he emphasized, that they should exhibit a 'solid, solemn, and scholastic character, that bespoke them at once to be the habitations

Fig. 12. 'A Vicarage Home, in correspondence with the architecture of the neighbouring church', from Papworth's *Rural Residences* (1818)

of men who were removed far beyond the ordinary pursuits of life'.[56] Some authors went further still, seeing the parsonage as an edifice no less important and, in many respects, only a little less sacred than the church it served. As John Mason Neale put it in 1859:

> The construction of a parsonage house is of almost as much import-ance to the tone of the parish as that of the church itself. Does it make no difference to the poor man, think you, whether his priest lives in such a number of such a row, like the physician or the lawyer; or whether he resides in a house set apart, not for him so much as for God?[57]

So it was that parsonages began to accrete ecclesiastical details and to ape ecclesiastical architecture. As early as 1816, the archi-tect J. B. Papworth argued that 'A Vicarage Home' should be designed 'in correspondence with the architecture of the neigh-bouring church', with 'parts of the design…selected from the church itself'. 'The practice of designing the residence of a cler-gyman with reference to the characteristics of the church to which it belongs', he concluded:

> is desirable, not only as relates to a tasteful advantage, but as it becomes another and visible link of connexion between the church itself and the pastor who is devoted to its duties; and also leads the spectator very naturally from contemplating the dwelling, to regard the pious character of its inhabitant.[58]

At Morwenstow in Cornwall the idiosyncratic Robert Hawker went one better, designing a parsonage 'with chimneys built to resemble the towers of the churches with which he had associ-ations' and a kitchen chimney apparently an exact replica of his mother's tomb.[59] But even less peculiar parsons engaged in equivalent architectural mimesis: making their homes more like their churches; hinting at their purposes with pointed gables,

Gothic windows, and other ecclesiastical rather than domestic details.[60]

School buildings possessed an equivalent importance and played a similar role. Indeed, as Nigel Yates has pointed out, to judge by the clerical correspondence of the period, in some parishes, 'the provision of day schools seems to have been regarded as of greater importance than either clerical housing or church restoration'.[61] There were, of course, good denominational reasons for this. Just as the different churches and sects competed with each other in the provision of places of worship, so elementary education was seen as a battleground for the souls of Britain's children. Yet, from our perspective, what's striking is the form that this competition took. They were not just

Fig. 13. School, church, and parsonage in John Sandford's *Parochialia* (1845)

building thousands of schools; each school was also a significant statement about the denomination it served. In that way, school architecture reproduced the wider debates about church architecture that we've been exploring over the last few chapters. How could it be otherwise, when, as John Sandford put it in his hugely influential tract, *Parochialia; or church, school, and parish* (1845), the parish school was intended to be 'a handmaid of the Church, and nursery for heaven'?[62]

In particular, it's worth noting the way in which the 1830s and 1840s saw school buildings become means of communicating denominational difference and theological principle. This was an assumption made manifest at the opening of the Leicester Nonconformist Proprietary School in 1837: an educational institution which had been established in direct competition with the recently founded—Anglican, and hence Gothic—Leicester Collegiate School. The headmaster of the Nonconformist institution declared that:

> He rejoiced greatly that they had adopted the Grecian style of Architecture in preference to the Gothic... To those whose associations fondly clung to the dark Monastic exploded institutions of our country, who love to dwell rather on the gloomy periods of our history, than to contemplate the blaze of light and knowledge which has since burst upon the world—to such persons he was aware the Gothic style of Architecture had great charms; but in an institution for the education of youth it was desirable that every association of the mind should be connected with a people who had carried literature to the highest point of perfection, whose love of liberty, of knowledge, of the fine arts, whose writings in History, in poetry had never been excelled, rather than with the superstitions of our Gothic ancestors who, with the exception of Architecture, were remarkable only for their ignorance and barbarism.[63]

With his condemnation of an architecture which he saw as synonymous with 'exploded monasticism', 'superstition', 'ignorance and barbarism', he spoke for many.

Even as he spoke, indeed, Anglican schools were becoming ever more dependent on Gothic models, seeing in neo-medievalism an appropriate architecture for education as well as worship, not least because of the message it was assumed to communicate. So at Lound in south Yorkshire, a school which opened in 1860 was hailed by the *Sheffield Times* as a building which was self-evidently 'distinct from the mere secular or every-day architecture of modern times, and having sufficient character to inform the passer-by that it has been reared for the service of the God of Charity'.[64] It was not just churches, therefore, that were intended to convey an idea: schools were similarly pressed into service as vehicles for a particular—and a particularly religious—message.

The ways in which both parsonages and schools were used gave an added impetus to this change. For they were often places of worship in their own right. We've already seen Hensley Henson deploy his vicarage garden as a location for temperance meetings and summer services alike. Even clerics like Ernest Geldart, vicar and visionary architect of **St Nicholas, Little Braxted,** in Essex—a building that fully embodies almost everything we've been exploring—did not confine his worship to the ornamented, decorated, illuminated, symbol-rich, text-covered, jewel-like church he had constructed. As he grew more infirm, Geldart obtained permission to use his parsonage for daily prayers and celebration of the Eucharist—and added a small, neo-medieval chapel to the house for just that purpose.[65] Schools were even more likely to be pressed into use as places of worship. In some parishes, they were regarded as less intimidating than the church and therefore more likely to be welcoming to working men.[66] In other places, like Danby in Cleveland, the church was inconveniently sited, so midweek services took place in the school. In still smaller, poorer parishes—like Staithes in North Yorkshire—the school, built in 1816, actually became a church, being licensed as a place of worship in 1849, and finally, formally rededicated as the mission church of St Peter the Fisherman in 1874.[67]

The architectural development, use, experience, and understanding of churches and churchyards, parsonages and parish schools consequently mirrored one another. They were all shaped by a new sense of what buildings could do, what they could mean, and how they might help to form people's religious faith. But they were also linked in another way—one that has been strangely neglected by British church historians and social historians alike, and one that architectural historians, until recently, would not have considered part of their province. They were linked by the novel sacred geography that was engendered by this new understanding of ecclesiastical architecture.

Fig. 14. Whitwalk, St Andrew's, Radcliffe in Lancashire, c.1910

The nineteenth-century development of religious processions is a subject that has been explored in depth and in detail and to great effect by historians of Continental Europe. Yet it has scarcely been touched on by historians of nineteenth-century Britain. This is all the more extraordinary given the wealth of evidence that exists and the numbers of people who participated in them. As Dorothy Entwistle has shown in one of the few serious studies of the phenomenon, in a typical Whit week procession in Hyde, near Manchester, it was estimated that up to 10,000 people participated, watched by around 12,000 others.[68] Larger conurbations had still more impressive numbers. And it was not just in the towns that these processions took place: for in some small villages, indeed, the annual school or church parade was the single biggest event of the year.

These processions were, in the main, Victorian innovations, first encouraged by the Church of England at the turn of the century and given a renewed impetus by the changes we've been exploring in the 1830s and 1840s.[69] They were soon copied by Roman Catholics, freed to parade in public by emancipation, and—even more remarkably—by many Nonconformist churches. By 1865, in Cardiff, 1,500 Anglican children were joined by hundreds of Nonconformists at a tea in the castle owned by the Marquess of Bute, himself a convert to Roman Catholicism only three years later;[70] in 1885, processions in Hyde were made up of seven Anglican parishes, fifteen Nonconformist chapels, and one Roman Catholic Church.[71]

These processions owed much to a new understanding of architecture and religious art. They were, as Paul O'Leary has observed in his study of processions in mid-nineteenth-century south Wales, attempts to capture public space; 'a process that served to "sacralise" spaces that were usually considered to be devoted to secular activities'.[72] And they would, as Robert Proctor has noted in his study of post-war Catholic churches, continue long into the twentieth century to be used as a way of turning the streets into a sort of sacred space, 'activated', in his words, 'by a spectacular processional movement', articulating a new religious geography.[73] Indeed, as the importance of symbolic communication became ever more stressed, so the iconography of these processions became ever more elaborate, with religious banners and books and flowers introduced from the 1850s onwards.[74]

Moreover, as Ronald Hutton has shown, these events were not simply attempts to recreate an old, lost, ritual year.[75] These were modern movements and modern moments—with the Whitsun walks growing in popularity once a bank holiday was declared in 1871, and many other processions making no pretence to be a revival, but rather reflecting modern conditions and—it must be said—celebrating modern buildings in the process.

The annual parish school feast is a good example of this. It was not, as Edward Cutts observed, 'an appointed church festival'; but it was, as he went on to note, 'a local occasion of some religious and social importance'. Indeed, as later reminiscences suggest, these 'Church Parades' were in many places 'the most exciting';[76] 'the chief event of the year'.[77] The school feast, wrote Cutts in 1860, is:

> fast taking on the character which used to belong to the old Village
> Feast; when it is held, as it often is, on the saint's day to whom the
> parish church is dedicated, it becomes the legitimate representative of
> the old local festival. In many parishes, it has all the good features of
> the old day of merry-making; the bells ring from early morning, and
> the parish makes a day's holiday; there is a service in church, to which
> the children march in procession with a band playing and flags flying;

Sunday-school teachers keep order along the line and the clergyman in his gown and bands, supported by the school committee, his chief parishioners brings up the rear.[78]

The school feast in Benjamin Armstrong's East Dereham was even more explicit in making the link between church, school, and parsonage. On 10 August 1853, he recorded 317 children marching with flags and streamers from the school house, to the church, and on then to the vicarage for tea and cake. Four years later, he noted, with approval, that houses along the route were now bedecked with banners.[79] The whole village had been transformed, in part and for a moment, into a sacred space.

This move was not uncontroversial, of course. Just as in Germany, say, or in Ireland, processions also offered opportunities for denominational conflict, even violence.[80] Within large multi-confessional towns, even the routes taken by different denominations were potentially problematic, with each church following a path dictated by custom, parish boundary, or the homes of important parishioners. The journalist William Haslam Mills recalled that in Ashton-under-Lyne, for instance, separate processions from different churches 'crossed one another at right angles and obtuse angles like caterpillars on a cabbage leaf'. On the morning of Whit Friday, he observed, 'Dissent was between the tram-lines and Church was on the pavement. In the afternoon it was Dissent on the pavement and Church between the tram-lines...Every year there occurred a moment at which in one of our meaner streets we "met the Catholics" face to face.'[81]

Processions themselves, and the religious iconography they increasingly accreted, were worrying in general for some Protestants and particularly alarming for those with a nose for ritualism. At Cuddesdon in Oxfordshire in the 1850s, for example, there were suggestions that clergymen had been seen processing 'in surplices, with Banners and Crosses, and chanting Hymns and Psalms'; there was even the accusation that 'two vergers' staves were carried, the heads of which terminated in small Crosses'.[82] Little wonder the place became a national scandal. As late as 1900, the incumbent of High Church St Alban's Holborn was forced to deny rumours that a donkey had been processed around the church as part of its Palm Sunday celebrations. 'I have been vicar here since December 7th, 1882,' he wrote, 'and during that time there has been no ass (that is, with four legs) in our church or led round it.'[83] But these controversies only emphasize the importance of processions: the fact that they were understood as communicative; the fact that they were believed to have a consequence.

They were consequential in two respects. In the first place, this linking together of school, church, churchyard, and parsonage—this enacted, embodied, sacred theatre, if you like—helped to entrench and communicate the idea that buildings had a special part to play in people's spiritual lives. It also broadcast this idea well beyond the precincts of the church itself. In that way, those historians who have seen religious organizations retreating back within their places of worship, seeking solace in an imagined past,[84] or who have argued—as Simon Green has argued—that this period saw 'the triumph of *worship* as the characteristic conception of organised religious experience' are quite wrong.[85] The built environment provided—and was intended to provide—all sorts of other opportunities for religious experience. A new understanding of the power of place meant that the streets themselves could now become sacralized—even if only for a few hours at a time.

Secondly, and perhaps more importantly, this new religious geography brought official religion closer to the religion of the everyday. As the historian Alexandra Walsham has argued, the Reformation did not so much desacralize the landscape as change its meanings.[86] In all sorts of ways—be it the Puritan fear of idolatry or a Latitudinarian distaste for enthusiasm—the official teachings of most Protestant denominations before the nineteenth century had been suspicious of popular belief, especially popular superstitions (as they were seen) about buildings or places. Yet this new Victorian understanding of both buildings and places could make use of these beliefs—and did. For some historians, like Bob Bushaway, the transmutation of Whitsun ales into Whitsun walks and processions, for example, is just about a crude form of social control, as festive beer drinking was replaced by the pious consumption of tea and cakes.[87] But, actually, something rather more interesting was happening—something more theological, more psychological, and something more material, too.

Folk beliefs had long associated places of worship with sites for magic and the uncanny. Francis Kilvert, for instance, recorded in 1871 that in a nearby village on New Year's Eve 'people used to go to the church door at midnight to hear the saints within call over the names of those who were to die within the year'.[88] In his study of Victorian magic the historian Karl Bell notes that churchyard soil—like holy water—was still believed to have special, curative powers, whilst each community had its own very particular topography of the supernatural, one that was often focused on church buildings. The people of Norwich, for instance, remained convinced that when three jackdaws were seen on the weathervane of the church of St Peter Mancroft, it presaged dreadful weather.[89] Changing ideas about death, dying, and the place of the dead also gave new impetus to some of these traditions. The late eighteenth and early nineteenth century witnessed a dramatic shift in attitudes: a new 'desire of the bereaved to visit the grave'; 'a growing feeling that the remains of the dead should not be disturbed'; a 'gravestone boom', which led to the erection of thousands of new memorials.[90] All this helped to place a new premium on the exterior as well as the interior of the church.

Moreover, as the historian Sarah Williams has shown, these ideas were not confined to rural or provincial people. Indeed, contemporaries were well aware that in some respects the capital was more conducive to such 'superstition' than elsewhere.[91] Thus, in Southwark, for example, it was considered good luck to get married in church or to attend the watchnight service on New Year's Eve. Certain churches, too, were considered especially propitious, with St Paul's, Kipling Street, singled out as a particularly fortunate place to tie the knot.[92] What these beliefs and practices reveal was the important place—the power—of churches and churchyards, of sacred architecture more generally, within the popular imagination. Long suppressed, or disregarded, these beliefs did not suddenly become orthodox—far from it. But the teachings of the church in many respects did grow closer to the traditional understanding of sacred buildings as places set apart, places that possessed power in their own right.

This was a long way from the Church's former understanding of buildings merely as receptacles for worship. So was the fact that the Church now encouraged a fully embodied form of participation through its use of processions. No longer was the worshipper, as it were, simply seen as a listener. Now, he or she was an active participant in a form of sacred drama, one that was enacted or performed throughout the town, throughout the village; inside the church and the school and even the parsonage; outside, even in the streets.

All of which, you'll be scarcely surprised to read, brings us back to Littlemore. It was here that Newman built a school as well as a church; here that he had a churchyard consecrated—and where a lychgate would eventually be built; here, too, that he organized an annual procession to mark the consecration of his church. Initially mobbed by protesting Protestants, it soon became an accepted part of village life. In Littlemore, Newman was doing no more than what scores of other clergymen would do across the century: erecting buildings that were designed to have an effect on their visitors and on the world around them; re-sacralizing the landscape and thereby seeking to reincorporate people within the architecture and the ethos of the Church.

4

Analysing

It cannot but be a matter of regret, to see the chapel of modern structure, belonging even to the Establishment, in the very richest districts, formed of mean materials...without a tower, without any character or feature appropriate to religion, or, in any respect, resembling the venerable fabrics of our forefathers.

Thomas Knox, *A Sermon Preached in the Parish Church of Tonbridge on Sunday, the 16th of March, 1834, in Aid of the Funds of the Incorporated Society for Promoting the Enlargement, Building and Repairing of Churches and Chapels* (London, 1834), p. 17

If the man who goes to his work, and returns from it morning and evening, passes his life without prayer and religion, will not this building be a witness against him? When the Sabbath-breaker, and the Gamester, and the Drunkard, and the Robber, and the violent Man, look up at it; will they not feel an evidence to their consciences that they are wrong, and that they must reform and amend to be saved.

John Collinson, *A Sermon Preached at the Opening of Gateshead Fell Church, October 30, 1825* (Newcastle, 1825), p. 16

It's worth lingering in Littlemore a little longer, not least to meet another exemplary figure in the transformation of ideas about church buildings. Here, on 29 September 1848 came the bishop of Oxford, Samuel Wilberforce. Known as a 'Soapy Sam' because of his smooth and somewhat slippery demeanour, Wilberforce is someone we have encountered already, and a man whose views perfectly encapsulate so many others' of the time. He came to consecrate a new chancel, built to cater for a growing number of worshippers and a still greater formality in worship. A lot had happened in the twelve years since 1836, when the church had first opened. John Henry Newman had founded a religious community at Littlemore, and then retreated from active life within it. He had, in 1843, resigned as vicar and preached his last sermon. Two years after that, in 1845, he had left Littlemore and the Church of England. To the delight of some, the horror of many, and the surprise of very few, he had converted to Roman Catholicism. Newman would go on to become a cardinal and is now halfway towards being a saint. In his sermon at the consecration of this new chancel, Wilberforce very deliberately mentioned none of this. Preaching on the feast day of St Michael and All Angels, he confined his comments to the angelic. Fearing controversy, he—unusually for him—drew no attention to the building itself. Fearing rancour, he—very wisely—forbore from addressing either Newman's work or his departure.[1] For us, however, the time has come to try and tie together the general and specific: Newman, his church, his parish, and the wider stories they are part of.

So far, I have very deliberately avoided recourse to grand narratives about the rise of Romanticism or professionalization or a transition to modernity as a way of explaining the transformation in ecclesiastical architecture which characterized the first few decades of Victoria's reign. I've also questioned the assumption that either the Cambridge Ecclesiologists or Oxford Tractarians single-handedly effected this change. Rather, what we've traced is literally more parochial but in reality more profound shifts: new ideas about the nature of architecture and of faith; a growing belief in the didactic and emotional power of the material world. These trends involved the rejection of late eighteenth-century attitudes and the embrace of architecture derived from a far more distant past. As the two quotations which open this chapter suggest, these notions were first articulated before either the Tractarians or the Ecclesiologists popularized them. Moreover, they were defined by people from a far broader range of theological backgrounds than many previous writers have noticed: people like John Collinson, antiquary and High Church Anglican; people like Thomas Knox, headmaster of Tonbridge (and a man far better known by posterity for his advocacy of cricket than his theology).

Another good example would be the bishop who preached at Littlemore on that saint's day in 1848 and so carefully avoided engaging with the difficult problems we have set ourselves to solve. Born an Evangelical—indeed born into one of the grandest Anglican Evangelical families in the country, Samuel Wilberforce became a liberal and then a High Church Tory and then something rather more *sui generis* than that. He celebrated the spirituality of the Evangelicals, but shocked them by his willingness to tolerate High Church ideals. He welcomed the Tractarians, but also harshly punished what he saw as their excesses—even prohibiting Pusey from preaching within the diocese of Oxford. As a reforming and activist bishop, Wilberforce oversaw the restoration and rebuilding of scores of churches. Littlemore was just one of perhaps fifty such buildings he consecrated between 1845 and 1853.

What's striking is that in both his public pronouncements and private writings, Bishop Wilberforce unselfconsciously articulated so many of the assumptions we have been exploring, despite the fact

that much of his work involved restraining the excesses of Tractarians and even though he believed many of his views would seem
'distinctly heretical' to the Ecclesiologists.[2] His personal notes inter-
sperse criticism of clergy who went fox hunting with all the sorts of
complaints about pews and galleries we've already encountered.
Again and again, he associates poor buildings with poor behaviour
and presumes that building or rebuilding will reawaken faith. His
greatest praise is for places where he finds 'the Church advancing in
the material building & spiritual'.[3] In his letters, too—and there are
many letters, for his son estimated he wrote nearly 6,500 a year—we
likewise find him insistent on the need to erect schools and parsonages, improve churchyards and burial places, remove pews and
galleries. Churches, he reiterates, must possess a proper 'eccles[ias-
tical] character' and must conform to the modern understanding of
'ecclesiastical architecture'.[4] This, it's clear, meant absorbing both the
idea of the church as a text and as a means of affecting the emotions.

Above all, in his sermons, Wilberforce sought to teach these
lessons to a wider public. Consecrating the new church of
St Catherine's in Bearwood, Berkshire, in 1846, for example, he
preached about the fundamental nature of a church. 'They
should,' he said:

> speak at once of their severed character; they should witness at once
> to the Christian's eye, that they are not houses for rest, for the lawful
> comforts or pleasure of this life, for its business, or its recreations;
> that they have to do with a higher life . . . they should, as far as may be,
> even by their material arrangements, shut out the world, its glare, its
> garishness, its artificial distinctions.

Here, indeed, is no sense of sublation: no sense of the church as a
place solely intended to hear the Word. Rather, here is the church
as a medium itself. And, he goes on, the model for this medium is

medieval; for medieval churches communicated and moved. 'The beauty of those temples was that not that of the earth, he concludes; 'every thing was meant to be symbolical; and as far, therefore, as it was truly symbolical, it fulfilled its purpose.'[5]

It's by looking again at people like Wilberforce—and Collinson and Knox and the others we'll encounter in this chapter—that we will be able to see *how* it was as well as *why* it was that churches changed in this period. Instead of studying church parties like the Tractarians, or insisting that religious buildings were simply reshaped by external, ethereal, disembodied trends, we will look at the individuals and the groups who actually built, rebuilt, restored, and renewed ecclesiastical architecture. We will also look at those who came to fear for the fabric of the parish church. Increasingly, and ironically, these were not assertive Protestants within Anglicanism or even Nonconformists without—for they were themselves seduced by these new notions about buildings. No: by the last few decades of the nineteenth century, the triumph of these ideas was such that other, very different people came to campaign against any further alterations to the holy edifices they had come to appreciate so much. In that way, the idea of the church as a text and as a place synonymous with the architecture of affect became highly problematic for the Churches themselves.

A broad coalition of people—all with somewhat different motivations, and each with rather different perspectives—made this change possible. In each parish, in every diocese, all across the country, a distinct set of circumstances and people participated in a general movement that transformed the churches of Britain. I will divide them into four types, acknowledging all the while that these capacious categories overlapped. Of course, others were involved—not least the worshipping communities these churches were intended to house. But, for the sake of simplicity, we will stick with just four.

The first of these is the group with which we've begun, the clergy—for they were, of course, key players: some motivated by strong aesthetic impulses; some by deep theological reasoning; all, in some respect or other, keen to use church buildings to reform church life—and especially to reform the place of the clergy within the parishes. As the historian Bill Jacob has argued, the 1820s and 1830s saw clergy of all theological dispositions increasingly keen to assert their own control over church buildings, something that can be measured in numerous attempts to reorder church buildings, removing box pews, installing eastward-facing benches, and reinstating the chancel.[6] This parochial reform was accompanied by and bound up with wider changes within the Church of England. What has come to be known as 'the diocesan revival' saw bishops like Wilberforce showing a desire to restructure the systems and improve the effectiveness of their organizations throughout each diocese.[7]

This increasing interest of the bishops in parochial matters was made manifest in the growing power of archdeacons like Henry Manning and Julius Hare, whose influence on the diocese of Chichester we have already noted. It was also found in the revival of the office of rural dean, as clergymen were appointed by bishops to oversee a collection of parishes grouped into a deanery. All this forced a renewed focus on the church building in parishes throughout the country. Archidiaconal visitations from the 1830s onwards, in particular, show an ever more intense interest not just in the stability but in the seemliness of church buildings. Writing in 1843, for instance, William Stonehouse, archdeacon of Stow in Lincolnshire, was typical of his time in prefacing his visitation returns with a condemnation of eighteenth-century practice and a celebration of what he called 'the revival of a better feeling as to decency' in worship and architecture in the previous few decades.[8] Again, it's worth re-emphasizing that this all began before either the Ecclesiologists or the Tractarians began agitating for such changes.

The Trollopian battles between clergy and laity which characterized some parishes in this period—the struggle between squire and parson, between parson and musicians, between parson and church wardens or parish clerks, between rector and curate, for that matter—these were struggles over space, over control of the church building, as well as over more finely grained doctrinal matters.

Hence the story Owen Chadwick outlines in his lovely little book, *Victorian Miniature*. Here, in Kettringham, Norfolk, was a fraught fight as the High Tory lord of the manor contended with the Low Church vicar—not just, indeed, not principally, about the nuances of belief, but about issues of applied theology: who could use the building and how, who could decorate it and how, and even who could be commemorated within it and how. The west gallery—with its inscription best read from the parson's pulpit, at which it must have been directed—still stands as a monument to a struggle for control that played itself out over the middle decades of the nineteenth century.[9]

Hence, too, the battle between the vicar of Aldeburgh in Suffolk and a single, elderly parishioner who refused to give up her chancel seat for a newly supplied, cassocked, and well-organized choir. 'Always the first person in the church on Sunday morning,' it was recorded, 'she marched up the centre aisle, followed by a meek but embarrassed husband, whom she motioned to precede her into the pew.'[10]

Hence, still more poignantly, the sad fate of many parish clerks. These were once amongst the leading figures in the neighbour-hood, seated in the focal point of the church at the bottom storey of a triple-decker pulpit or behind a reading desk, second only to the parson. But now, increasingly, as the furiously Tractarian Frederick Oakeley put it, with enormous satisfaction, the clerk found himself 'dethroned from his ancient pre-eminence'. At Oakeley's own church—the pioneering ritualist All Saints chapel in London's Margaret Street—the poor clerk was displaced earlier than most, finding that he had 'no alternative but to subside into the general body of the congregation, and there assert his ancient right in the only way which was left to him, by reciting the responses with vociferous obtrusiveness'. This contest of space was also, of course, a contest of sound.[11]

It was a contest that was not just found in London and was not merely confined to famous churches or notorious cases. It also went on long after the 1830s. There were riots in the small Oxfordshire village of Blockley in the 1870s when the new vicar sought to exercise control over the church bells: sacralizing what had become seen as a purely secular sound.[12] In Rochdale in the 1850s and 1860s, by contrast, it was opponents of the new dispensation who found themselves under attack. Hamlet Nicholson, a cobbler turned druggist turned tobacconist, now remembered—when he is remembered at all—as the inventor of the modern cricket ball, hoped to go down in history as the man who fought ritualism in Rochdale Parish Church.[13] He opposed the removal of 'one of the finest old polished black oak three-decker pulpits' and the introduction of an organ chamber. He condemned the 'intoning, monotoning, singing of the psalms for the day, bowing and crossing, genuflexions, processions and recessions'. For his pains, he was 'jostled and pushed by the Choristers', insulted and kicked by the superintendent of the Sunday school, and even—on one memorable Sunday— thumped by the vicar, and in church too. It was all to no avail: the innovations continued—and Nicholson could find no way of effectively opposing them. He drew on old Reformation rhetoric—on the language and imagery of Foxe's Book of Martyrs—but the pace of change just quickened. 'Lighted candles', he expostulated in a traditional piece of Protestant polemic, were symbols of the 'rack, the faggot, and the fire; the horrors of Smithfield'. Yet these familiar tropes, it seems, no longer had their old purchase on the popular imagination. Indeed, they simply showed that he had become as willing to see the church in symbolic terms as those he opposed. It was oddly symbolic, too, that the event which precipitated his departure from the place was when a churchwarden struck him with the offertory box—another liturgical innovation.[14]

This struggle for control was fought out in buildings and with buildings and through buildings. But it was also articulated with the other means open to clergy in the parishes: their words. Sermons and publications, special events and special services all helped to broadcast the new understanding of architecture and the material world more generally. Children were inducted into it through Church schools, Sunday schools, and choirs, as well as through the Whitwalks and processions we've already looked at. The symbolism of flowers, too, was emphasized in a wide variety of media.[15] Bindweed 'represents sin', explained one tract; 'the Golden Candlestick was intended as a type. It represented the

Fig. 15. St John's Church, Woodbridge

Church,' explained another.[16] And there were many more besides. In that way, the typological, symbolic view which had come to prominence in the 1830s was perpetuated long afterwards. Sermons to adults—especially, as we have already seen, those preached at the consecration of churches—were intended to serve a somewhat similar purpose. Indeed, the changed ideas about architecture we have been uncovering can be traced in the changed registers and references used in these set-piece occasions of clerical oratory.

By the beginning of the nineteenth century, most of these consecration sermons followed a familiar formula, tracing the development of sacred space from the Old Testament onwards and then emphasizing the uses of the building which had now been constructed. High Churchmen tended to assert the importance of liturgy; those lower down the scale preferred to focus on preaching. Even those few who mentioned symbolism tended to argue that it had no bearing on modern churches: Solomon's Temple 'was typical of spiritual and better things'; a church, by contrast, was simply a place to worship.[17] Even those who thought about emotions tended to emphasize sound rather than sight, absence very much more than presence: praising churches which 'affect us pious with their simplicity; or by their silence'.[18] 'Fail not, brethren,' observed one remnant of this tradition at a consecration in 1846, 'to mark *wherein consists the right adorning of a Christian* temple. It consists not in outward magnificence, nor in internal decoration; but in the presence of God—in spiritual worship—in the preaching Christ.'[19] The church in which he declaimed these words—St John's, in Woodbridge, Suffolk—reflected this view. At its heart and centre stage was an old-fashioned triple-decker pulpit. But its Gothic form, its apse, and its magnificent spire also hinted at a loosening of Puritan opposition to architectural effect. Sure enough, within a few decades, even here, the pulpit was gone, a choir had moved into the chancel, and the altar became the focus of attention. Sermons also changed. Newman's controversial and strikingly innovative words at Littlemore, when he attempted to inculcate a symbolic, typological interpretation of the building, were just the first of many. His curate, Isaac Williams, did the same at the consecration of his own church in Llangorwen in 1841, as did Bishop Samuel Wilberforce.[20] As time went on, so did many other less *parti pris* preachers. In this way, the churches were reinterpreted for the people.

The consecration was a single event. Clergy had, however, other means of reinforcing this message, not least of which was an entirely new invention: the parish magazine. First formalized in the 1850s, these were soon ubiquitous, combining local news with material which was nationally distributed. 'Clergymen', as Jane Platt observes in her standard work on the subject, 'saw them as a form of outreach which travelled with them and their lay district visitors into all sorts of homes around the parish.'[21] They were usually prefaced with an image of the church, and often contained details about the building. It's also worth noting the ways in which the more generic 'inserts'—pages of copy bought from specialist publishing houses—drew attention to architecture, its meanings and its effects. The *Old Church Porch*, which we've encountered a couple of times already, was just one of these inserts, albeit a relatively short-lived, relatively ritualist one. It was filled with essays and pieces of serial fiction, many—as the title of the journal suggests—written with one intention: to explain the function and meaning of ornaments and structure alike. 'How holy, deep, and full of meaning are symbols of the Church,' observed one meditation on 'Our Church Window'; 'how in every outward type is the hidden reality distinguishable, if only rightly sought for'.[22] Week by week, even those who did not attend church nonetheless might come to understand the building in the way their clergy hoped they would.

Church guidebooks likewise provided a way of explaining these buildings. Often produced to mark the opening or reopening, they were in many cases subsequently reprinted or used as the basis for later guides, thus prolonging their life—and propagating the message they were first written to convey.[23] Sometimes, as at the elaborately decorated and utterly remarkable church at Cockayne-Hatley in Bedfordshire, this simply meant identifying the sources for the architectural details and furnishings it included: with the chancel window 'copied from the east window of Wilbraham church in Cambridgeshire'; a roof with bosses from Biggleswade and a cross from Trinity College Cambridge; and woodwork taken from the Abbey of Alne and the church of Malines in France; together with chairs copied from Glastonbury and stalls 'placed in the nave by an arrangement somewhat similar to the antient [sic] church of St Clement, Rome'.[24] Increasingly, however, the clerical authors of these guides tried to evoke still deeper meanings. Describing the radically restored, effectively rebuilt church of St Peter, Hascombe, Surrey in 1885, for instance, the rector declared he was writing for two sorts of readers: his parishioners, that they 'might enter the better into the teaching which its present decoration is intended to convey', and those strangers who might need to be persuaded that 'the restoration and adornment of our churches is not a mere aesthetic exercise, but a work mediately yet surely tending to the good of souls'. Every detail, therefore, is explained, interpreted, and shown to convey a spiritual truth.[25] Rather wonderfully, many of these interpretations are repeated even today on the church website.[26] In that way, some lost lessons taught by the Victorians still live on.

There was, though, never a complete clerical takeover of the church. Indeed, most clergymen did not have the resources to work alone in rebuilding or refitting their places of worship. Above all, they relied on money from our second group of actors—laymen and laywomen: sometimes, in England, working through the Incorporated Church Building Society, which helped to build hundreds of new churches; sometimes through the state, which spent £3 million on new churches in England, and smaller, though nonetheless still significant amounts in Ireland and Scotland, too.[27] More than anything else, they depended on individual lay patrons. These included smaller benefactors like the cast of people Francis Kilvert recalled in his diaries: Miss Newton, who gave a text to the church of Bredwardine and a banner to Brobury; Mrs Prodgers, who became the scandal of the parish when she paid for a new east window in Kington St Michael and had herself and her children included 'in the most prominent position'.[28] They also included immensely wealthy figures like the first Marquess of Ripon, an eccentric, Masonic, Roman Catholic convert, whose church at Studley Royal is, in the architectural historian Joe Mordaunt Crook's words, 'a Gothic portent of the New Jerusalem…an elaborate exercise in iconography', a monument to its patron, and, with an 'attendant choir school', a monument too to a 'new paternalism'.[29]

As the complex case of Studley Royal—which is both a memorial to its patron and also a densely packed religious text in its own right—makes quite plain, it would be wrong to say that lay people built solely for secular reasons, of course; just as it would be wrong to assume that the professionally religious built only for purely theological purposes. A complex web of interrelated impulses doubtless impelled both clergy and laity. Moreover, if we are to take seriously the challenge to think religiously about religion— the challenge with which this book began—then we need to do more than assume that changes in the wider world were simply, uncomplicatedly reproduced within church buildings.[30]

Nevertheless, it is true to say that some of the changes in church architecture were intended to respond to the ways in which public and domestic buildings also changed at the same time. Indeed, as one writer put it in 1887, although the 'Catholic Revival' was 'one of the prime factors' in 'transforming the appearance' of churches, it was also aided by 'the gradual advance' and 'general perception of brightness, smartness, and outward decency' that he believed had transformed Victorian society more generally.[31]

It's certainly the case that advocates for church-building programmes like Beresford Hope saw wider developments as a justification for their efforts. A pioneering Ecclesiologist and patron of **All Saints Margaret Street** in London—the church which succeeded Frederick Oakeley's chapel—he argued that amongst the reasons for rebuilding was the poor comparison many churches made with other newer, bigger, grander institutions. 'Our public works and our public buildings become day to day more vast and more lofty,' he wrote in 1861:

> The giant hotel replaces the gloomy and obscure tavern, and the public library throws into the shade the few hoarded volumes in the corner. The cramped stage-coach, with its handful of squeezed travellers, has been annihilated by the train with its hundreds of well-housed passengers. The intellectual expenditure of artistic invention, and the physical expenditure equally characterise the structures of the day.

Beresford Hope saw this general trend as a particular challenge to the church: 'Shall God then only be forgotten?' he went on:

> Shall we be told that we ought to make our homes and our town-halls, our theatres and our hotels, our shops and our legislative chambers, lofty and wide, glorious in painting and carved work, and glittering with costly materials, and that the House of the Lord alone is to remain small and mean?[32]

As visitors can still see from the sumptuous church he built, his answer was a definite, undeniable, unignorable no.

ALL SAINTS CHURCH, MARGARET-STREET, CAVENDISH-SQUARE.—FROM A DRAWING BY MR. MURRAY.

Fig. 16. All Saints Margaret Street

More than this, the assumptions that underlay many of these secular buildings were directly—and indirectly—formative for sacred architecture. In her book on nineteenth-century American churches, Jeanne Halgren Kilde has shown that the design of theatres and fashions in domestic furnishings were critical in reshaping church architecture in the 1880s—especially amongst Evangelicals suspicious of the clerical and Catholic associations that had grown up around more traditional, Gothic churches.[33] A parallel process was undertaken in Britain a generation before. The reordering of many churches, dividing up the building into discrete and well-defined units—the chancel, the organ chamber, the choir stalls, the nave—replaced a generalized congregational space with the sort of highly differentiated plan that increasingly characterized many Victorian buildings, from country houses to hospitals. The bodily discipline expected in church—the sitting, kneeling, silent movement, and congregational singing—likewise resembled the growing regulation of the body that was also being practised in clinics, schools, houses, and even prisons.

Perhaps above all—and, certainly, most revealingly—the notion that buildings could and should communicate was also articulated by school builders in the Victorian period, with Edward Thring, pioneering headmaster of Uppingham, famously observing that school buildings should 'speak the truth, the honourable truth', whilst the founding warden of Radley rather alarmingly claimed that everything within his school—from the curriculum to the soft furnishings—was directly inspired by the Athanasian Creed.[34] The emotional effect of architecture was a commonplace of the era, and something which also came to shape prison and asylum architecture. Moreover, as Colleen McDannell has argued in her wonderful history of *The Christian Home in Victorian America*, 'the creation of emotion and sentiment' was an important part of domestic architecture too.[35] This was, in short, not an exclusively clerical process of architectural reform.

A third group of people also played a necessarily pivotal part in reshaping Victorian church architecture, alongside the clergy and laity who used these places. They were, of course, the architects. Although this book is not about them—and will not devote much space to them—it is worth remarking on their importance, because this was, in many respects, an innovation.[36] True enough, architects like Wren and Hawksmoor and Gibbs had helped transform church buildings in the late seventeenth and early eighteenth centuries. But never before had so many churches been built.

Never before, too, had there been so many architects—and, more to the point, so many architects who specialized in church building. The architects who emerged in the 1830s and 1840s—architects like George Gilbert Scott, who restored more than a dozen cathedrals and built or rebuilt hundreds of parish churches—were representatives of a new breed of expert, increasingly and self-consciously professional, and using their specialist knowledge of historical architecture to bolster their professional claims.[37]

As the architectural historian Neil Levine has shown, this change can be found at work in two rather different buildings, Pugin's Church of **St Giles, Cheadle,** and Henri Labrouste's Bibliothèque Sainte-Geneviève in Paris. In both cases, Pugin and Labrouste turned their back on the settled, familiar authority of classical architecture in favour of an approach in which construction was not concealed but was rather expressed—and expressed using forms derived from history. It's worth noting, too, that this is a process that transcends style; that makes style, in a rather surprising sense, a second-order issue. Levine has traced this transformation in a series of essays, revealing that the 1830s saw a radical shift in architecture all across Europe. 'A new and broader awareness and understanding of architecture's history', he writes, 'opened up possibilities previously considered only in marginal ways.' No longer would architects seek justification for their work solely by reference to scientific principle, biological analogy, or the classical canons. Architecture was increasingly seen as the decoration of construction rather than the construction of decoration. Above all, as Levine asserts, 'history replaced nature as the basis for generating architectural forms'.[38]

NORTH AISLE, SHOWING THE LADY CHAPEL, &c.

Fig. 17. St Giles, Cheadle

Pugin and Labrouste were by no means alone—indeed, for all their innovative genius they were representative. The 1830s and 1840s did indeed see the collapse of the eighteenth-century classical canon and its replacement by an architecture which used all sorts of history as a sourcebook for new forms of design. The problem was, of course, that architects trained almost exclusively in the principles of Vitruvius, Palladio, and—increasingly—ancient Greek examples, were ill-prepared to understand the buildings of other eras. It was here that the fourth and last of our groups comes in. For the importance of antiquaries to the reimagining of architecture is hard to overstate, however much it has been disregarded since. They were critical in shaping what the historian Rosemary Sweet terms a 'new mode of perception' in the years leading up to the Victorian era.[39] It was antiquaries who had first begun to establish the core principles that would underpin the transformation in church architecture this book is about. They included men like John Milner, who helped to shape the understanding of architecture as a system of signs and symbols, a sort of text;[40] men like James Bentham, who helped establish the idea of an architecture of affect, with Gothic, in his words, an architecture in which all the elements 'concur in affecting the imagination with pleasure and delight, at the same time that they inspire awe and devotions'.[41]

Above all, the work of antiquaries—some of whom were architects, some clerics, and some simply interested amateurs— helped to systematize forms of architecture that had previously been seen as chaotic, unsystematic, and unintelligible. Antiquaries, in particular, drew up taxonomies of the Gothic, developing the terminology of Early English, Decorated, and Perpendicular— or First, Second, and Third Pointed—that would structure all subsequent thinking on the subject.[42] This taxonomic mode of thought enabled architects to reproduce medieval architecture, and their clients to understand what was being reproduced. Taxonomy enabled them to break buildings down into their component parts. Architectural training became a process of learning how to draw the details of medieval buildings and the analysis of architectural design became, to a certain extent, the identification of the origins for this or that idea. 'I think, Sir,' said one of G. F. Bodley's pupils as he looked over a new plan, 'that comes from such and such a place.' 'I see', said Bodley, 'the ass knoweth his master's crib.'[43]

It was not just those erecting new buildings who were shaped by this new mode of taxonomic, almost deconstructive architectural analysis. This approach similarly shaped encounters with older church buildings, which were also broken down into their component parts; analysed for evidence of style and date; compared and contrasted to agreed models of the type.[44] One of the most important contributions of the Ecclesiologists and the other societies set up in the 1830s and 1840s was precisely this: popularizing taxonomy and thus training people how to see—to experience and make sense of—a medieval church. In 1841, for instance, the Oxford Architectural Society produced proformas for church visitors to fill in. A short while afterwards, the Cambridge Camden Society began publishing a still more exhaustive 'church scheme'— a lengthy document which encouraged Ecclesiologists to move systematically through each church, starting inside with the chancel and east windows and working through the interior before beginning the analysis of the outside. Details and dating were everything—with the observer enjoined to pay particular attention to the tracery, the mouldings, the existence or otherwise of features like sedilia (seats for the clergy), lavabos (places for priests to wash their hands during the Mass), and the like.[45]

The effect of this was remarkable—and can be seen to have had an effect on each of the three other groups I have identified. As Rhona Richman Kenneally points out in what is, remarkably, the only serious study of the subject, the church scheme's seminal influence can be discerned in the work of architects like George Edmund Street, whose sketchbooks faithfully follow the analytical, taxonomic framework suggested by the Ecclesiologists' proformas.[46] This influence can also be felt in guides to church buildings themselves: books like the history of St Mary's Callington in Cornwall, which structured its tour of the church fabric precisely in terms dictated by the same schemes.[47]

The impact of this new way of seeing can be witnessed, too, in the changing language used by the newly activist archdeacons as they inspected—or undertook 'visitations' of—the churches under their charge. Here, for example, is Archdeacon Butler, a High Churchman of the old school, in his returns of 1823–4, with the twelfth-century church at Alfreton described as 'An ancient stone building consisting of spacious nave, south aisle and chancel.' Here he is on the eleventh-century church in Allestree: 'An ancient stone building consisting of spacious nave, south aisle and chancel.'[48] Exactly the same words for entirely different buildings—and I could go on, for he was keen on this phraseology, and repeated it often, apparently indifferent to what the churches he described actually look like. Yet here is Archdeacon Bonney, another old-fashioned High Churchman, in his visitation twenty years later, in 1845: St Peter at Gowts, he reports, is in 'Transition Early English'; St Margaret's Huttoft, he observes, has 'A very interesting early English tower at the West end of the nave, with an additional story of Transition Decorated.'[49] A revolution in perception had taken place.

This new understanding of history and of architecture, this new sense of what a church should contain and how it should be experienced, had consequences for how churches were then built and restored; for what churches were assumed to be and what it was hoped they would do. It helped to create an ideal type of church—almost a Platonic idea—against which reality could be measured. Indeed, so attractive was this ideal type that it helped to shape real churches in tangible ways. As Nicholas Orme has noted, the fashion for churches to acquire dedications grew out of this, with most modern names—be they St Mary's, All Saints, or something more exotic—simply the product of

Victorian wish fulfilment; 'a mixture', in his words, 'of ancient truth with modern inventions, guesses, and errors'.[50] As Christopher Herbert has observed, it also led to a fruitless and fictitious search for fittings like Easter sepulchres, assumed to have been part of the normal appurtenances of any parish church. The result was that 'many objects which had never actually been Easter Sepulchres were redefined to fulfil that aspiration'.[51]

More strikingly still, churches were built in imitation of these ideals—and, still more remarkably, others were 'restored' to the image of what should be rather than what actually was or ever had been. 'To restore a building is not to preserve it, to repair, or to rebuild it,' wrote the French architect Eugène Viollet-le-Duc; 'it is to reinstate it in a condition of completeness which may have never existed at any given time.'[52] The result could be—and often was—massive rebuilding in the name of restoration. This accounts, for instance, for transformations like those at the Round Church in Cambridge, which was wholly reconstructed in the 1840s, as the Ecclesiologists attempted to return it to its supposedly ideal form. It explains, too, the way in which St Albans Abbey was rebuilt in the years after 1878, as Perpendicular Gothic was replaced by conjectural reconstructions of earlier styles. Here we can see that a new sense of historicism combined with the new belief that church architecture served an almost missionary purpose to remake a building utterly, as it was changed into what its rebuilders believed it should look like—and should always have looked like.

Not everyone was convinced, of course. We've already noted—at some length—the ways in which many critics saw this return to a Gothic past as anathema. For some Protestants, it was unacceptably Catholic. For some Catholics it was not nearly

Tridentine—and, hence, baroque—enough. For many radicals, churches—especially ancient churches—were far from being embodiments of an ideal faith or time. For the radical poet Thomas Cooper, for instance, Lincoln Cathedral was not a bastion of religion; it was rather a 'Great sepulchre of haughty gloom and grandeur . . . The tomb of regal priests who banqueted on joys wrung from the peasants' woes.'[53] Yet many Nonconformist churches did begin to embrace a historically inflected architecture, an architecture that harked back to the medieval past. Think, for instance, of Oxford, with its Dissenting Gothic Colleges of Mansfield and Manchester, or the Wesley Memorial Church—topped off, just as the Ecclesiologists recommended, and just as Keble had done at Hursley, with a golden weathercock, which

Fig. 18. Mill Hill Unitarian Chapel, Leeds

'bids us watch and pray and endure hardness', as Neale and Webb put it.[54] Think, too, of the magnificent neo-medieval **Mill Hill Unitarian Chapel** in Leeds, erected in 1848 and modelled in plan and style after the recently rebuilt Leeds Parish Church.[55] Even low-cost, temporary, expressly evangelistic buildings, like the numerous 'tin tabernacles' mass-produced from the 1850s onwards, even they expressed their purpose and their meaning by embracing—almost universally—Gothic details and Gothic ornament.[56]

As this suggests, the search for an ideal-type church emphatically did not result in a backward-looking, atavistic architecture, much less a naïve attempt to revive the rural parish of medieval England. These were modern buildings—heated and lit and furnished with the latest technology. Even the music was modern, for, as the pioneering organ builder John Baron put it, unforgettably and surely undeniably, 'Every man of progress, even if only semi-musical, must feel an interest in the great triumph of mechanical art and musical science exhibited by a large and really good organ.'[57] Those writers who see in this Gothic Revival a necessarily reactionary movement are consequently quite wrong.

Rather, this ideal type was exactly that—a type, a type of building designed to achieve certain effects and assumed to possess certain characteristics. Above all, the creation of this typology helped to change the meaning of the word church. A Gothic church, with stained glass, and medieval or neo-medieval fittings; a church designed to communicate and to evoke emotions; a church with a certain place in the landscape or townscape: this became the yardstick against which all other ecclesiastical buildings were judged. Sometimes, there was outright rejection. In his marvellous memoirs of Lancashire in the 1880s, for instance, William

Fig. 19. West Croydon Congregational Church

Haslam Mills recalled the pride with which his Congregationalist chapel disavowed—'on principle', as he put it—'the certificated beauty of stained glass or of stone aisles and prostrate attitudes'.[58] But other congregations and even some other Congregationalists differed.

Take the Congregationalists of Croydon, for example, and their London Road Church of 1865. As the historian Jeremy Morris has shown, at the foundation-stone laying it was made quite plain that this was intended to be neither a 'chapel' nor a 'meeting house', but a 'church'. 'Ours . . . is a church,' declaimed the speaker:

> although to some it may savour of affectedness, or of pretension to adopt this title in preference to the one generally given to

Nonconformist places of worship, we prefer this word, and purposely designate our buildings by this name, to which we shall adhere, not only because it is an ecclesiastical structure, but as more truly significant of the purpose of its erection.[59]

Twenty years later, they would go one better, erecting a substantial neo-Gothic church, complete with 'Croydon's most ambitious spire'.[60]

Where the Congregationalists of Croydon led, others soon followed. For this turn towards an ideal type of church also suited some Methodists, like the architect F. J. Jobson, who argued for Gothic architecture on similarly typological grounds. 'Who has not felt', he asked:

the uncertainty of apprehension, and the incongruity of ideas, arising from the sight of a Chapel in Roman or Grecian Architecture when he entered a city or town for the first time? On looking upon the building (unless an inscription board was on it) he could not tell whether it was a Concert-room, a Theatre, a Town-hall, or a Chapel. But who, on seeing a Gothic chapel, has had any difficulties in determining its appointed purpose? Its ecclesiastical form made known its use, at first sight, and without any possibility of mistake.

This was not Ecclesiology. Indeed, Jobson hoped that 'the day will never come when painted scenes and sculptured figures shall be introduced into Methodist chapels', and he was clear that medieval facades should not be paired with medieval plans, for 'Methodism—in a word—requires *Chapels*, and *not* Churches'. But it was a typological argument for style, and one that depended on assumptions about architecture as, in Jobson's words, 'the outward and visible representation of Christian worship'.[61]

So it was that theology, history, and architecture; clergy, laity, architects, and antiquaries; Anglicans and Nonconformists: all converged to produce a widely accepted understanding of what a church should look like, what it should feel like, how it should function. Conceived by Anglicans in the early Victorian period, by the end of the nineteenth century, it was such a commonly held idea that it influenced all manner of different denominations. This ideal type of church, I've argued, was built on two assumptions: the first about architecture, the second about time. It was assumed that architecture was a vehicle of communication and an engine of emotion. It was also assumed that history provided a guide to how this had worked in the past and an authority for how it should work in the future. There were, however, inherent tensions in this apparent consensus; tensions—denominational, theological, architectural, and, perhaps above all, historical—that were to prove increasingly problematic.

This was true for all sorts of church buildings—churches old and new, churches restored and churches freshly erected. For new-built churches, the appeal to past architecture was necessarily bound up with what the architectural historian Joe Mordaunt Crook has called the 'Dilemma of Style'.[62] Seeking an architecture which would communicate and move, and with the whole of human history to choose from, architects and their clients were faced with an impossible range of choice. Little wonder, as the architect Thomas Graham Jackson complained in 1873, that, in the course of a single generation, Victorian architects had 'twice run through all those varieties of Gothic architecture which represent the steady growth of four centuries'.[63]

If this was a problem for churches being built, then it was still more problematic for those being restored. What priority should govern this process? Which features should be retained and which removed? Which style should be used? How could a church remain faithful to its past and to its purpose in the present? And what about the future? As the historian Chris Miele, amongst others, has shown, this debate about restoration was critical for Victorian architecture. And one can see why: for new churches were not just modelled aesthetically after older, medieval examples. They were also interpreted in light of them. As we've seen, it was perhaps above all the antiquaries who had taught Victorians to look for meaning in Gothic churches and to be moved by them too.

More importantly, there was a theological as well as an architectural dilemma here. All could agree that these ancient churches were important. Yet why they were important—for what they housed, what they did, or for what they were—remained a vexed and apparently insoluble question. Ecclesiology was built on antiquarianism, but for its proponents it was important not to confuse the two approaches. 'There is no greater mistake, in my judgement, than to identify ecclesiastical architecture with archaeology,' wrote the parson Thomas Chamberlain in 1856. 'Ecclesiastical architecture must of all the sciences be the most living.'[64] Increasingly, especially in older churches, however, antiquarianism came to trump Ecclesiology and, with it, architecture came to trump theology, as the form of the building itself came to be emphasized over and above its function as a church. This was an implicitly secularizing process—one that can be traced, not just in buildings, but also in the treatment of their contents. An example uncovered by the archaeologist Kate Giles is a good case in point.

Pickering in Yorkshire in the early 1850s was just one of many churches undertaking serious restoration. It was also one of many in which medieval wall paintings were uncovered in the process—indeed, a few years later, in 1858, the architectural magazine the *Builder* would observe that 'the discovery of painting on walls of churches is now of daily occurrence'.[65] Pickering, however, was special and different. The pictures discovered were extraordinary. They were also deeply alarming to the Low Church incumbent, John Ponsonby. Ponsonby wanted them whitewashed again, defending his actions in the following words:

> I am at a loss to conceive how a clergyman could, even with a shew of consistency read to his congregation the Homily on Peril of Idolatry, and at the same time approve of having the Crucifixion scene and Legends of Popish saints represented by a painting (old or new) on the wall before his eyes.

Moreover, he feared that these pictures had been given new importance by the rise of ritualism and the efforts of the Tractarians, 'whose effect' he went on:

> is in fact … to adopt every Romish symbol and practice which the law will admit, and so degrade the Church to Romish principles … When I look upon these pictures and reflect upon the superstitious errors once associated with them, and when I find upon the authority of the martyred Cranmer and the Sainted Jewel that the having of such things in a Christian Sanctuary is a (wilful) violation of God's word and commandment, and contrary to the usage of the primitive Church … I protest accordingly.

Now, all this is terribly familiar stuff—think of Peter Maurice's horror at Littlemore or the aspersions cast on the Ecclesiologists by Frederick Close that we've already encountered. And, in truth, Ponsonby's attitudes were not just old-fashioned Puritanism; they also reflected—just as Maurice's and Close's polemics reflected—a renewed opposition to the new sense that had developed of buildings as active participants in people's faith.

What's more striking about this moment, however, is the archbishop of York's response to Ponsonby's protest. For in his letter to the vicar of Pickering, it is clear that the claims of history outweighed any theological qualms. 'As relics of a past age,' the archbishop observed, 'I should not be willing to obliterate and destroy them...I should be as much opposed to the risk of danger in this respect as any one could be, but I cannot concur with your fears on this behalf.' Here, the prelate makes an important move: he recognizes the historical importance of the images, but he cannot conceive that they have any religious function. They are to be preserved for their own sake; and not for the sake of their spiritual effects—for they are believed to have none.[66] As the years went on, so this attitude became acceptable not just for the details of a church, but for whole churches. The buildings were valued for what they communicated and how they made visitors feel. But what they communicated, increasingly, was history; and what they evoked was a sense of the past rather than the religious present.

Fig. 20. St John the Baptist, Inglesham

Chris Miele is again a good guide to this process—and he offers us an excellent example of its secularizing effects in his analysis of **Inglesham Church** in Wiltshire, a building often identified as one of the great success stories of Victorian church conservation after its restoration of 1888–9. 'The results', he writes, 'are barely perceptible; the church was left nestling in its snug churchyard like an accent in an eighteenth-century watercolour.' Yet, this freezing of time, he concludes, is problematic. It is an:

> act of conservation which enshrines the very decay of the church fabric...a commentary on the decay of the institution of the Church...More than that even, because the scrupulous preservation of the physical form arrests the church at a particular historical moment, it connotes a similar end to the building's spiritual mission. At Inglesham, the church—perhaps even the Church—lies off the beaten path, and the ideology of its conservation implies that is where it should be.[67]

I don't think Miele exaggerates. Indeed, we could go further and note the way in which this approach to historic churches—one which places the emphasis on the word *historic*—tends to leave the church and the faith it was built to articulate a thing of the past. It was a process only exacerbated as the nineteenth century gave way to the twentieth, and the historicism of the Victorians made way for modernism. The aftermath of all this and the development of churches since 1900 are the subject of Chapter 5.

5

Revisiting

If you are going to build a church
you are going to create a thing which speaks.
It will speak of meanings, and of values,
and it will go on speaking.
And if it speaks of the wrong values
it will go on destroying.
There is a responsibility here.

> Robert Maguire, 'Meaning and Understanding', in Peter
> Hammond, ed., *Towards a Church Architecture*
> (London, 1962), pp. 65–77, p. 66

If there is one simple method of saving the Church's mission, it is
probably the decision to abandon church buildings.

> Michael Winter, *Mission or Mortar: a study in new pastoral
> structures* (London, 1973), p. 24

It was a splendid, unforgettable occasion. Three bishops, more
than 300 clergymen, and a choir of still more hundreds processing slowly through the city singing psalms. The date was
30 June 1863. The place was Hereford, and the reason for all this
activity was the reopening of the cathedral following a long and
costly restoration campaign. Over two decades the edifice had
been reordered, rebuilt, and was looking better than it had for
centuries. At its centre, and at the heart of the restoration

Fig. 21. Hereford Cathedral Screen

effort, stood a brand-new, brilliantly gilded, lavishly ornamented, eight-tonne metal structure: a choir screen, designed by the pre-eminent architect of the era, George Gilbert Scott, and constructed by his trusted collaborator, Francis Skidmore, a man widely recognized as the greatest ironworker of the century. Journalists reporting the reopening were struck by the ironwork's beauty, its skilful composition and construction, and by the sympathetic way in which it framed and embellished the cathedral. For the *Illustrated London News*, this great Gothic screen was nothing less than 'the most noble work of modern times'.[1]

Times change, however; so do tastes. Scott and Skidmore's screen was destined to remain in place for a little over a century. By the 1920s, it was being dismissed as 'unsuitable' in guidebooks.[2] By the 1930s it had become the subject of indignant letters to the press. In 1939, the Council for the Care of Churches—the national body responsible for cathedral conservation—was also calling for its removal.[3] Writing in August 1965, the dean of Hereford expressed his own horror at a structure he believed to be characterized by its 'incongruity and over-obtrusiveness'.[4] The gilding and the ornamentation, the elaborate neo-medieval design: in the nineteenth century, they had been seen as beautiful—and, more important, as appropriate. Appropriately enough, indeed, the screen had been understood as a sort of text, filled with figures that 'Everyone can understand...at a glance'; covered in images whose 'meaning may be felt without the aid of any inscriptions'.[5] Yet, by the 1960s all this now seemed superfluous, meaningless, even wrong. In March 1967, eighteen months after the dean's expostulation, the offending structure was finally taken down, never to return. 'The screen was removed a few days ago,' wrote the architectural historian Alec Clifton-Taylor. 'I sat rejoicing. The improvement is almost unbelievable.'[6]

Fast forward twenty years, and attitudes had changed again. A revival of interest in all things Victorian combined with a growing disillusionment with the modern movement in architecture and a growing distaste for many of the recent reorderings of Britain's churches to make many regret the removal of the screen. Dismantled, stored in boxes in a Battersea warehouse, and visibly decaying, it seemed to symbolize everything that had gone wrong with the twentieth century's treatment of historic buildings. In 1993, a campaign was started to raise funds for the screen's restoration. Slowly, painstakingly, conservators took apart the 30,000 individual components; they then cleaned, repaired, and replaced much of its fabric. It was repainted, regilded, and made to shine again. In 2001, after the most expensive conservation project ever undertaken by the museum, the Hereford screen was installed at the V&A. It is now exhibited to visitors as 'one of the monuments of High Victorian art and a masterpiece in the Gothic Revival style'.[7]

Although the Hereford screen is undeniably remarkable, its story is certainly not. It traces a familiar arc—from the enthusiasm of the Victorians to the condemnation of their successors to the resurrection of interest in their art towards the end of the twentieth century. It would be easy—and not wholly wrong—to tell this as a heroic epic, as the conservation movement triumphs over philistinism and the Church comes to appreciate its Victorian inheritance. But, of course, it is all rather more complicated than that—it is *always* more complicated than that. The Victorians themselves can just as easily be seen as vandals—indeed, many Victorians themselves were appalled by the nineteenth-century restoration of Hereford Cathedral, screen and all. Likewise the dean who, in the 1960s, wanted to rid himself of this striking piece of Victoriana was, in his own terms, scarcely a philistine. The screen, he argued, was not just unsightly; it was also a bar to the proper use of the cathedral space. Both he and his nineteenth-century predecessors, then, were equally acting in good faith, making decisions that seemed right at the time. These are not the villains that a good epic needs.

Moreover, it's worth asking who and where are the heroes in this story? Before we become too complacent about our own treatment of historic churches, it is salutary to be reminded that what happened in Hereford is still happening today. Indeed, it is happening with an ever greater intensity, for, as the bishop of Dorchester recently put it, 'we are currently seeing the greatest alterations to the interiors of our churches since the late nineteenth century'.[8] Thousands of churches and cathedrals are being reordered, and, in the process, the furniture, fittings, and fixtures the Victorians installed are being moved, or removed, all across the country. Perhaps the most vulnerable architecture of the present day, writes the director of the Victorian Society, is 'unfashionable, Victorian ritualist church interiors'. 'Little', he concludes, 'could be further from the spirit of the age.'[9] And, as if to confirm his point, at a meeting of the Church of England's General Synod in July 2015, Canon Timothy Allen—the man responsible for church conservation in the diocese of St Edmundsbury and Ipswich—unequivocally asserted that 'The three great banes which hold back more effective use of church buildings as an instrument of mission and growth are the following: blocked gutters, bats and the Victorian Society.'[10] Little wonder that one expert, Richard Halsey of the Cambridge Historic Churches Trust, should complain at a conference on 'Piety in Peril' in 2013 that current developments amount to 'Reversing the Ecclesiologist, Tractarian concept of sacred space'.[11]

There is, then, no happy ending. But nor, for that matter, is there a simple narrative arc to follow either. Indeed, on closer examination, our story turns out to be even more complicated—and, I'd suggest, even more compelling. For although it's clear that attitudes to the aesthetics of the Victorian church would change and keep on changing in the twentieth and twenty-first centuries, the basic assumptions which had governed Victorian church building continued and continue to have a defining importance for ecclesiastical architecture. The notion of church buildings which teach, move, and help sacralize the landscape has never gone away. If anything, recent years have seen these ideas reinforced rather than undermined.

It would be easy to ignore or overlook this continuity—and most scholars have. An obsession with the externals of style has led to a neglect of the ideas that underpinned church building more generally. In this final chapter, we will see that both those who argued for the removal and those who argued for the restoration of the Hereford screen, both those who wanted to preserve and those who wanted to reform, reorder, or even destroy nineteenth-century churches more generally, were all participating in a discussion that the Victorians themselves had started—and, as a result, ended up using ideas and developing concepts first articulated in the nineteenth century. Looking at taste alone—simply telling a story of how architectural fashions change—hides this truth. It also conceals the fact that we too are involved in this story and part of this ongoing discussion. In that way, just as I suggested at the start of this book, we can see that we are still experiencing the Victorian church. The problem is that these ideas are now so ubiquitous we don't even notice them. As a result, we fail to understand the sacred space bequeathed to us: what it is, why it was built, and how it might still speak to us.

The victory of Victorian values—or, at any rate, of the particular consensus that we have been exploring in this book—can be measured by the way in which these ideas had almost wholly triumphed over much remaining resistance from Anglican Evangelicals and many Nonconformists by the turn of the twentieth century. Visiting St Jude's in Kensington in 1891, the archbishop of Canterbury, E. W. Benson, was struck by what he found: 'Here is an Evangelical congregation and minister,' he wrote; yet here was a 'cross on the altar and a white cloth with a lace border always remaining on it and a piscine [a bowl or niche for washing the communion vessels] and a surplice choir'. 'Any one of these things,' he noted, 'would have been deadly popery' in his youth.[12] It was true, for what has sometimes been described as a process of 'levelling up' was indeed well under way by then. The number of Anglican churches using candles, for instance, increased from 581 in 1882 to 4,765 by 1901. Over the same thirty-year period, the number with ministers wearing vestments rose from 336 to 2,158. Crosses and flowers—so controversial a generation before—became common, and surpliced choirs became commonplace.[13] Many Nonconformists proved equally allured, with the Congregationalists, for example, celebrating a new chapel in Great Yarmouth in 1938 as a place which 'combines the richly prized intimacy of our Free Church worship with the reverence and dignity associated with Anglican buildings. The appearance of the choir in their simple black gowns enhances this impression.'[14] That the architect of this chapel was F. W. Lawrence, a man obsessed with sacred symbolism and the emotional effect of his architecture, only enhances the sense that the Victorian consensus lasted long into the subsequent century. Indeed, as Basil Clarke put it, in the Edwardian era, 'The theory of designing and adorning a church was still what it had been in the days of the Ecclesiologists.'[15]

Still more remarkably, these aesthetic assumptions lasted long after that. At the 1965 New York World's Fair, complained one contemporary, the model 'City of the Future' sought to reimagine all forms of architecture—all forms, that is, except for ecclesiastical architecture; for the church at the heart of this futurist vision was recognizably, inevitably, a Gothic one.[16] Little wonder: the late nineteenth-century Gothic Revival, argues the historian Gavin Stamp, 'became an orthodoxy which lasted for over half a century, even beyond the Great War'.[17] True enough, there remained some denominations and individuals who rejected all of this, insisting on plain Puritanism, just as there had been in the nineteenth century. True, too, even those who continued to embrace Gothic idioms often defended this in new ways. At Liverpool Cathedral, for instance, begun in 1904 and finally finished in 1978, Giles Gilbert Scott offered an enormous piece of neo-medievalism, but one which stressed the importance of space rather than the significance of surface for its effect. 'Don't look at my arches, or the tracery of the windows, or the carved ornamentation,' he wrote; 'look at my spaces.' But he still argued in true Victorian style that this was a building which communicated and which was intended to shape the emotional life of its users through its 'solemnity' and 'mystery'.[18] And, of course, its Gothic form spoke of continuity, too, showing just how hard it was to reimagine the fundamentals of ecclesiastical architecture for much of the twentieth century. As Mrs Poultridge puts it in T. S. Eliot's pageant of 1934, The Rock, 'I do believe that if the Church gives up Gothic, it may come to disestablishment, or re-union, or nonconformity, or almost anything.'[19]

Although the interwar period saw some attempts to reject the nineteenth century, Victorianism proved hard to overturn. 'In the first half of the century,' writes one expert, 'the dominant philosophical force in the Church of England was that of Anglican Catholicism, whose preferred architecture was a stripped-down continuing perpendicular Gothic.'[20] This is, of course, precisely the tradition we have watched emerge. And even apparent alternatives proved little threat to the status quo. The ultra-ritualist Anglicans of the interwar period, for example, tended to dismiss the Gothic Revival, embracing instead what became known as the 'Back to Baroque Movement': 'not an attempt to get back to what we were before the Reformation', as N. P. Williams put it in his magnificently titled *Too Much Stiffness* of 1917; but *'an attempt to get forward to what we should have been if the Reformation (in its more destructive aspects) had not happened'.*[21] Other churches wanted something more self-consciously contemporary, and employed architects like Nugent Cachemaille-Day to 'cast away the unconvincing and artificial frills of the less good work of the last century'.[22]

But it must be said that the Baroque Revival was short-lived and, in any event, its proponents tended to approach their work in exactly the same way that the Victorians had done, by reference to some very familiar assumptions about how churches worked and what ecclesiastical architecture was expected to do.[23] Many of the more modern churches, too, were characterized by traditional plans, generic symbolism, a familiar type of emotional economy, and a particular kind of place within their town or village. As his biographer notes, even the self-consciously contemporary Cachemaille-Day 'recognized the tenacity of the Gothic tradition'.[24] In that way, even when appearances apparently changed, the basic underlying ideas did not.

As late as 1966, when the writer Bryan Little surveyed recent Roman Catholic church building, he concluded that even in the last decade and a half, many new churches had remained resolutely 'traditional in style', the product of a 'desire for a place of worship which would "look like a church"'. Here was the triumph of the Victorians indeed, but it was one that Little believed increasingly came at a cost. 'Pastorally,' he suggested, these churches were 'valuable', but they were 'not buildings of the type one finds mentioned in books on modern church architecture. In the context of this country's "contemporary" religious architecture they have little meaning.'[25]

The dilemma identified by Little was a real one and one made all the more acute by a twofold transformation of taste in post-war Britain. On the one hand, there was the modern movement in architecture—a broad and disputatious category, to be sure, but one that evidently described a new sensibility and a new aesthetic. For modernists, modernity was to be expressed in modern materials and modern styles. Indeed, a functional approach would transcend style altogether, producing an architecture driven by the needs of users and the zeitgeist. 'The nineteenth-century Gothic Revival', wrote one pundit in his study of *The Modern Church*, published in 1957, 'has lost its meaning for the scientific spirit of the age.'[26] On the other hand, there was a new approach to liturgy: one that looked back to early Christian practice rather than the ideals of the Middle Ages; one that saw fixed structures and tightly disciplined congregations as anathema, a break with authentic Christian spirituality.

All this seemed to challenge the Victorian status quo. 'The majority of Gothic-revival churches', declared the architect-priest Peter Hammond in his hugely influential book of 1960, *Liturgy and Architecture*:

> are unsuitable for worship not simply because they are often full of unlovely ecclesiastical furniture and sentimental stained-glass, or because they have ill-proportioned altars and dreadful sculptured reredoses. Their unsuitability is due above all to the fact that they are planned in accordance with an understanding of the liturgy which is fundamentally at variance with modern biblical and liturgical scholarship.[27]

The result of this change in taste was not just a series of new churches, often built with experimental plans and materials in explicitly modern styles, but also, necessarily, the reordering of older churches.

It was within this context, of course, that the Hereford screen was removed, and it was just one of many such changes. Across the country, pews were removed, altars relocated, Victorian painting whitewashed—and much more besides. For Roman Catholics, reeling from the aftershocks of Vatican II, that reforming Church Council of 1962–5, with its vernacular liturgy and new conception of worship, the change was staggering. But many Protestants were in many respects equally iconoclastic. 'The ordering and re-ordering of churches', wrote the prolific Anglican commentator Gilbert Cope in 1962, 'must... proceed on the basis that these buildings are functional power-houses and not old curiosity shops.'[28] At their most radical, writers were willing to contemplate closing churches altogether, seeking to replace them with more flexible, free-form, multifunctional spaces. It was this that prompted Michael Winter's comment, quoted at the start of the chapter, that the Church should simply shut its churches. It was this, too, which helped to justify the decision to demolish redundant churches. By 1976, a church was being knocked down every nine days.[29]

For contemporaries, this seemed like a revolution, a transformation every bit as complete as the Victorians had effected—and these comparisons were picked up on at the time. Writing in 1960, the historian Peter Anson claimed that the changes advocated by reformers comprehensively undid the legacy of the nineteenth century, returning ecclesiastical architecture to the ideas which had animated the pre-Victorian church. 'The pendulum had swung from one end to another,' he concluded. 'All those rigid principles set forth by Pugin and the ecclesiologists in the eighteen-forties and -fifties were thrown overboard. The reversal was complete.' 'To-day,' he concluded, 'we have got back to the "auditory church" of Sir Christopher Wren.'[30] Nor was he the only author of the time to draw on these analogies, with the cleric Stephen Smalley coupling an attack on the 'disaster' of nineteenth-century church building with a claim that his own vision of modern ecclesiastical architecture should be read as 'a "tract for the times"';[31] the architect Nigel Melhuish quoting Ruskin and Morris;[32] and Peter Hammond depicting himself as a latter-day Pugin, hoping to write:

> a volume of Contrasts, consisting largely of photographs and scriptural quotations, in which evangelical qualities such as humility, sincerity, truthfulness, poverty of spirit, etc., would be illustrated from the secular architecture of the last thirty years or so; while the whole catalogue of deadly sins—pride, sloth, luxury and the rest—would be illustrated from the ecclesiastical buildings of the same period.[33]

Readers were expected to understand that at the start of the Victorian era Pugin's Contrasts had boldly made the argument for Gothic in a somewhat similar way, and to see this new, modern, rational dispensation as the unravelling of all that.

Yet the very fact that this comparison was being made is intriguing. It suggests that, in some respects, far from being a clean break with the past, the reformers of the 1960s could not escape—indeed, that they remained overshadowed by, and some-what in thrall to—their Victorian predecessors. The more one looks, indeed, the more one can see that for all the bravado, for all the claims of revolution, and for all the apparent antagonism and rejection of tradition, much remained intact.

Take the radical church reformer Nicolas Stacey, for example. As rector of Woolwich between 1960 and 1968, he was in many respects the poster boy for religious reform. He was featured in the colour supplements, he appeared on television, and he was a popular writer for the newspapers. Above all else, church buildings were the instruments he chose to effect his changes. He hated the 'Victorian monstrosity' in which he had trained for the priesthood and loathed the 'ugly red-brick Victorian parish church' in which he served his curacy. At the end of the 1950s, he had argued that three-quarters of Anglican churches should be closed and then demolished. The remainder should be converted into multifunctional social centres. In South London, he sought to achieve just that, hoping to 'make Woolwich Parish church the most exciting multi-purpose centre in the country', by turning much of the fabric over to offices, a cafe, and even 'the swing-ingest nightclub in London' in the crypt. It was an unquestionably comprehensive transformation—one which was intended to undo much of what the Victorians had intended in order to create a building 'to meet twentieth-century needs'.

This, again, all sounds very much like a radical rejection of all the ideas we have been exploring, and all the changes that the Victorians made. But it is worth digging deeper. Stacey's focus on the church building reflected the ongoing belief, inherited from the nineteenth century, that architecture did something, that it helped shape faith. The reordering at Woolwich, he argued, transformed the church from a building which 'proclaimed that God was dead' into one that 'spoke of the majesty and power and love of God'. The removal of pews and the installation of carpets, he claimed:

> altered the entire atmosphere of the building. Worshippers had become so accustomed to cold and draughty churches with their hard flagstone floors and uncomfortable pews, that they did not realize that the very furniture makes it almost impossible to generate that sense of peace and quiet which enables one to hear the 'still small voice'.

The aesthetic is different; but the approach is not—nor was the way in which Stacey measured its success. Just like the Victorians, he assumed that the sheer number of people now entering the building was an index of its renewed importance, and hoped that its new outward appearance would 'slowly alter people's attitude to the Church' as a whole.[34]

A curious combination of traditional content in a modern form can be found in even the most apparently profound rethinking of church architecture in the 1960s. In a wonderful irony, modern architecture and liturgical change actually served to heighten the didactic and emotive importance of buildings. The result was a surprising tension, even a paradox, in the arguments made by reformers, who insisted on functionalism, but then conceded that part of the church's function was indeed to articulate theology and help shape faith. So we find Peter Hammond, unarguably the leading figure in this movement, dismissing 'the old pictorial approach to architecture' and the Victorian attempt to '"express" this and "symbolize" that', in the same short essay on 'A Radical Approach to Church Architecture' in which he rearticulates the idea of architecture as a 'living language', something that 'can never be dissociated from meaning'.[35] For him, the goal was very similar to what the Victorians had wanted: 'the recovery of an authentic language of symbols'.[36] So too, one of Hammond's chief critics, Peter Smith, who argued in the early 1970s that previous reformers had not gone far enough, proved keen both to attack architecture 'attempting to preach "sermons in stone"' and at the same time to advocate buildings which functioned as 'effective ... profound symbols'.[37] Likewise, in his pioneering work on *The Modern Church*, Edward Mills argued for a return to 'the "auditorium" type of plan', and a rejection of 'mock classic or pseudo-Gothic monuments'; but also for buildings which would 'speak' to the modern world. 'The test of whether a work is good or bad', he concluded, 'is whether it inspires the right emotion.'[38]

Such conceptual ambiguity was universal. It was the product of a multitude of different factors, not least the growing interest of modern architects in communicating with the public and developing an architecture which was, in the words of one important pair of practitioners, 'poetry without rhetoric'.[39] The post-war period saw theologians, too, increasingly attracted to symbolic analysis. 'It has been said that theology is suffering from a rush of symbols to the brain,' observed one writer in 1960.[40] Above all, assumptions about the very nature of the church building clearly remained intact, whatever the wider debates about the form this should take.

The more sophisticated the analysis, the more likely it was that this surprising truth was recognized—as it was by the pioneering architectural practice of Maguire and Murray, responsible for many of the most important and interesting new churches of the period. Writing on 'Material Fabric and Symbolic Pattern', Keith Murray even quoted John Mason Neale and Benjamin Webb and argued for a renewed appreciation of their work. 'They were', he concluded, 'defending not particular symbolic forms but the symbolic way itself.'[41] It was this symbolism he—and others—sought to create in the churches that they designed and built.

The rejection—even the destruction—of Victorian churches was consequently defended in terms which would have been entirely familiar to the Victorians. Nor was it just the most aggressively avant-garde who argued in this way, although they were pleased to find that others agreed with them:

A very ordinary, traditionalist and entirely uncranky vicar, with a barn of a Victorian-Gothic church, said to me recently, 'I shall never begin to get my people to see themselves as the Body of Christ until the entire lay-out of this building has been changed.' I am sure he was quite right . . . The church building is a prime aid, or a prime hindrance to the building up of the Body of Christ. And what the building says so often shouts something entirely contrary to all that we are seeking to express through the liturgy. And the building will always win—unless and until we can make it say something else.[42]

So wrote the Bishop of Woolwich in 1962: a controversial figure reporting on the views of a much less turbulent priest, and both of them parroting phrases that had first been articulated at least 120 years before. The notion that Christians were both formed and informed by their church buildings was clearly a very long-lived and long-lasting one.

This helps to explain why those who removed the Hereford screen were also simultaneously responsible for packing the cathedral with a whole range of new symbols. The screen was taken out, as we have seen, because it was felt to be 'meaningless'; because it acted as a barrier to modern worship. Yet, at precisely the same time, the very same people were introducing new symbolism, new meanings, new messages: 'hassocks with emblematic designs', 'more elaborate' floral decorations, and much more besides; all intended 'to meet modern requirements and a changing outlook'. Both the removal of the screen and the installation of these new symbolic instruments sprang from the same impulse: 'new ideas for the nineteen-sixties' which were in reality old ideas of the 1830s and 1840s.[43]

Still more remarkably, those who opposed these changes also drew on the language and ideology of the nineteenth century.

This was precisely what self-defined traditionalists wanted, of course; and throughout the twentieth century there were ongoing attempts to defend and even extend the Victorian approach to church buildings and parish life. Hence the pious children colouring and cutting out paper chasubles in High Church Sunday schools across the land. Hence, too, the forest of statues and banners that sprang up in Anglo-Catholic churches—and in even churches of more Evangelical hue, like the Low Church St Saviour's, Ilford, which in 1976 still celebrated its architecture as a sort of text, its 'white walls for His white life, and hangings blue/As Mary's robe'.[44]

The impact of liturgical reform—and especially the iconoclasm associated with Vatican II—may even have strengthened this tradition. The closure of churches and the stripping of altars allowed Anglicans like the flamboyant Brian Brindley, vicar of Holy Trinity Reading, to fill his previously sparsely furnished church with a rood screen by Pugin thrown out by the Roman Catholic cathedral in Birmingham, a high altar from the Anglican church of St Paul's, and a pulpit from All Saints, Oxford, the whole creating an effect described in the *Buildings of England* as 'altogether the Highest of the High'.[45] 'At no time had good church furniture and ornaments been so freely available,' observes the historian Anthony Symondson. 'Never before had so much lace been seen in Anglican chancels.'[46] Within this world, the old assumptions about the role and function of the church building remained apparently unassailable.

Similar continuities can be discerned in the attitudes of those who otherwise appeared to take a diametrically different approach to the subject. The late nineteenth century, as Chapter 4 suggested, gave rise to an understanding of the church as an art object, worth preserving for its own sake and not for its religious functions. Such a sensibility was only heightened by modernist trends in town planning, which tended, in the historian Otto Saumarez Smith's words, to give ecclesiastical architecture 'a central, indeed a dominating position', yet only at the price of rendering it 'deconsecrated, aestheticized and abstracted by the plan'.[47] This was the natural outgrowth of those late Victorian ideas.

The same was true for many of those who campaigned to preserve churches, and who sought to challenge the changes that were transforming their appearance. For conservationists of the twentieth century also inherited many of the attitudes of their nineteenth-century predecessors. Thomas Hardy's distinction between the cleric for whom 'the church is a workshop' and the antiquary for whom 'it is a relic' remained as true in 1960 as it was in 1906, when he first made it.[48] Fiercely opposed to those who wished to rip out pews and reorder buildings so that they became more obviously contemporary, campaigners like John Schofield echoed the rhetoric of Victorian conservationists. 'The tendency', he wrote in 1977, 'is always to make an ancient building less, to reduce what it has to say.' 'Out go mystery, subtlety, profundity, sympathy. And with them spirituality too.' Instead, he argued, 'We want to let old churches, in all their many riches of art and intellect and Spirit, speak for themselves.'[49] It might have been William Morris writing—and, indeed, Schofield was writing on behalf of the Society for the Protection of Ancient Buildings, which had been founded by Morris a century before. Just as late nineteenth-century writers and campaigners celebrated churches for their form rather more than their function, for their history instead of their active role in fostering faith, so many twentieth-century conservationists and preservationists hoped to stop the

Fig. 22. St Bartholomew's, East Ham

clock, ensuring that churches were 'fossilised', as one writer recently put it, 'in their largely Victorian state'.[50]

It has proved hard—indeed apparently impossible—to escape the Victorian church. Even today, the notion that buildings should communicate and that they should move us emotionally has not wholly dissipated. The slew of books on how to 'read' a church reveals the continuation of that Victorian idea of the church as text.[51] The ongoing sense of the church as somehow active, somehow set apart, can similarly be seen in the ways that many congregations have transformed the architecturally reticent, multifunctional buildings erected in the aftermath of the 1960s. Take St Bartholomew's, East Ham, for example:

a brick and glass construction, consecrated in 1983; a piece of 'deliberately undemonstrative architecture', effectively embody-ing the Church's desire to eschew the excesses of the past and embrace new architecture and new ideas. It's worth noting, how-ever, that even this bare building was intended to be symbolic, expressing a 'message that the Church of England was the church of the whole parish, churchgoers or not'. Still more intriguing—and revealing—is the response of those who actually used it. The congregation overruled rector and architect alike by insisting that the plain exterior wall should be ornamented by a sculpture of the Holy Family, marking this out as a sacred structure. Later still, a cross would be added, addressing an absence of symbolism which church members deeply regretted. 'We didn't even know it was a church at first, did we?' complained one parishioner.[52] That the nineteenth century helped establish our idea of what a church would look like explains much about this and many other places. 'In many ways,' writes Carola Hicks, in her recent study of Cam-bridgeshire churches, 'we are Victorians' in our attitudes to our church buildings.[53]

This ongoing influence can even be traced in some of the most dramatic and destructive reorderings undertaken by churches in the last thirty years. It's clear, for instance, that the work of the most influential Anglican exponent of church reordering, Richard Giles, should be seen as the continuation of ideas first pro-pounded in the 1950s and 1960s rather than as a significant break with the past. As such, he marks continuity, rather than change—and with it, an unacknowledged, perhaps even some-what shameful debt to the nineteenth-century past.

Giles's book, Re-Pitching the Tent, published in 1996 and then again in 1999, was widely read and revered as a radical intervention in debate. So was his work in remaking churches, like St Jude's Peterborough, where 'he took a really rather ordinary twentieth-century red-brick church and turned it into a Le Corbusier-type space for worship'.[54] His approach was summed up in his work at St Thomas's Huddersfield: 'a gloomy and overlarge Victorian "masterpiece"' by George Gilbert Scott,[55] which he detested and sought to reform by stripping out the pews and other fittings, installing new, contemporary designs, and escaping what he elsewhere described as the 'unholy influence' of Victorian aesthetics.[56] In truth, none of this was really new: it was all taken straight from the writings of Peter Hammond and Gilbert Cope, who had, after all, called for churches to be 'the Tent of God' rather than a 'stronghold of the Establishment' as long ago as 1962.[57] For all Giles's claims, therefore—and for the excitement at the new furniture and new liturgies that went with these claims—his work, like that of his predecessors, remained necessarily in dialogue with the past. Indeed, his books and his buildings were saturated with the assumptions he had inherited from the Victorian past. His arguments—that church buildings 'speak', that they can be active evangelists on the streets, that they 'are not *primarily* architectural forms. They are rather theological statements'—are exactly those made by people as far back as the 1830s.

Little wonder we're confused about churches. If even the most apparently iconoclastic of figures—a man renowned for his 'uncompromising vision and radically obdurate way of getting things done'—turns out to be parroting phrases that are more than a century old, then what hope do we have of producing a genuinely contemporary, wholly original approach to church architecture and design?[58] How are we to make churches for and of our own times?

Our current confusion is rather wonderfully illustrated by the Church of St Nicholas in Durham, scene of an important reordering undertaken in the early 1980s by the then vicar—and future archbishop of Canterbury—George Carey. Hundreds of thousands of pounds and a thirteen-month building campaign left the place unrecognizable, with worship reoriented, the Victorian fittings removed, and entirely new furniture installed. Against the criticism of this transformation levelled by conservationists, who wished to preserve the nineteenth-century interior, the church prominently displayed a banner reading 'it is people that matter, not buildings'.[59] Yet, of course, the very act of reordering, and the willingness to raise so much money, suggested just how important the building actually was to its users. The old arrangement, argued Carey, was 'a major stumbling block to the gospel'. The new dispensation was intended to communicate and to evangelize. The resonance with Victorian ideas about buildings is inescapable. In his book on St Nicholas, Lord Carey recalled his encounters with visitors to the church: '"What—no pews?" was the usual comment. But when it was explained that we had chosen chairs because they were more adaptable than pews, they left well pleased that a church was taking active steps to reach the world with the gospel.'[60] That people still expected to find pews in a church is telling. That stacking chairs could be seen as key instruments in the evangelization of England by a church community which argued that people mattered more than buildings is equally remarkable. Both tell us much about our ambiguous inheritance from the Victorian past.

That the Churches now find themselves responsible for large numbers of often very old buildings and a diminishing number of often very old worshippers only makes the matter more complex.

As the title of an influential study by the Diocese of Norwich puts it, church buildings are both *A source of delight and a cause of anxiety* (2003).[61] Although there has been much church building and still more reordering in the last few decades, there has also been significant church closure. From 1969 to 2013 1,873 Anglican churches were closed, one-fifth of which were demolished.[62] The Free Churches have been even more willing to offload surplus buildings. In the county of Oxfordshire alone, while the Church of England shut seventeen places of worship, the other denominations closed more than 100.[63]

Moreover, there are those who actively welcome this cull. In the 1970s, Michael Winter was in fact far from alone in arguing that 'If there is one simple method of saving the Church's mission, it is probably the decision to abandon church buildings.'[64] It's a call that has become ever more insistent. 'We must do to our churches what Beeching did to the railways,' argues the controversial cleric Giles Fraser in a typical piece written for *The Guardian* in 2015.[65] This is not just a matter of money—although the cost of propping up ancient and sometimes decaying architecture is an important part of the context for these discussions. There is also a theological component to their arguments. For Fraser, an iconoclastic liberal, preserving church buildings is a form of idolatry. For Sally Gaze, another Anglican—but an Evangelical one this time—churches are often little more than 'transitional objects', not unlike a child's soft toy, which the mature Christian needs to give up.[66] Richard Giles makes the point most plainly when he argues that churches must always seek to escape any form of conservationism, any attempt to preserve their form, and any campaign to avoid modernization and the appropriately contemporary reordering that goes with it. 'What is absolutely

Fig. 23. St Benedict's Church, Manchester, now the Manchester Climbing Centre

non-negotiable for the Church', he concludes, 'is that preservation is not an option.'[67] It is better, he observes, to close a building than to be forced to preserve its Victorian features.

In recent years, churches have explored some alternatives to closure. There is the idea of the 'festival church': a building which is mothballed for most of the year, but opened up for high holy days and special occasions.[68] There are also multiple ways of reusing old churches and chapels—from offices to homes, from bars and restaurants, from clubs to a rather marvellous climbing centre at St Benedict, Manchester.[69] As the secularist and columnist Simon Jenkins succinctly put it, 'England's churches can survive—but the religion will have to go.'[70] Somewhere between these two poles is the increasingly popular attempt to do exactly what Nicolas Stacey did in the 1960s and convert churches into multipurpose buildings, with space shared between the secular and sacred, as they are turned into what the Diocese of Oxford has called 'community hubs'. It is this process, above all, that has led to perhaps the most intriguing change in the landscape of ecclesiastical architecture, one which has seen churches kept open but profoundly transformed inside, with pews ripped out, sofas installed, and—as one expert puts it—places of worship made 'indistinguishable from a doctor's surgery or even some sort of domestic interior'.[71] Strikingly even this radical change, this undoing of the Gothic Revival, is defended as the 're-medievalization of the church', as buildings are supposedly returned to some ancient, shared concept of space.[72] In that way, the rhetoric recurs even as the aesthetics are altered beyond all recognition.

Is this, then, the future? A few precious Victorian jewels preserved unchanged for ever; other churches comprehensively refitted—either as state-of-the-art liturgical spaces or multifunctional 'community hubs'; still more deconsecrated, sold off, or simply left to moulder away. That certainly seems to be the message delivered by a recent enquiry, published in 2015 by the Church of England, the denomination which possesses the single largest collection of places of worship and which has responsibility for the most churches recognized as architecturally important. It's a remarkable report: one that reiterates so many of the themes that have run throughout this book: the notion of churches which 'have the capacity to speak of the living God'; the idea of places which 'assist in proclaiming the gospel just by being there'; the concept of structures which 'help us to experience the presence of God'.[73] It also helps us to understand the direction that many Anglicans at any rate expect the Church to travel: closing more buildings; reusing more; preserving the best and turning others into places of occasional, sporadic, 'festival' worship.

Yet it's worthwhile wondering whether this has to be the case—and whether these are the best outcomes that we can expect. There are two problems with much of what is currently said about church buildings. The first is architectural. The second is historical. We need to take each in turn.

Architecturally, as the theologian David Brown has observed, many of these developments grow out of a strongly instrumentalized understanding of buildings. 'Church architecture', he argues, 'is often seen merely as one particular means of facilitating some general strategy such as the communication of the faith.'[74] Buildings, in other words, are seen as a means to achieve some specified end, rather than as ends in themselves. So strong is this instrumentalization that it even overcomes experiential evidence to the contrary. Take Richard Giles, for instance. His key text, Re-Pitching the Tent, begins with a revealing anecdote. Visiting a Cornish church, he found it full and thriving—'a model Christian community'. Yet he was 'troubled' by the architecture and its fittings: 'Its unaltered building', he wrote, 'spoke more loudly than its energetic priest.' It was 'a church fit only for the heritage trail'; a building which spoke of 'a geriatric God incarcerated in an old folks' home'.[75] That the church was working; that it was attracting worshippers; that it sustained a 'model Christian community': none of this apparently mattered. The building was, for Giles, failing in its purpose, even if all the evidence suggested otherwise, because it was not, in his mind, saying the right things in the right way.

The same is true in many of those places which have reordered or rebuilt, assuming that the greatest barrier to churchgoing is the church building.[76] The results have often been disappointing. As one expert puts it, there is a sense that some people 'may be blaming the pews, irrationally, for reduced congregational support or, equally irrationally, hoping their replacement with comfortable chairs will magically solve more fundamental problems'.[77] In reality, even those volumes published to advocate just such a change are hard-pressed to find evidence of anything of the sort happening. Typical is the rueful observation made by representatives of St Helen's in Abingdon, Oxfordshire, which was reordered to encourage the 'renewal of the congregation' and the creation of 'an area that could be used by the community'. Encouragingly, they do believe there have been benefits, and they note in particular that more people are now crossing the threshold. More dispiritingly, however, they 'are currently unsure of how much the additional uses are contributing to the mission of the church and the sustainability of the building'.[78]

Brown is surely right to see these attitudes as the product of a particular theology. But even more than that, they are the result of a historical process: the outcome of a change that dates back to the Victorians. This instrumentalization, this assumption that churches perform certain functions, this sense that they move and communicate as well as house and accommodate, this is all, as we've seen again and again, an inheritance from the nineteenth century. The Victorians were the first to propound this view and it's their understanding—even their terminology—that we continue to use. Yet all the changes we are currently experiencing are being undertaken as though this were not the case, as though we were somehow breaking free from the past. The result is a terrible conceptual confusion, one that is reshaping churches across the land. The Victorians are seen as the problem. But they are seen as the problem for the wrong reasons. Those who would reform or reorder the church look at nineteenth-century buildings and fittings and see inflexible space, a building that fails to communicate contemporary values. What they don't see is that this thoroughly instrumentalized perspective is fundamentally Victorian, too; and it's one that is shared with many congregations, visitors, and those who barely ever darken the door of a church.

This provides every church or chapel with an enormous opportunity. Instead of seeing our Victorian heritage as an obstacle to mission, we should seek to build on the common sense of what a church is and what it does, a common sense that is shared with many of those outside worshipping communities. The Victorians have provided us with certain cues that suggest sacred space. They have also given a model of how to interpret it. The Victorians, in other words, have taught us how to experience the church. True enough, many of those who come into a church have never been exposed to the theological or architectural language which would enable them to read it as a text. It's true too that 'the traditional "body-language" of the church no longer seems so pertinent...discomfort is no longer so appropriate'.[79] But the fact that many people arrive still expecting to understand the building, expecting to be moved by it—the fact that they instrumentalize it—is in many respects encouraging. It suggests that there is a chance of using churches to do exactly the things that the Victorians had intended them to do. The church in that way actively becomes a form of education, a means of mission. The instrumentalization need no longer be implicit, unacknowledged, disregarded. It can now be made manifest—and used. It means a rather different response to our inheritance from the one that has characterized so much debate for so long. It means working with the grain of these buildings, rather than against them. It means accepting them for what they are instead of wishing that away.

Visiting **Leeds Parish Church** in 2002, a writer for *Church Building*, the pre-eminent publication in the field, was unimpressed. None of the features that had so enraptured many Victorians captured him. 'It might be asking the impossible,' he wrote:

> but St Peter's should be stripped out—and its beautiful ground floor pews recycled...Surely St Peter's is a church loved by its congregation—and no doubt by the Victorian Society—but we cannot worship in a free, unfettered and joyous way while fixed into the building like this.[80]

But need that be so? Perhaps a better way would be to recognize that it is indeed a building 'loved by its congregation', and a building built to express some very particular ideas, to do some very particular things. Over the last century and a half new ideas have also been incorporated and new experiences generated as a result. Instead of taking these away, might it not be worth seeking to add to them? Instead of dismissing the church as utterly outmoded, is it not possible to work with and to reinterpret what they already have? Certainly, that is how Stephen Oliver, then rector of Leeds, came to understand the place. Arriving in 1991, he was alarmed to find an inflexible Victorian museum-piece. Writing three years later, in 1994, however, he observed:

> My initial fears concerning the building have not been realized. The daunting pulpit whilst being 'high and lifted up' enables the preacher to enjoy a surprisingly intimate relation with the congregation.

The elevation of the Chancel, but in sight of the majority of the congregation, allows for that essential sense of unity in the celebration of the Eucharist.[81]

Working with the building, in other words, he came to see its opportunities, not its limitations.

The same is surely possible for so many of the churches and chapels that surround us, that we worship in, live in, or merely drive by or walk past. Whether the products of the nineteenth century or sometime later, all of them were built for different times and different people. They were also built for different tastes. Much has changed—and much continues to change. Yet the impact of the Victorian revolution in church architecture has never wholly dissipated. It continued to shape buildings long into the twentieth century, and still seems to have a purchase on the popular imagination today. More importantly, the mode of experiencing ecclesiastical architecture pioneered in the first few decades of the nineteenth century has remained surprisingly enduring. Even those who radically reject the Victorians have proved incapable of finding another way of understanding the church. This may be a problem. It may very well be that such instrumentalization is theologically flawed. But it also presents an opportunity: to use churches to do what the Victorians intended them to do; to teach, to preach, to move, to convert, to lead people closer to God.

Just a little way out of Oxford—not to the south, like Littlemore, but to the north, about six miles from the centre of the city—is a church I know quite well, not least because I often officiate at services there. St Mary the Virgin in Kidlington is not Victorian. It finds its way into Simon Jenkins's *Thousand Best Churches* because of its medieval origins, its magnificent spire,

Fig. 24. St Mary's Kidlington

and its thirteenth-century woodwork. Visitors and worshippers alike admire the grand view from the great west door to the ancient stained-glass window at the east end, interrupted only by an open Gothic screen. Opinions are more divided about the modern, plastic, brightly blue-coloured chairs, put in as part of a reordering in the 1970s; and Jenkins—for one—is not completely convinced by the statues introduced at the same time, which he sees as 'mawkish'.[82]

Both the antiquity of the structure and the modernity of many of the fittings make the nineteenth century seem very far away and rather irrelevant. Yet, of course, everything in this place is, in fact, Victorian in one way or another. Had we visited Kidlington

200 years ago, we would have a found a very different church—an auditory church, with a pulpit in the middle of the north wall, surrounded by galleries on the other three sides. The chancel and most of the rest of the church were separated from the nave by plaster walls; a plaster ceiling hid the medieval roof and cut off the tops of the windows. It was the Victorians who restored the place, turning it into something we now recognize—and experience—as a church.[83] It was the Victorians who reoriented the place, turning all eyes to the east; the Victorians who refurnished it; even the Victorians who discovered and then effaced some 'indescribably accurate drawings' of the seven deadly sins on the walls.[84] Those Victorian values led to the introduction of new symbolism and ultimately to the removal of pews and their replacement with new chairs.

It's worth remembering this, not just because it's good history, but because it reminds us of the unfinished revolution the Victorians began: turning churches from preaching boxes into something more; into something almost sacramental. Now unlocked and open every day—just as the Victorians would have wanted—St Mary's Kidlington, like so many other churches, remains a memorial to this change; and, much more than that, an invitation to reinterpret it—to experience it—anew.

Afterword

Seeing for Yourself

What sort of church, I wonder?
The path is a grassy mat,
And grass is drowning the headstones
Sloping this way and that.
'Cathedral Glass' in the windows,
A roof of unsuitable slate—
Restored with a vengeance, for certain,
In eighteen-eighty-eight.

John Betjeman, 'A Lincolnshire Church', in his
Collected Poems (London, 2006), p. 141[1]

To most people today a church is a puzzling place.

Simon Jenkins, *England's Thousand Best Churches*
(London, 1999), p. ix

In his splendid guide to *England's Thousand Best Churches*, Simon Jenkins identifies sixty-six Victorian churches that are especially worth visiting. This is certainly an underestimate, and in truth, of course, almost all the other 934 were reshaped—sometimes radically—in the nineteenth century. The following suggestions, therefore, are just that—suggestive examples. They should not be seen as either prescriptive or even representative.

Rather, they are illustrative, intended to exhibit some of the themes that we have explored. I have also excluded several of the buildings mentioned in the text because they are closed to the public—or, at any rate, are frequently inaccessible. With one exception, churches that have been radically reordered are not mentioned either. This applies, alas, even to Littlemore, which until recently was an embodiment of the process we have been exploring. It was extended soon after construction in 1836; then given a tower. With its walled graveyard, lychgate, neighbouring school, and even its yew tree, it embodied so many of my arguments. Now, however, it is rarely open and there are plans to develop the site by extension or extensive reordering. Like numerous other churches, it thus has no place on this shortish list.

St Mary's Whitby

Climb the 199 steps from the town to the church, set on a rocky promontory high above the harbour, and you will enter a building which is marvellously evoked in the clipped tones of Nikolaus Pevsner. This is, he writes, 'a wonderful jumble of medieval and Georgian when one walks round it, but when one enters it, hard to believe and impossible not to love'.[2]

Originally built in the early twelfth century, the parish church of Whitby was extended in the thirteenth and fourteenth centuries. It is a glorious example of the way in which the auditory church overwrote the principles which had been embodied in medieval architecture. Filled with box pews and galleries, it was everything that the Victorians would come to hate; but it clearly worked for the Georgians. As early as 1625, the local lords of the manor built a gallery—the Cholmley pew—which cut off the connection between nave and chancel and set a trend which was to find its fulfilment in the early nineteenth century. With the population growing and tourists starting to arrive, the church became congested. Successive waves of galleries were built from the 1690s onwards, with large windows installed to light them and a massive triple-decker pulpit erected in 1778. In 1819 a huge north extension was opened, transforming a cruciform plan into something more like a square. It too was filled with galleries and pews.

This was one of the very few churches to survive the Victorians more or less intact. True enough, it did not escape wholly untouched: the pulpit was moved; some stained glass, by the noted artist Charles Kempe, replaced previously clear glazing. But, in essence, this is the apotheosis of the eighteenth century—and, especially, of the late eighteenth century—which turned old churches into preaching rooms. That this was entirely compatible with a fondness for medieval architecture is made plain by the porch of the early 1820s, which preserves the old Norman arch and coupled it with some vaguely 'Gothick' windows. The northern extension is likewise lit by some pretty pointed fenestration. These stylistic allusions were not, however, combined by any attempt to recreate the medieval plan, and reveal an eclectic approach to the Gothic that would be condemned by many Victorians. In that way, St Mary's doesn't simply preserve the old idea of the auditory church, but also shows that stylistic change—even an acceptance of Gothic—is not sufficient to explain the transformation in architectural ideas which would characterize the Victorian era.

Plockton Church

Many of the purpose-built churches of the two or three decades after 1780 are now closed, converted, or so profoundly altered that they provide a poor guide to the prehistory of the Victorian church. Even those that have survived, comparatively untouched, are always vulnerable. In 2013 it looked as though the small church of Plockton, in Ross and Cromarty, would be sold, and—like a neighbouring church building—be turned into housing. Fortunately, however, the Free Church of Scotland—more popularly known as the Wee Frees—was able to buy the place and it continues to be used as a place of worship, preserving the building and granting us a rare insight into the basic principles of church architecture in the early nineteenth century.

Opened in 1827, this was just one of the group known as Telford Churches which were built by the British government in the Highlands of Scotland. Responding to a perceived crisis in faith, the state underwrote the scheme, using plans for churches, manses, and schools published by the engineer Thomas Telford. Across the road from the church in Plockton, indeed, you can still see the manse—one of the smaller ones, as befitted this tiny fishing community. The church is not unchanged; indeed, it was extended and the woodwork elaborated and replaced over the years. It is carpeted, heated, and electrically lit. Nonetheless, it remains fascinating because it highlights two key themes; themes that we have also seen in Whitby. In the first place, it shows us how these functional churches worked. With its raised central pulpit, its galleries, and its tall, clear-glass windows, there is no mystery here; rather, it is a box perfectly designed for preaching in. Secondly, this should not be taken to mean that its designers wholly eschewed architectural effect. Note the arched and mullioned windows, the vestigial bell-cote on the gable. These are visual cues, designed to link even this most functional building back to older churches. Importantly, however, these details were intended to possess no more meaning than that.

To see how the Victorians transformed even the architecture of the Presbyterian Scots, you need to get on the train, travel across the moors, and visit Inverness, where great Gothic basilicas like the East Church, built two decades later, in 1852–3, reveal the impact of new ideas about buildings: what they could do and what they were meant to say. At the East Church—remarkably, a Wee Free church—there are still galleries; still a central pulpit. But all this is now clad in neo-medieval forms. In the 1890s, it would be topped off with a great Gothic-traceried window. It is a remarkable change of tone, one that reflected a new paradigm—a changed understanding and experience of church architecture.

St John the Baptist Drumcree

There are very few Roman Catholic churches from the late eighteenth and early nineteenth centuries that I can recommend. This is partly because few were built: anti-Catholic legislation and anti-papist public opinion made building tricky. More importantly still, most of those churches and chapels which were built before the Victorian era were profoundly transformed by the Victorians. The little Catholic chapel of St Mary's, Hampstead, for instance, was consecrated—galleries and all—in 1816, but then 'adorned' in 1822, 'beautified' in 1840, 'repaired and improved' in 1850, 'embellished and again repaired' in the 1860s, 'altered and beautified' in 1878, and 'embellished' again in 1916.[3] It was, in other words, left all but unrecognizable in a typically nineteenth-century attempt to transform a plain Georgian church into a typically Victorian medium for communication and a means of shaping faith.

That we still possess St John the Baptist Drumcree—and that, because it is part of the Ulster Folk Museum, it will be preserved in perpetuity—is thus little short of providential. Built in 1783, when the discriminatory Penal Laws were still in force, it is outwardly very reserved, signalling its function with a diminutive gable cross and arched windows, not unlike those on the church at Plockton. Inside, too, it is plain—and, most fascinatingly, planned in accordance with many of the same principles that would inform Telford's designs. With galleries on three sides and benches facing north, south, and east, the only thing that distinguishes it from a Presbyterian chapel is the fact that the focus on the long, fourth wall is an altar rather than a pulpit. Here again, function rather than symbolism or any search for meaning dictates form.

To get a sense of how this could be done with more money and more self-confidence, you need only travel to St Malachy's Church in nearby Belfast. Built in the early 1840s, it has a sort of Gothic exterior, and inside, as the historian C. E. B. Brett puts it, 'it is as though a wedding-cake had been turned inside-out'.[4] Yet despite all the sugar-coating, here is a similar idea: a rectangle with galleries to the north, west, and south; its altar set in the centre of the long east wall. It owes nothing to genuine medieval precedent and everything to a sensible pursuit of convenience and practicality. The Victorians would come to hate it.

Back at St John the Baptist Drumcree, meanwhile, it's worth noting that the nineteenth century even left its mark here: building a (now demolished) tower; installing an organ; adding ornamentation;

replacing the old, dirt floor with flagstones and—that great desideratum of Victorian church builders—encaustic tiles.

St Giles Cheadle

A wholly new idea of the church is embodied in the Roman Catholic St Giles Cheadle, built at exactly the same time as St Malachy's, but representing a revolution in architectural understanding. Designed by the dedicated, pugnacious, polemical, and surprisingly persuasive Augustus Pugin, it dominates the streetscape of this small Staffordshire town, and was later joined by a school, convent, and presbytery. The streets around would also come to be filled with regular processions. It is, in short, a perfect picture of exactly what this book has been about.

In part, St Giles was new because it was determinedly old: modelled, as it was, after the decorated Gothic churches of the thirteenth century. But this was no museum piece. As Rosemary Hill, Pugin's biographer, puts it, 'there was never anything quite like Cheadle in the Middle Ages'.[5] No: what St Giles expressed above all was a new sensibility. Here was a building that shut out the world, capturing the visitor for itself. The church, in Pevsner's words, is 'decorated wherever decoration could find a place'.[6] Its small, stained-glass windows make it dark; but the gilding, the marble, the encaustic tiles, the stencilling, and the paintings make it glitter nonetheless. At the consecration in 1846, the Catholic journal *The Tablet* got to the heart of the matter, observing:

> The effect upon the mind—even if one's experience of churches has not been confined to the miserable barns, stables and meeting houses which are our lot in and about London, but has extended itself to some of the Continental churches and cathedrals—is indeed magical.

The first view, while it elevates and exalts, overpowers the mind alike by its novelty and magnificence. When it becomes more familiar, and the disturbance, from a sense of novelty in ecclesiastical decoration, vanishes, the grandeur and beauty, elevating, refining, and sublimating the thoughts and feelings of the soul, remain behind.[7]

It was exactly this effect—this architecture of affect—that many Victorians would seek to achieve in their own churches.

Visiting St Giles in 1846, another church builder, and something of a sceptic about Pugin's passion, was nevertheless impressed. John Henry Newman wrote that it was 'the most splendid building I ever saw...I could not help saying to myself *Porta Coeli* [Gate of Heaven].'[8] Happily, the church was spared the most profound effects of Vatican II and has been beautifully preserved. It is still a moving place today.

Leeds Parish Church and Mill Hill Chapel

Just before St Giles was opened, the charismatic vicar of Leeds W. F. Hook constructed his own new idea of a church: then the parish church, now renamed Leeds Minster. His architect was R. D. Chantrell, a figure—like Hook—from an older, pre-Victorian generation. The building reflects this; a tendency that was exacerbated by the complexity of rebuilding on the site, and on the plan, of the old church. As a result, Leeds retains many features that would come to be seen as objectionable. It has galleries, a tremendous, vertiginous pulpit, and Gothic details that could not be mistaken for anything but the work of the nineteenth century.

Now cut off from the city by large roads and railway lines, it would be easy to walk past this church. That it was so soon condemned by the Ecclesiologists, who far preferred the more

Fig. 25. Leeds Parish Church

'correct' St Saviour's, founded by E. B. Pusey, and built only a ten-minute stroll away, might also deter us from visiting. But Leeds Minster is a revealing building—and well worth a trip. In the first place, of course, it reveals the way in which people began to rethink church architecture *before* the Ecclesiologists. Hook was an old High Churchman; he was neither Ecclesiological nor, for that matter, Tractarian. Leeds, then, speaks of the broad coalition of people who, from the 1830s onwards, transformed church building. Secondly, and just as importantly, the Minster is an example of what this new dispensation amounted to. The key point was not that they embraced Gothic (this had been done before), but rather that they saw this architecture as a means of conveying a message. Hook declared that 'a standing church is a kind of standing sermon'.[9] The sharp distinction between the sanctuary and the rest of the church, the emblems and images in the stained-glass windows, the other ornamentation: this all turned the church into a text; something designed to be read.

The impact of this change can be felt in the centre of the city, at Mill Hill Unitarian Chapel, opened in 1847. Here we see the abandonment of the old Dissenting classicism, which had characterized Nonconformists architecture for decades. In its place came a commitment to the Gothic, with a plan derived from the Anglican parish church—the Minster down the road. Its architect, Henry Bowman, might well have condemned his contemporaries' obsession with a symbolic interpretation of architecture, but his clients seem to have disregarded his advice.[10] As the historian Edward Royle points out, the choice of Gothic architecture was in and of itself symbolic, designed to assert a long-held belief that this congregation—and not the nearby Anglicans—were the *real* Church of England.[11] Succeeding generations would pursue this theme to its logical conclusion. Almost without realizing it, once the new idea of the church had been accepted, it began to encourage ever greater elaboration. Stained-glass windows by the finest artists—Morris, Clayton and Bell, Powells—were installed from the 1870s. Mosaic panels elaborated the east end in 1876. A reredos of Christ and the Prophets by the fashionable firm of Salviati appeared in 1884. In that way, this bastion of Nonconformists faith likewise became legible: a building which spoke.

All Saints Margaret Street Westminster

Built to replace the proprietary chapel that Frederick Oakeley had modelled after Newman's church at Littlemore, All Saints was intended to be an ideal that still others would in turn go on to imitate. It was the product of a collaboration between three men: the antiquary Sir Stephen Glynne, famous for his detailed notes on church architecture; Alexander Beresford Hope, a fabulously wealthy philanthropist, who was a leading light amongst the Ecclesiologists; and William Butterfield, a Tractarian architect who would go on to build that great cathedral of the Oxford Movement, Keble College. Squeezed onto a tiny, inconveniently shaped site, they managed to fit in church, clergy house, and choir school.

It is, though, the interior that impresses—or, oppresses, depending on your point of view. Every inch is ornamented. 'From everywhere the praise of the Lord is drummed into you,' as the *Buildings of England* guide observes.[12] Even those spots left blank by the architect were soon to be filled with mosaic work, paintings, and other elaborations. This has an obvious effect on anyone who enters the church. Finding yourself shut away from the bustle of central London, in a completely enclosed space, even the empty church has an impact. Everywhere you look there is something calling for your attention. Here is the architecture of affect indeed.

In an important article, the architectural historian Michael Hall has also suggested how this structure can be understood as well as felt. This is a building filled with narrative, he argues: from the great painted cycles on the walls to the images in the stained-glass windows. Even the profusion of colourful marbles, the striated walls, and the structural polychromy of the brickwork had a story to tell, evoking as they did the geological record.[13]

In 1847, before the project got under way, Butterfield had reordered the old building. 'Margaret Chapel looks most wonderfully well,' Beresford Hope wrote to Gladstone; 'Butterfield has really made a most religious place of it.'[14] When, twelve years later, in 1859, the church was finally consecrated, its reception was rather more ambivalent. Butterfield had not got his way over everything. Beresford Hope was openly critical. Fashion had moved on. But the building still speaks of this attempt to create a most 'religious place': a building somehow imbued with and able to imbue spiritual truths.

St Nicholas Little Braxted

All Saints Margaret Street was a famous, fashionable, metropolitan minster. Just over fifty miles away, and almost thirty years later, a rather less well-known church was transformed. Little Braxted is a magical little building: originally Norman, and restored by Ewan Christian in 1856, it is one of the smallest churches in

Fig. 26. Little Braxted Church

Essex. In 1881, it came into the possession of Ernest Geldart, an extraordinary architect and Anglican priest, who would, over the next half decade, devote his considerable energies, his undoubted enthusiasm, and his remarkable talents to the place.

Geldart, the author of *The Art of Garnishing Churches at Christmas and Other Festivals* (London, 1882), and, later, of *A Manual of Church Decoration and Symbolism* (Oxford, 1899), enforced the whole programme of church reform we have been exploring in this book. From the moment he arrived, he insisted on weekly communion and a weekly offertory. He introduced vestments, candles, flowers, and new liturgical music. He extended his church, building a new north aisle and a vestry, enlarging the organ, and filling the windows with stained glass. He installed a screen to separate the tiny chancel from the not much bigger nave. And he painted; painted and stencilled, embellishing the walls with ornaments and also with theological texts. Three large pictures, for instance, show the Nativity, the Apostle's Creed, and three trees representing knowledge, healing, and life. The chancel is ornamented with symbols of Christ and of his crucifixion, whilst the reredos is a typological study, revealing the Old Testament forerunners of the Eucharist.

In 1885 a contemporary observed that 'the church has undergone a complete change in its interior, and scarcely an inch of space is left of its walls which has not been artistically adorned with stencil work or paintings representing religious subjects'.[15] It's true—and, of course, not everyone liked it. There were the familiar complaints from many who saw this as idolatrous, papistical, or simply effeminate. Nonetheless, St Nicholas—and the nearby rectory, with its adjoining chapel—does speak of the profound transformation that had occurred over the century.

Geldart's vision, expressed in his church and in his guide to the church, written as though its author was the old Norman window in the chancel, demonstrates just how potent the new under-standing of ecclesiastical architecture could be. Moreover, the fact that succeeding decades would see even Evangelical churches embrace many of these reforms reveals their surprisingly wide-ranging attraction and power.

St John the Baptist Inglesham

Set down a potholed, one-track lane, just off the A361 between Lechlade-on-Thames and Highworth in Wiltshire, Inglesham Church is probably easier—and certainly much more pleasant—to visit by foot for walkers following a nearby path along the river. Originally built by the Saxons and then extended in the thirteenth century, it's a tiny little place, almost lost behind a wall and the accumulated mounds of earth raised by centuries of burials in its churchyard. Stone- and slate-built, with its rubble walls enclosed in lime-washed roughcast, it looks very much at home here; as much a part of the landscape as the nearby clumps of trees. Inside, though, it's extraordinary: a time capsule, frozen, it almost seems, in the late eighteenth century. Here is a jumble of screens and box pews—some in front, some behind, and some to the side of a small, raised pulpit.

Inglesham plays its part in our story for two reasons. In the first place, it gives us another glimpse of what preceded the Victorian revolution in church architecture—and it reminds us, too, that not every building was equally affected by that change. Some through choice, and others—as in this case—through poverty, retained older assumptions and ancient arrangements. Secondly, and more particularly, this church exemplifies the way in which many people in the late nineteenth century came to celebrate churches not as active agents of mission in the present but as evidence of times past. In 1887, William Morris's Society for the Protection of Ancient Buildings launched an *Appeal for the Preservation of Inglesham Church*: an appeal that, significantly, did not attach a dedication or saint's name to the place and which couched its argument exclusively in terms derived from archaeology and anti-quarianism rather than religion. Even clerical supporters followed suit, with the Archdeacon of Bristol, for instance, arguing that Inglesham deserved preservation because 'The chancel walls and nave arcade...are such as art students can ill afford to lose.'[16]

There followed the painstaking restoration by the architect J. T. Micklethwaite: a process designed to arrest decay but to leave the structure and the fittings as unchanged as possible. Of course, this did involve some change—and there has been more since. Micklethwaite, for instance, had not expected to find any significant wall paintings. In fact, as any visitor can see, the church was littered with them, and now reveals work stretching from the early thirteenth to the early nineteenth century. Since 1979, when it was declared redundant, there has been an ongoing project to stabilize and then reveal these relics of the church's past. In that way, the church has become a very different sort of text: a palimpsest on which history has been inscribed. That is certainly how its admirers approach it, with the chaplain of Lampeter for one celebrating it on his popular blog in exactly these terms. 'The church', he writes, 'is no longer used for worship and that has preserved a lot of its atmosphere.' Another commentator agrees, going on to complain that there is a cross on the altar, destroying the period feel.[17] Thus today does archaeology trump faith.

NOTES

Frontmatter

1. F. W. Farrar, *The Lord's Prayer: sermons preached in Westminster Abbey* (London, 1893), p. 5. The cynic might also note that he said very much the same thing in several other publications. See, for instance, F. W. Farrar, *Families of Speech: four lectures delivered before the Royal Institution of Great Britain* (London, 1870), p. ix.

Introduction

1. G. A. Bremner, *Imperial Gothic: religious architecture and High Anglican culture in the British Empire c.1840–70* (New Haven, CT and London, 2012).
2. Matthew Arnold and Dominic Barberi, quoted in Henry Tristram, 'Littlemore', in *Newman and Littlemore: a centenary anthology and appeal* (Littlemore, 1945), pp. 9–20, p. 9.
3. Jennifer Sherwood and Nikolaus Pevsner, *The Buildings of England: Oxfordshire* (London, 1974), p. 688. In fairness, they do note it was 'of striking proportions'.
4. A. J. B. Beresford Hope, *The Worship of the Church of England* (2nd edn; London, 1875), p. 11.
5. H. M. Colvin, *A Dictionary of British Architects, 1600–1840* (New Haven, CT and London, 2008), p. 1066.
6. J. H. Newman, 'On the Introduction of Rationalistic Principles into Revealed Religion', in *Essays, Critical and Historical* (2 vols; London, 1871).
7. Peter Maurice, *The Popery of Oxford Confronted, Disavowed, and Repudiated* (London, 1837), p. 53; Peter Maurice, *Postscript to the Popery of Oxford: the number of the name of the beast* (London, 1851), p. 14.
8. So busy was he with this campaigning, he begged to be allowed to be a non-resident vicar. See, Ronald and Margaret Pugh, eds, *The Diocese Books of Samuel Wilberforce* (Oxford, 2008), p. 329.

9. Peter Maurice, *The Ritualists or Non-Natural Catholics: their origins, progress, and principles explained and elucidated with illustrations and a copious index* (London, 1870), pp. v, 150; *Postscript to the Popery of Oxford*, p. 14; see also pp. 11–12.

10. Alan Munden, *A Cheltenham Gamaliel: Dean Close of Cheltenham* (Cheltenham, 1997), pp. 1, 19, 26. The slippers are mocked in J. H. Newman, *Loss and Gain: the story of a convert* (1848; Leominster, 2014), p. 27.

11. Francis Close, *The 'Restoration of Churches' Is the Restoration of Popery* (4th edn; London, 1845).

12. Francis Close, *Church Architecture Scripturally Considered, from the Earliest Ages to the Present Time* (London, 1844), pp. 79–80, 20–1.

13. Henry Liddon, quoted in Michael Hall, *George Frederick Bodley and the Later Gothic Revival in Britain and America* (New Haven, CT and London, 2014), p. 342.

14. *The Times*, 2 July 1888, p. 9.

15. Peter Howell, 'Newman's Church at Littlemore', *Oxford Art Journal* 6 (1983), pp. 51–6, pp. 53, 54; James Patrick, 'Newman, Pugin, and Gothic', *Victorian Studies* 24 (1981), pp. 185–207.

16. *Views and Details of Littlemore Church Near Oxford* (Oxford, 1840); *Elevations, Sections, and Details of the Church of St Mary the Virgin at Littlemore* (Oxford, 1845).

17. Thomas Mozley, *Reminiscences: chiefly of Oriel College and the Oxford Movement* (2 vols; London, 1882), vol. i, p. 346; Patrick, 'Newman, Pugin, and Gothic', p. 191.

18. Howell, 'Newman's Church at Littlemore', pp. 51–6.

19. Quoted in R. D. Middleton, *Newman and Bloxam: an Oxford friendship* (London, 1947), p. 35.

20. Fredrick Oakeley, *Historical Notes on the Tractarian Movement* (London, 1865), p. 98.

21. Thomas Leach, *A Short Sketch of the Tractarian Upheaval* (London, 1887), p. 126; compare with Mozley, *Reminiscences*, p. 390.

22. Close, *Restoration of Churches*, p. 4.

23. A. G. Lough, *John Mason Neale. Priest Extraordinary* (1975), p. 55.

24. Janet Mayo, *A History of Ecclesiastical Dress* (London, 1984), p. 102.

25. George Herring, *The Oxford Movement in Practice: the Tractarian parochial world from the 1830s to the 1870s* (Oxford, 2016), pp. 91, 200.

26. G. W. Herring, 'Tractarianism to Ritualism: a study of some aspects of Tractarianism outside Oxford, from the time of Newman's conversion in 1845, until the first Ritual Commission in 1867' (DPhil, Oxford, 1984),

p. 304; see also his 'Tractarians and Ritualists', *Ecclesiology Today* 29 (September 2000), pp. 51–60.

27. Owen Chadwick, *The Victorian Church* (2 vols; 3rd edn; London, 1987) vol. i, p. 213.

28. Quoted in Jeremy Morris, 'The Regional Growth of Tractarianism: some reflections', in Paul Vaiss, ed., *From Oxford to the People: reconsidering Newman and the Oxford Movement* (Leominster, 1996), pp. 141–59, p. 145. Though see Herring, *Oxford Movement*, p. 193 for a more sceptical account of this.

29. See, for example, Geoffrey Rowell, *The Vision Glorious: themes and personalities of the Catholic Revival in Anglicanism* (Oxford, 1983), ch. 3.

30. Quoted in James Bettley, 'The Reverend Ernest Geldart (1848–1929) and Late Nineteenth-Century Church Decoration' (PhD, Courtauld Institute, 1999), p. 121.

31. Christopher Webster and John Elliott, eds, *'A Church as It Should Be': the Cambridge Camden Society and its influence* (Donington, 2000); Dale Adelmann, *The Contribution of Cambridge Ecclesiologists to the Revival of Anglican Choral Worship, 1839–62* (Aldershot, 1997).

32. Rowell, *The Vision Glorious*, ch. 5.

33. J. Mordaunt Crook, 'The Restoration of the Temple Church: ecclesiology and recrimination', *Architectural History* 8 (1965), pp. 39–51, p. 43.

34. Chris Miele, 'Gothic Sign, Protestant Realia: Templars, Ecclesiologists and the round churches at Cambridge and London', *Architectural History* 53 (2010), pp. 191–215, p. 198.

35. William Whyte, 'Restoration and Recrimination: the Temple Church in the nineteenth century', in Robin Griffith-Jones and David Park, eds, *The Temple Church: history, art, and architecture* (Woodbridge, 2010), pp. 195–210.

36. Middleton, *Newman and Bloxam*, p 43. See Robin Darwall-Smith, 'The Monks of Magdalen, 1688–1854', in L. W. B. Brockliss, ed., *Magdalen College Oxford: a history* (Oxford, 2008), pp. 253–386, p. 339.

37. See, for example, Clyde Binfield, '"We Claim Our Part in the Great Inheritance": the message of four Congregational buildings', in Keith Robbins, ed., *Protestant Evangelicalism: Britain, Ireland, Germany and America, c.1750–c.1950: essays in honour of W. R. Ward, Studies in Church History Subsidia 7* (Oxford, 1990), pp. 201–23; *The Contexting of a Chapel Architect: James Cubitt, 1836–1912* (London, 2001); Stewart J. Brown, 'Scotland and the Oxford Movement', S. J. Brown and P. Nockles, eds, *The Oxford Movement: Europe and the wider world 1830–1930* (Cambridge, 2012), pp. 56–77.

38. J. Ewing Ritchie, *The Religious Life of London* (London, 1870), p. 81.

39. Walter Walsh, *The History of the Romeward Movement of the Church of England, 1833–1864* (London, 1900), p. 255.

40. *Church of the People* 1:5 (March 1854), p. 75.

41. Alexandrina Buchanan, *Robert Willis and the Foundation of Architectural History* (Cambridge, 2013), p. 280.

42. Sarah Foot, 'Has Ecclesiastical History Lost the Plot?', *Studies in Church History* 49 (2013), pp. 1–25.

43. Mary Carruthers, *The Craft of Thought: meditation, rhetoric, and the making of images, 400–1200* (Cambridge, 1999), p. 263.

44. Stuart J. Brown, *The National Churches of England, Ireland, and Scotland 1801–1846* (Oxford, 2001).

45. David W. Bebbington, *Evangelicalism in Modern Britain: history from the 1730s to the 1980s* (London, 1988), p. 75.

46. Peter B. Nockles, *The Oxford Movement in Context: Anglican High Church-manship 1760–1857* (Cambridge, 1994), p. 307.

47. Nigel Yates, *Anglican Ritualism in Victorian Britain, 1830–1910* (Oxford, 1999), p. 375.

48. Bebbington, *Evangelicalism in Modern Britain*, p. 95.

49. Basil Clarke, *Church Builders of the Nineteenth Century: a study of the Gothic Revival in England* (Newton Abbott, 1969), p. 11.

50. Jeffrey Chipps Smith, *Sensuous Worship: Jesuits and the art of the early Catholic Reformation* (Princeton, NJ and Oxford, 2002); David Morgan, *The Embodied Eye: religious visual culture and the social life of feeling* (Berkeley, CA, 2012); Jane Garnett and Gervase Rosser, *Spectacular Miracles: transforming images in Italy from the Renaissance to the present* (London, 2013).

51. Key texts include James Stevens Curl's *Piety Proclaimed: an introduction to places of worship in Victorian England* (London, 2002) and the first-rate collection of essays, *Victorian Church: architecture and society*, ed. Chris Brooks and Andrew Saint (Manchester, 1995). *The Faber Book of Victorian Churches*, ed. Ian Sutton and Peter Howell (London, 1989) provides a gazetteer of buildings and is consequently ideal for church visiting. Basil Clarke, *Church Builders of the Nineteenth Century: a study of the Gothic Revival in England* (Newton Abbott, 1969), has, in many respects, stood the test of time, though for a survey of how more recent writings have changed some of our perspectives, see William Whyte, 'Ecclesiastical Gothic Revivalism', in Joanne Parker and Corinna Wagner, eds, *The Oxford Handbook of Victorian Medievalism* (Oxford, forthcoming). Nigel Yates

was, for many years, the acknowledged expert on the subject, and two of his books are central to any serious study of the subject: *Buildings, Faith, and Worship: the liturgical arrangement of Anglican Churches 1600–1900* (Oxford, 2001) and—with a broader focus—*Liturgical Space: Christian worship and church buildings in Western Europe 1500–2000* (Aldershot, 2008). Two older books are also worth consulting for the special knowledge they bring to bear on the subject: G. W. O. Addleshaw and Frederick Etchells, *The Architectural Setting of Anglican Worship* (London, 1948) and Peter Anson, *Fashions in Church Furnishings, 1840–1940* (London, 1960).

52. Andrew Saint, 'The Conundrum of "By"', in Malcolm Airs and William Whyte, eds, *Architectural History after Colvin* (Donington, 2013), pp. 58–70.

53. See Anne Bordeleau, *Charles Robert Cockerell, Architect in Time: reflections around anachronistic drawings* (Aldershot, 2014), for a similar observation.

54. William Whyte, 'The Success of Sir Howard Colvin and the Curious Failure of Architectural History', in Airs and Whyte, eds, *Architectural History after Colvin*, pp. 1–17.

55. 'Ignore the ideas,' writes Dominic Erdozain, 'and the history of religion becomes an exercise in describing what went on in and around churches, followed by brittle speculations as to why all the activity eventually dissipated.' Dominic Erdozain, *The Problem of Pleasure: sport, recreation, and the crisis of Victorian religion* (Woodbridge, 2010), p. 19.

56. Herring, *Oxford Movement*, p. 250.

57. David Morgan, 'Preface' to *Religion and Material Culture: the matter of belief* (London and New York, 2010), p. xiv.

58. Yates, *Anglican Ritualism in Victorian Britain*, Dominic Janes, *Victorian Reformation: the fight over idolatry in the Church of England, 1840–1860* (Oxford, 2005).

59. Bebbington, *Evangelicalism in Modern Britain*, p. 75.

60. S. J. D. Green, *Religion in the Age of Decline: organisation and experience in industrial Yorkshire, 1870–1920* (Cambridge, 2003), p. 89.

61. Samuel Wilberforce, *A Sermon Preached March 4, 1847, the Day of the Consecration of the Church of St James Woolsthorpe* (London, 1847), p. 18.

62. James Vernon, *Distant Strangers: how Britain became modern* (Berkeley, CA, 2014).

63. Stefan Muthesius, 'Provinciality and the Victorians: church design in nineteenth-century East Anglia', in T. A. Heslop, Elizabeth Mellings, and Margrit Thøfner, eds, *Art, Faith and Place in East Anglia: from prehistory to the present* (Woodbridge, 2012), pp. 209–39, p. 213.

Chapter 1

1. For the ways in which it fits within Newman's wider sense of the church building as the embodiment of the sacramental principle, see George Herring, *The Oxford Movement in Practice: the Tractarian parochial world from the 1830s to the 1870s* (Oxford, 2016), pp. 74–5.
2. Charles Daubeney, *A Sermon Preached at the Consecration of Christ Church in the Parish of North Bradley* (London, 1825), pp. 30, 23.
3. Jelinger Symons, *A Sermon Preached at the Consecration of the New Church at Hackney, on Saturday, July 15, 1797* (London, 1797), p. 3.
4. John Henry Newman, *Sermons, 1824–43: vol. iv*, ed. Francis J. McGrath (Oxford, 2011), pp. 236–43.
5. William Whyte, 'Ecclesiastical Gothic Revivalism', in Joanne Parker and Corinna Wagner, eds, *The Oxford Handbook of Victorian Medievalism* (Oxford, forthcoming). See also Anne Bordeleau, *Charles Robert Cockerell, Architect in Time: reflections around anachronistic drawings* (Aldershot, 2014), pp. 128–39.
6. Peter Maurice, *The Popery of Oxford Confronted, Disavowed, and Repudiated* (London, 1837), p. 53.
7. Peter Maurice, *Postscript to the Popery of Oxford: the number of the name of the beast* (London, 1851), p. 23.
8. Maurice, *Postscript to the Popery of Oxford*, pp. 45–6.
9. Walter Walsh, *The History of the Romeward Movement of the Church of England, 1833–1864* (London, 1900), p. 255.
10. James Patrick, 'Newman, Pugin, and Gothic', *Victorian Studies* 24 (1981), pp. 185–207, p. 197.
11. Ian Ker, *John Henry Newman: a biography* (Oxford, 2010), p. 339.
12. Wendel Mayer, 'A Tale of Two Cities', *Journal of Ecclesiastical History* 61 (2010), pp. 746–62.
13. J. H. Newman, *Loss and Gain: the story of a convert* (1848; Leominster, 2014).
14. Ker, *Newman*, 317. See also Newman, *Loss and Gain*, p. 87.
15. Isaac Williams, *A Sermon Preached at the Consecration of the Church of Llangorwen in the Diocese of St David's December 16, MDCCCXLI* (Aberystwyth, 1841); *The Cathedral, or the Catholic and Apostolic Church in England* (5th edn; Oxford, 1848), p. v.
16. Pierre de la Ruffinière du Prey, *Hawksmoor's London Churches: architecture and theology* (Chicago, 2000).
17. Terry Friedman, *The Eighteenth-Century Church in Britain* (New Haven, CT and London, 2011).

18. A classic example is J. C. Atkinson, *Forty Years in a Moorland Parish* (London, 1891), pp. 44–5.
19. John Martin (1847) in Chris Pickford, ed., *Bedfordshire Churches in the Nineteenth Century: part 1*, Bedfordshire Historical Record Society 73, 1994, p. 153.
20. See, for example, J. S. Purvis, *The Condition of Yorkshire Church Fabrics, 1300–1800* (London and York, 1958); Nigel Yates, *Buildings, Faith, and Worship: the liturgical arrangement of Anglican Churches 1600–1900* (Oxford, 2001).
21. Jeremy Gregory and Jeffrey S. Chamberlain, eds, *The National Church in Local Perspective: the Church of England and the regions 1660–1800* (Woodbridge, 2002).
22. Henry Addington, *Some Account of the Abbey of St Peter and St Paul at Dorchester, Oxfordshire* (Oxford, 1845), p. 2.
23. Joseph Skelton, *Skelton's Engraved Illustrations of the Principal Antiquities of Oxfordshire, from Original Drawings* (Oxford, 1823), Dorchester Hundred, p. 4.
24. Nicholas Doggett, 'The Dissolution and After: church and people, 635–2005', in Kate Tiller, ed., *Dorchester Abbey: church and people, 635–2005* (Stonesfield, 2005), pp. 39–48, p. 47. See also Geoffrey Tyack's marvellous chapter in the same volume.
25. Warwick Rodwell, *Dorchester Abbey, Oxfordshire: the archaeology and architecture of a cathedral, monastery and parish church* (Oxford, 2009), chs. 8–9.
26. G. W. O. Addleshaw and Frederick Etchells, *The Architectural Setting of Anglican Worship* (London, 1948), pp. 179–200.
27. Richard L. Bushman, *The Refinement of America: persons, houses, cities* (New York, 1992), pp. 172–80.
28. Louis P. Nelson, *The Beauty of Holiness: Anglicanism and architecture in colonial South Carolina* (Chapel Hill, NC, 2008), pp. 174, 345.
29. Jan Maria Albers, 'Seeds of Contention: society, politics, and the Church of England in Lancashire, 1689–1790' (PhD, Yale University, 1988), p. 55.
30. John Martin Robinson, *James Wyatt (1746–1813): architect to George III* (New Haven, CT and London, 2012), pp. 189–91.
31. *The Manchester Guide: a brief historical description of the towns of Manchester and Salford, the public buildings, and the charitable and literary institutions* (Manchester, 1804), pp. 114–15.
32. W. F. Pocock, *Designs for Churches and Chapels of Various Dimensions and Styles Consisting of Plans, Elevations, and Sections: with estimates. Also some designs for altars, pulpits, and steeples* (London, 1835), p. 9.

33. *Ordnance Survey Memoirs, vol. i: Parishes of County Armagh 1835–8*, ed. Angelique Day and Patrick McWilliams (Belfast, 1990), p. 29.
34. Quoted in Alastair Rowan, 'Wardour Castle Chapel', *Country Life* CXLIV (1968), pp. 908–16, p. 909.
35. [Jane Panton], *Fresh Leaves and Green Pastures* (London, 1909), p. 60.
36. Antony Jaggard, 'Lulworth Castle Chapel', *Archaeological Journal* 140 (1983), pp. 48–52, p. 51.
37. Damie Stillman, 'Church Architecture in Neo-Classical England', *Journal of the Society of Architectural History* 38 (1979), pp. 103–19, pp. 110–11.
38. Nigel Yates, *Liturgical Space: Christian worship and church buildings in Western Europe, 1500–2000* (Aldershot, 2008), p. 111.
39. Thomas Rawlins, *Familiar Architecture; or, original designs of homes for gentlemen and tradesmen, parsonages, summer retreats, banqueting-rooms, and churches* (London, 1795), pp. 25–6.
40. Michael Port, *Six Hundred New Churches: the Church Building Commission, 1818–1856* (2nd edn; Reading, 2006).
41. Philip Aspin, 'Architecture and Identity in the English Gothic Revival, 1800–1850' (DPhil, Oxford University, 2013).
42. Simon Bradley, 'The Gothic Revival and the Church of England, 1790–1840' (PhD, London University, 1996).
43. Addleshaw and Etchells, *Architectural Setting of Anglican Worship*, p. 203.
44. Arthur Burns, *The Diocesan Revival in the Church of England, c.1800–1870* (Oxford, 1999), p. 116; see also Chris Brooks and Andrew Saint, eds, *The Victorian Church: architecture and society* (London, 1995).
45. J. M. Neale, *Ayton Priory; or the restored monastery* (London, 1843), p. i.
46. Quoted in Friedman, *Eighteenth Century Church*, p. 259.
47. Barbara Kiefer Lewalski and Estelle Haan, eds, *The Complete Works of John Milton: vol. iii, the shorter poems* (Oxford, 2012), p. 36.
48. Philip Aspin, '"Our Ancient Architecture": contesting cathedrals and late Georgian England', *Architectural History* 54 (2011), pp. 213–32.
49. See Port, *Six Hundred New Churches* and Timothy V. Parry, 'The Incorporated Church Building Society, 1818–1851' (MLitt thesis, Oxford University, 1984).
50. William Whyte, 'Shaping Material Reform: pressure groups in Great Britain and Ireland, 1780–1920', in Peter Jan Margry and Jan de Maeyer, eds, *The Dynamics of Religious Reform in Church, State and Society in Northern Europe, c.1780–c.1920: vol. vi, material reform* (forthcoming).
51. *Ecclesiologist* VIII (February 1846), p. 52.

52. J. M. Neale and Benjamin Webb, *The Symbolism of Churches and Church Ornaments: a translation of the first book of the* Rationale Divinorum Officiorum, *written by William Durandus* (Leeds, 1843), pp. vii, xxiv, cxxx.

53. Michael Bright, *Cities Built to Music: aesthetic theories of the Victorian Gothic Revival* (Columbus, OH, 1984), p. 287.

54. *Christian Remembrancer* 2 (1841), p. 387.

55. W. B. T. Jones, 'On Uniformity, Considered as a Principle in Gothic Architecture', in *Proceedings of the Oxford Society for Promoting the Study of Gothic Architecture*, 26 February 1845, pp. 35–6 and 14 May 1845, pp. 44–53.

56. E. A. Freeman, 'Development of Roman and Gothick Architecture and Their Moral and Symbolical Teaching', *Proceedings of the Oxford Society for Promoting the Study of Gothic Architecture*, 12 November 1845, p. 25; *Ecclesiologist* 5 (1846), p. 181.

57. T. H. Lowe, *A Few Thoughts on the Interior Arrangements of Churches* (Exeter, 1842), pp. 21–2.

58. William Bardwell, *Temples, Ancient and Modern; or, notes on church architecture* (London, 1837), pp. 14, 29, 51–2, 61.

59. Charles Anderson, *Ancient Models; or, hints on church-building* (2nd edn; London, 1841), p. 121.

60. Charlotte M. Yonge, *John Keble's Parishes: a history of Hursley and Otterbourne* (London, 1898), pp. 116–20.

61. Manning, *Charge*, p. 8. *Methodist Review* 24 (1842), pp. 458–68, p. 463.

62. Julius Charles Hare, *Charges to the Clergy of the Archdeaconry of Lewes, Delivered at the Ordinary Visitations from the Year 1840 to 1854* (3 vols; Cambridge, 1856), vol. i, pp. 20–2.

63. The following paragraphs draw heavily on my 'Sacred Space as Sacred Text: church and chapel building in Victorian Britain', in Joe Sterrett and Peter Thomas, eds, *Sacred Text–Sacred Space: architectural, literary, and spiritual convergences in England and Wales* (Leiden, 2011), pp. 247–67.

64. George Ayliffe Poole, *The Appropriate Character of Church Architecture* (Leeds, 1842), p. 18.

65. G. F. Bodley, *The Modes in Which Religious Life and Thought May Be Influenced by Art* (London, 1881), p. 5.

66. George Wightwick, *The Palace of Architecture: a romance of art and history* (London, 1840), p. 128.

67. John Ruskin, *Collected Works*, ed. E. J. Cook and A. Wedderburn (London, 1903–9), vol. x, p. 206.

68. Quoted in Michael Brooks, 'Describing Buildings: John Ruskin and architectural prose', *Prose Studies* 3:3 (1980), pp. 241–53, p. 241.

69. Ruskin, *Works*, vol. x, p. 112.

70. James Fergusson, *An Historical Inquiry into the True Principles of Beauty in Art* (London, 1849), pp. 121–2.

71. J. T. Micklethwaite, *Modern Parish Churches, Their Plan, Design and Furniture* (London, 1874), pp. 2, 5–6.

72. Joseph Gwilt, *An Encyclopaedia of Architecture, Historical, Theoretical, and Practical* (2nd edn; London, 1851), p. 824.

73. Neil Levine, 'The Book and the Building: Hugo's Theory of Architecture and Labrouste's Bibliothèque Ste-Geneviève', in Robin Middleton, ed., *The Beaux-Arts and Nineteenth-Century French Architecture* (London, 1982), pp. 138–73.

74. Francis Close, *The Footsteps of Error Traced through a Period of Twenty-Five Years; or, superstition the parent of modern doubt* (London, 1863), p. 7.

75. *Athenaeum* (1843), p. 188.

76. J. A. Tabor, *Nonconformist Protest against the Popery of Modern Dissent, as Displayed in Architectural Imitations of Roman Catholic Churches* (Colchester, 1863), pp. 4–5.

77. Tabor, *Nonconformist Protest*, pp. 4–5.

78. Alexander Thomson, 'On the Unsuitableness of Gothic Architecture to Modern Circumstances', in Gavin Stamp, ed., *The Light of Truth and Beauty: the lectures of Alexander 'Greek' Thomson, 1817–75* (Glasgow, 1999), p. 58.

79. J. C. Carlile, *C. H. Spurgeon: an interpretative biography* (London, 1933), p. 155.

80. Anthony Jones, *Welsh Chapels* (Stroud, 1996), p. 62.

81. James Cubitt, *Church Design for Congregations* (London, 1870), p. 8.

82. Anthony John Harding, 'Development and Symbol in the Thought of S. T. Coleridge, J. C. Hare, and John Sterling', *Studies in Romanticism* 18 (1979), pp. 29–48, p. 30.

83. Herbert L. Sussman, *Fact into Figure: typology in Carlyle, Ruskin, and the Pre-Raphaelite Brotherhood* (Columbus, OH, 1979); George P. Landow, *Victorian Types, Victorian Shadows: biblical typology in Victorian literature, art and thought* (Boston, MA, 1980).

84. Walter A. Gray, *The Symbolism of Churches and Their Ornaments, a Lecture* (London, 1857), p. 5.

85. Kirstie Blair, 'Church Architecture, Tractarian Poetry and the Forms of Faith', in Victoria Morgan and Clare Williams, eds, *Shaping Belief: culture, politics, and religion in nineteenth-century writing* (Liverpool, 2008), pp. 129–45, p. 129.

86. See also *Old Church Porch* 1 (1854), p. 272.

87. James Skinner, *Why Do We Prize Externals in the Service of God?* (London, 1855), p. 15.

88. A. W. N. Pugin, *The Present State of Ecclesiastical Architecture in England* (London, 1843), p. 81.

89. Janet Mayo, *A History of Ecclesiastical Dress* (London, 1984), p. 104.

90. *The Holy Flower Show in Belgravia, or Puseyism at a Discount* (London, 1857). See also J. F. Biscoe and H. F. B. Mackay, *A Tractarian at Work: a memoir of Dean Randall* (London, 1932), pp. 55, 64.

91. [Charles Maurice Davies], *Orthodox London: or, phases of religious life in the Church of England, by the author of 'Unorthodox London'* (London, 1875), p. 238.

92. Davies, *Orthodox London*, p. 240.

93. See also Anthony Trollope, *The Last Chronicle of Barset* (1867; Oxford, 2013), p. 131.

94. William Peace, *The Reformation and the Cross: a letter to the Right Reverend the Lord Bishop of Oxford* (London, 1859), p. 39.

95. John Unwin, ed., *Earnest Christianity Illustrated: or, selections from the journal of the Rev. J. Caughey. With a brief sketch of Mr. Caughey's life* (London, 1857), p. 42.

Chapter 2

1. Nikolaus Pevsner, *The Buildings of England: Staffordshire* (London, 1974), pp. 137–8; though he does note its Ecclesiological correctness.

2. <http://www.greatwyrleyparish.org.uk/> (accessed 13 October 2015).

3. William Gresley, *God's House a House of Prayer* (Lichfield, 1845), pp. 4–8.

4. Geoffrey K. Brandwood, 'Appendix: a Camdenian roll-call', in Christopher Webster and John Elliott, eds, *'A Church as It Should Be': the Cambridge Camden Society and its influence* (Donington, 2000), pp. 359–454, p. 398.

5. S. A. Skinner, 'Gresley, William (1801–1876)', *Oxford Dictionary of National Biography* (Oxford, 2004).

6. *Speech of the Rev Robert McGhee on Auricular Confession* (Brighton Protestant Tracts 16, 1853), p. 19.

7. John Harvey, *Image of the Invisible: the visualization of religion in the Welsh Nonconformist tradition* (Cardiff, 1999), pp. 15, 19.

8. William Peace, *The Reformation and the Cross: a letter to the Right Reverend the Lord Bishop of Oxford* (London, 1859), pp. 4–5.

9. David Morgan, *The Embodied Eye: religious visual culture and the social life of feeling* (Berkeley, CA, 2012), pp. 168–70.

10. Victoria George, *Whitewash and the New Aesthetic of the Protestant Reformation* (London, 2012).

11. Christopher Wren, *Parentalia: or, memoirs of the family of the Wrens; viz. of Mathew bishop of Ely, Christopher dean of Windsor, &c. but chiefly of Sir Christopher Wren* (London, 1750), p. 320.

12. Quoted in Catherine Hall, *Macaulay and Son: architects of imperial Britain* (New Haven, CT and London, 2011), pp. 179–80.

13. This paragraph relies heavily on William Whyte, 'Sacred Space as Sacred Text: church and chapel building in Victorian Britain', in Joe Sterrett and Peter Thomas, eds, *Sacred Text–Sacred Space: architectural, literary, and spiritual convergences in England and Wales* (Leiden, 2011), pp. 247–67.

14. Judges 7:1.

15. 'Jerubbaal', *Manchester College Chapel Windows* (Manchester, 1895). See also *Inquirer*, 16 March 1895, p. 170.

16. Francis Close, *A Sermon, Addressed to the Female Chartists of Cheltenham* (London, 1839).

17. Francis Close, *A Sermon, Addressed to the Chartists of Cheltenham* (London, 1839), pp. 23, 24.

18. Francis Close, *The 'Restoration of Churches' Is the Restoration of Popery* (4th edn; London, 1845), p. 17.

19. Close, *The 'Restoration of Churches'*, p. 4.

20. H. J. Spencer, 'Christmas, Henry (1811–1868)', *Oxford Dictionary of National Biography* (Oxford, 2004).

21. Quoted in Dominic Janes, *Victorian Reformation: the fight over idolatry in the Church of England, 1840–1860* (New York, 2009), p. 30.

22. Quoted in Michael Bright, *Cities Built to Music: aesthetic theories of the Victorian Gothic Revival* (Columbus, OH, 1984), p. 190.

23. John E. Toews, 'Church and State', in Gareth Stedman Jones and Gregory Claeys, eds, *The Cambridge History of Nineteenth-Century Political Thought* (Cambridge, 2011), pp. 603–48, pp. 607, 611.

24. Peter Maurice, *The Ritualists or Non-Natural Catholics: their origins, progress, and principles explained and elucidated with illustrations and a copious index* (London, 1870), p. 75.

25. See also Francis E. Paget, *Milford Malvoisin: or pews and pewholders* (London, 1842).

26. Francis E. Paget, *St Antholin's; or, churches old and new. A tale for the times* (London, 1841), p. 39.

27. John Mason Neale, *Ayton Priory; or the restored monastery* (London, 1843), p. 147.

28. Neale, *Ayton Priory*, p. 145.
29. Gladstone, *Church Principles*, pp. 84, 68.
30. Thomas Chamberlain, *The Chancel: an appeal for its proper use addressed to architects, church-restorers and the clergy generally* (London, 1856), p. 18.
31. A. W. N. Pugin, *The Present State of Ecclesiastical Architecture in England* (London, 1843), p. 105.
32. William Henry Teale, 'Introduction', in William Henry Teale, ed., *Seven Sermons Preached at the Consecration and Re-Opening of the Parish Church of Leeds* (Leeds, 1841), pp. i–lx, p. xiv.
33. Alexander Beresford Hope, *The English Cathedral of the Nineteenth Century* (London, 1861), p. 250.
34. Paul Thompson, *William Butterfield* (London, 1971), p. 33.
35. Henry Edward Manning, *A Charge Delivered at the Ordinary Visitation of the Archdeaconry of Chichester* (London, 1842), p. 17.
36. Julius Charles Hare, *Charges to the Clergy of the Archdeaconry of Lewes, Delivered at the Ordinary Visitations from the Year 1840 to 1854* (3 vols; Cambridge, 1856), vol. i, p. 55.
37. J. Mordaunt Crook, *The Dilemma of Style: architectural ideas from the picturesque to the post-modern* (London, 1987), p. 63.
38. Matthew Hyde, review of L. A. S. Butler, ed., *Sir Stephen Glynne's Church Notes for Cumbria*, in *Ecclesiology Today* 45 (January 2012), pp. 92–3, p. 93.
39. E. W. Godwin, *A Handbook of Floral Decoration for Churches* (London, 1865), p. 5.
40. C. S. Armstrong, ed., *Under the Parson's Nose: further extracts from the diary of the Revd B. J. Armstrong MA (Cantab), vicar of East Dereham, 1850–1888* (Dereham, 2012), p. 209.
41. George Field, *Chromatography: or a treatise on colours and pigments, and of their powers in painting* (London, 1841), p. 15.
42. George Herring, *The Oxford Movement in Practice: the Tractarian parochial world from the 1830s to the 1870s* (Oxford, 2016), p. 245.
43. Hare, *Charges to the Clergy of the Archdeaconry of Lewes*, vol. i, p. 13.
44. R. K. Pugh and J. F. A. Mason, *The Letter-Books of Samuel Wilberforce, 1843–68* (Oxford, 1970), p. 73.
45. Anthony Edwards, 'The Churches of E. B. Lamb: an exercise in centralised planning', *Ecclesiology Today* 42 (2010), pp. 29–48, p. 42.
46. Richard Glover, *The Golden Decade of a Favoured Town, Biographical Sketches of Celebrated Characters Connected with Cheltenham from 1843 to 1853, by Contem Ignotus* (London, 1884), p. 44.

47. Quoted in Richard Cullen Rath, 'No Corner for the Devil to Hide', in Jonathan Sterne, ed., *The Sound Studies Reader* (New York and London, 2012), pp. 130–40, p. 132.

48. William Bardwell, *Temples, Ancient and Modern; or, notes on church architecture* (London, 1837), p. 213.

49. Robert T. Beyer, *Sounds of Our Times: two hundred years of acoustics* (New York, 1999), pp. 48–9, 158–9.

50. John W. Baldwin, *Paris, 1200* (Stanford, CA, 2010), p. 147.

51. Barry Blesser and Linda-Ruth Salter, *Spaces Speak, Are You Listening? Experiencing aural architecture* (Cambridge, MA and London, 2007), p. 93.

52. John Unwin, ed., *Earnest Christianity Illustrated; or, sections from the journal of the Rev James Caughey* (London, 1857), pp. 21, 395–6.

53. Walter Hillsman, 'The Victorian Revival of Plainsong in English: its usage under Tractarians and ritualists', *Studies in Church History* 28 (1992), pp. 405–15.

54. Nicholas Thistlethwaite, *The Making of the Victorian Organ* (Cambridge, 1990), p. 321.

55. See also Herring, *The Oxford Movement in Practice*, pp. 75–9.

56. Mark M. Smith, *Listening to Nineteenth-Century America* (Chapel Hill, NC and London, 2001), pp. 97–8.

57. John W. W. H. Molyneaux, *A Letter Addressed to the Bishop of Ely* (Sudbury, 1856), p. 38.

58. Complaints about behaviour in box pews: N. S. Harding, ed., *A Stow Visitation: being notes on the churches in the Archdeaconry of Stow 1845* (London, 1845), p. 12. On the improvement in behaviour following restoration, see Ronald and Margaret Pugh, eds, *The Diocese Books of Samuel Wilberforce* (Oxford, 2008), p. 237.

59. Charlotte M. Yonge, *John Keble's Parishes: a history of Hursley and Otterbourne* (London, 1898), p. 122.

60. Thomas James, in *Ecclesiologist* 8 (1848), p. 177.

61. *Old Church Porch* 1 (1854), p. 87.

62. *Church of the People*, 1:8 (October 1856), p. 126.

63. Gresley, *God's House a House of Prayer*, pp. 14, 11.

64. J. H. Markland, *On the Reverence Due to Holy Places* (London, 1845), p. 11.

65. *Free and Open Church Advocate* 2 (1874–5), p. 87 (15 November 1874).

66. John William Burgon, *The Oxford Diocesan Conference; and romanizing within the Church of England, two sermons* (Oxford, 1873), p. 33. See also Glover, *The Golden Decade of a Favoured Town*, p. 12.

67. John William Burgon, *To Educate Young Women like Young Men, and with Young Men, a Thing Inexpedient and Immodest: a sermon preached before the*

University of Oxford in the chapel of New College on Trinity Sunday (June 8th 1884) (Oxford, 1884).

68. Paget, *St Antholin's*, pp. 12–13.

69. And can be found most obviously in Paget, *St Antholin's*, p. 68.

70. See, for instance, Jan Maria Albers, 'Seeds of Contention: society, politics, and the Church of England in Lancashire, 1689–1790' (PhD, Yale University, 1988), p. 59.

71. *Church of the People* 2 (1858–60), p. 330.

72. *Free and Open Church Advocate* 2 (1874–5), p. 241 (15 December 1875).

73. *Church of the People* 2 (1858–60), p. 52.

74. *Free and Open Church Advocate* 2 (1874–5), p. 70 (15 October 1874).

75. Quoted in Armstrong, *Under the Parson's Nose*, p. 322.

76. Quoted in Chris Pickford, *Bedfordshire Churches in the Nineteenth Century: vol. i* (Bedford, 1993), p. 317.

77. Quoted in Chris Pickford, *Bedfordshire Churches in the Nineteenth Century: vol. ii* (Bedford, 1998), p. 484.

78. Chris Pickford, *Bedfordshire Churches in the Nineteenth Century: vol. iii* (Bedford, 2000), p. 633.

79. Pickford, *Bedfordshire Churches, vol. iii*, p. 672. See G. A. Poole, *Churches: their structure, arrangement and decoration* (London, 1846), p. 71.

80. *Free and Open Church Advocate* 2 (1874–5), p. 20 (14 March 1874).

81. J. Frewen Moor, *A Guide to the Village of Hursley, the Home of Keble, Author of the 'The Christian Year'* (Winchester, 1899), p. 12.

82. Pugh and Pugh, *Diocese Books of Samuel Wilberforce*, p. 246.

83. *Why Are Our Churches Closed? An argument against closed churches; or, an appeal to those in authority to open the houses of God throughout this Christian land. By a layman* (Oxford, 1858), pp. 19–20.

Chapter 3

1. Owen Chadwick, *Hensley Henson: a study in the friction between Church and State* (Oxford, 1983), p. 54.

2. Herbert Hensley Henson, *Retrospect of an Unimportant Life* (3 vols; Oxford, 1942–50): it might, of course, be noted that—however 'unimportant'—he still devoted three substantial volumes to his life.

3. S. J. D. Green, *Religion in the Age of Decline: organisation and experience in industrial Yorkshire, 1870–1920* (Cambridge, 1996), p. 105.

4. Nigel Yates, *Anglican Ritualism in Victorian Britain, 1830–1910* (Oxford, 1999); James Bentley, *Ritualism and Politics in Victorian Britain: the attempt to legislate for belief* (Oxford, 1978).

5. K. D. M. Snell and Paul Ell, *Rival Jerusalems: the geography of Victorian religion* (Cambridge, 2000). For an important local study, see for instance, Kate Tiller, *Church and Chapel in Oxfordshire 1851: the return of the census of religious worship* (Oxford, 1987).

6. Richard Yates, *The Church in Danger: a statement of the cause, and of the probable means of averting that danger attempted; in a letter* (London, 1815), p. 77.

7. Quoted in Owen Chadwick, *The Victorian Church* (2 vols; 3rd edn; London, 1987), vol. i, p. 366.

8. *Church Builder* 1 (1862–3), p. 101.

9. James Ewing Ritchie, *The Religious Life of London* (London, 1870), p. 82.

10. F. C. Mather, 'Georgian Churchmanship Reconsidered: some variations in Anglican public worship 1714–1830', *Journal of Ecclesiastical History* 36 (1985), pp. 255–83, p. 278.

11. R. W. Ambler, *Churches, Chapels and the Parish Communities of Lincolnshire, 1660–1900, History of Lincolnshire* 11 (2000), p. 183.

12. Peter Maurice, *Sequel to the Ritualists or Non-Natural Catholics* (Yarnton, 1875), p. 43.

13. Mark A. Smith, *Religion in Industrial Society: Oldham and Saddleworth, 1740–1865* (Oxford, 1994), p. 49.

14. Ambler, *Churches, Chapels and the Parish*, p. 184.

15. C. S. Armstrong, ed., *Under the Parson's Nose: further extracts from the diary of the Revd B. J. Armstrong MA (Cantab.), vicar of East Dereham 1850–1888* (Dereham, 2012), p. 110.

16. *Church of the People* 1:6 (April 1854), p. 81.

17. John W. H. Molyneaux, *A Letter Addressed to the Lord Bishop of Ely* (Sudbury, 1856), p. 33.

18. Sabina Sutherland, ed., *The Church Inspection Notebook of Archdeacon James Randall 1855–1873 and Other Records*, Berkshire Record Society 21 (2015), p. xix.

19. Charles Booth, *The Life and Labour of the People in London: third series, religious influences* (7 vols; London, 1902), vol. i, pp. 34–5.

20. Armstrong, *Under the Parson's Nose*, p. 134.

21. Revd James Skinner in *Church of the People* 1:8 (October 1856), p. 126.

22. W. S. F. Pickering, *Anglo-Catholicism: a study in religious ambiguity* (London, 2008), p. 88.

23. Anthony Trollope, *The Last Chronicle of Barset* (1867; Oxford, 2013), p. 184.

24. Armstrong, *Under the Parson's Nose*, p. 41.

25. Ambler, *Churches, Chapels and the Parish*, p. 187.

26. A. J. B. Beresford Hope, *The Worship of the Church of England* (2nd edn; London, 1875), p. 26.

27. Frances Knight, *The Nineteenth-Century Church and English Society* (Cambridge, 1995), pp. 89–90; see also Margaret Houlbrooke, *Rite out of Time: a study of the ancient rite of churching and its survival in the twenty-century* (Donington, 2011).

28. S. C. Williams, *Religious Belief and Popular Culture in Southwark, c.1880–1939* (Oxford, 1999), p. 87.

29. Armstrong, *Under the Parson's Nose*, p. 191.

30. Knight, *The Nineteenth-Century Church*, p. 71.

31. John Baron, *Scudamore Organs, or, practical hints respecting organs for village churches and small chancels* (London, 1858), p. 38.

32. Frances Paget, *The Curate of Cumberworth: and The Vicar of Roost, by the Author of 'The Owlet of Owlstone Edge'* (London, 1859).

33. Edward Stuart, *The Pew System, the Chief Hindrance to the Church's Work in Towns: a sermon preached at Christ Church, St Pancras, Advent 1851* (London, 1851), pp. 9–11.

34. *Why Are Our Churches Closed? An argument against closed churches; or, an appeal to those in authority to open the houses of God throughout this Christian land. By a layman* (Oxford, 1858), pp. 13–14.

35. *Free and Open Church Chronology Including Authorities & Landmarks of the Movement* (London, 1892).

36. *Why Are Our Churches Closed?*, p. 17.

37. Molyneaux, *A Letter Addressed to the Lord Bishop of Ely*, p. 27.

38. *Free and Open Church Advocate* (15 October 1874), p. 76.

39. See especially, Julie Rugg, *Churchyard and Cemetery: tradition and modernity in rural North Yorkshire* (Manchester and New York, 2013). For other perspectives, see Keith Snell, 'Gravestones, Belonging and Local Attachment in England, 1700–2000', *Past and Present*, 179 (2003), pp. 97–134, and for a very broad—though conventionally secularizing—account, Thomas W. Laqueur, *The Work of the Dead: a cultural history of mortal remains* (Princeton, NJ and Oxford, 2015), ch. 5.

40. Armstrong, *Under the Parson's Nose*, p. 163.

41. R. K. Pugh and J. F. A. Mason, eds, *The Letter-Books of Samuel Wilberforce, 1843–68* (Oxford, 1970), p. 352.

42. Julie Rugg, Fiona Stirling, and Andy Claydon, 'Churchyard and Cemetery in an English Industrial City: Sheffield, 1740–1900', *Urban History* 41 (2014), pp. 627–46.

43. Quoted in Rugg, *Churchyard and Cemetery*, p. 16.

44. For a useful short and accessible survey of the relationship between churchyards and yew trees, see E. R. Yarham, 'Britain's Veteran Churchyard Yews', *Irish Forestry* 23 (1966), pp. 22–7.

45. Chris Pickford, *Bedfordshire Churches in the Nineteenth Century: vol. i* (Bedford, 1993), p. 118.

46. Isaac Williams, *A Sermon Preached at the Consecration of the Church of Llangorwen* (Aberystwyth, 1841), p. 16.

47. A. W. N. Pugin, *The Present State of Ecclesiastical Architecture in England* (London, 1843), p. 19.

48. Paget, *The Curate of Cumberworth*, p. 261.

49. As Stefan Muthesius points out, this also affected the design of lodges and chapels in cemeteries. See his 'Provinciality and the Victorians: church design in nineteenth-century East Anglia', in T. A. Heslop, Elizabeth Mellings, Margrit Thøfner, eds, *Art, Faith, and Place in East Anglia: from prehistory to the present* (Woodbridge, 2012), pp. 209–39, p. 213.

50. John Frewen Moor, *The Birth Place, Home, Churches, and Other Places Connected with the Author of 'The Christian Year'* (Winchester, 1867), p. 123.

51. F. E. Paget, *A Tract upon Tomb-Stones or, suggestions for the consideration of persons intending to set up that kind of monument to the memory of deceased friends* (Rugeley, 1843).

52. Hope, *The Worship of the Church of England*, p. 26.

53. William Plomer, ed., *Kilvert's Diary, 1870–1879* (1944; Harmondsworth, 1984), p. 32.

54. Edward L. Cutts, *An Essay on the Christmas Decoration of the Churches* (London, 1863), p. 43.

55. George Neale Barrow, *A Sermon Preached at the Consecration of Christ Church at Jeffries' Hill, Hanham* (Bristol, 1842), p. 18.

56. Pugin, *The Present State of Ecclesiastical Architecture*, pp. 102, 104.

57. Quoted in G. W. Herring, 'Tractarianism to Ritualism: a study of some aspects of Tractarianism outside Oxford, from the time of Newman's conversion in 1845, until the first Ritual Commission in 1867' (DPhil, Oxford University, 1984), p. 66.

58. 'A Vicarage Home, in Correspondence with the Architecture of the Neighbouring Church', in *The Repository of Arts, Literature, Fashions, Manufactures, &c* II:10 (1 October 1816), p. 187, reprinted in J. B. Papworth, *Rural Residences* (London, 1818), p. 45. See also Anthony Jennings, 'The Influence of the Victorian Parsonage on English Domestic Architecture', *Transactions of the Ancient Monuments Society* 58 (2014), pp. 114–33, p. 129.

59. Francis James Bettley, 'The Reverend Ernest Geldart (1848–1929) and Late Nineteenth-Century Church Decoration' (PhD, Courtauld Institute, 1999), p. 51.

60. See, for instance, Richard Olney, *Church and Community in South London: St Saviour's Denmark Park, 1881–1905* (Studley, 2011), p. vii.

61. Frances Yates, 'Developments in the Parishes, 1850–1920', in Glanmor Williams, William Jacob, Nigel Yates, and Frances Knight, *The Welsh Church from Reformation to Disestablishment, 1603–1920* (Cardiff, 2007), pp. 309–98, p. 364.

62. John Sandford, *Parochialia; or church, school, and parish* (London, 1845), p. 73.

63. Malcolm Seaborne, *The English School: its architecture and organisation, 1370–1870* (London, 1971), pp. 188–9.

64. Seaborne, *The English School*, p. 212.

65. Bettley, 'The Reverend Ernest Geldart'.

66. Molyneaux, *Letter Addressed to the Lord Bishop of Ely*, p. 35.

67. David Clark, *Between Pulpit and Pew: folk religion in a North Yorkshire fishing village* (Cambridge, 1982), p. 58.

68. Dorothy Entwistle, 'The Whit Walks of Hyde: glorious spectacle, religious witness, and celebration of a custom', *Journal of Religious History* 31 (2012), pp. 204–33, pp. 214–15.

69. The first in Manchester seems to have been held in 1801. See William E. A. Axon, *The Annals of Manchester: a chronological record from the earliest times to the end of 1885* (London, 1886), p. 128.

70. Paul O'Leary, *Claiming the Streets: processions and urban culture in South Wales, c.1830–1880* (Cardiff, 2012), p. 129.

71. Entwistle, 'The Whit Walks of Hyde', p. 212.

72. O'Leary, *Claiming the Streets*, p. 123.

73. Robert Proctor, *Building the Modern Church: Roman Catholic church architecture in Britain, 1955 to 1975* (Aldershot, 2014), p. 272.

74. Entwistle, 'The Whit Walks of Hyde', p. 216.

75. Ronald Hutton, *The Stations of the Sun: a history of the ritual year in Britain* (Oxford, 2001), p. 287. The reinvention of Rogationtide processions in some parishes in the 1860s can perhaps be seen as an exception to this general rule.

76. Alfred T. Ridel, *Ninfield in the Nineties* (1955; Ninfield, 1980), p. 131. This from East Sussex.

77. Louise Jermy, *The Memories of a Working Woman* (Norwich, 1934). This from Hampshire in the 1880s.

78. Cutts, *Christian Decoration*, p. 55.

79. Armstrong, *Under the Parson's Nose*, pp. 25, 112.

80. Oliver Zimmer, 'Beneath the "Culture War": Corpus Christi processions and mutual accommodation in the Second German Empire', *Journal of Modern History* 82 (2010), pp. 288–334.

81. William Haslam Mills, *Grey Pastures* (London, 1924), pp. 27–8.

82. E. A. Litton, *Address to the Bishop of Oxford of the Rev E. A. Litton and Other Clergymen of the Diocese, Together with His Lordship's Reply* (Oxford, 1859), pp. 1, 9.

83. Quoted in G. I. T. Machin, 'The Last Victorian Anti-Ritualist Campaign', *Victorian Studies* 25 (1982), pp. 277–302, p. 290.

84. See, for instance, K. S. Inglis, *Churches and the Working Classes in Victorian England* (London, 1963), p. 24.

85. Green, *Religion in the Age of Decline*, p. 295.

86. Alexandra Walsham, *The Reformation of the Landscape: religion, identity, and memory in early modern Britain and Ireland* (Oxford, 2011).

87. Bob Bushaway, *By Rite: custom, ceremony and community in England 1700–1880* (London, 1981), pp. 174–5.

88. Plomer, ed., *Kilvert's Diary* p. 229.

89. Karl Bell, *The Magical Imagination: magic and modernity in urban England, 1780–1914* (Cambridge, 2012), pp. 56, 63.

90. Sarah Tarlow, *Bereavement and Commemoration: an archaeology of mortality* (Oxford, 1999), p. 127.

91. Armstrong, *Under the Parson's Nose*, p. 282.

92. Williams, *Religious Belief and Popular Culture*, p. 91.

Chapter 4

1. Samuel Wilberforce, *Union with Christ: the condition of communion with the angels and saints, a sermon preached at the consecration of the new chancel of the Church of St Mary the Virgin and St Nicholas, Littlemore* (Oxford, 1848).

2. R. K. Pugh and J. F. A. Mason, eds, *The Letter-Books of Samuel Wilberforce, 1843–68* (Oxford, 1970), p. 8.

3. Ronald and Margaret Pugh, eds, *The Diocese Books of Samuel Wilberforce* (Oxford, 2008), 304. The parish in question was the pioneering ritualist one of Wantage.

4. Pugh and Mason, *The Letter-Books of Samuel Wilberforce*, pp. 22, 73.

5. Samuel Wilberforce, *A Sermon Preached at the Consecration of St Catherine's Church, Bear Wood, April 23, 1846* (London, 1846), pp. 9, 12.

6. W. M. Jacob, 'Sacred Space in the Long Eighteenth Century: seating in churches', *Ecclesiology Today* 44 (July 2011), pp. 3–16, p. 3.

7. Arthur Burns, *The Diocesan Revival in the Church of England, c.1800–1870* (Oxford, 1999).

8. N. S. Harding, ed., *A Stow Visitation: being notes on the churches in the Archdeaconry of Stow 1845* (Lincoln, 1940), p. 11.

9. Owen Chadwick, *Victorian Miniature* (Cambridge, 1960).

10. Christopher Turner, 'The Decline of the Gallery Tradition', in Christopher Turner, ed., *The Gallery Tradition: aspects of Georgian psalmody* (Ketton, 1997), pp. 71–80, p. 77.

11. Frederick Oakeley, *Historical Notes on the Tractarian Movement* (London, 1865), p. 63.

12. A. W. Exell and Norah M. Marshall, eds, *Autobiography of Richard Boswell Belcher of Banbury and Blockley* (Blockley, 1976), p. 16.

13. See, for instance, <http://manchesterhistory.net/rochdale/nicholson.html> (accessed 19 October 2015).

14. Hamlet Nicholson, *An Autobiography and Full Historical Account of Hamlet Nicholson in His Opposition to Ritualism at the Rochdale Parish Church* (Rochdale, 1892), pp. 24, 27, 28.

15. From the 1850s onwards, for instance, the Church of St Katharine Cree hosted an annual flower sermon at Whitsun. It was not alone. *Illustrated London News* 60 (1872), p. 508.

16. John Bruster, *The Beautiful Valley and the Lilies: a children's flower sermon* (London, 1888), p. 2; W. Meynell Williams, *The Almond Blossoms: the thirty-fourth flower sermon preached at St Katharine Cree Church on Whit-Tuesday, 1886* (London, 1886), p. 5.

17. John Tucker, *The Church, a Spiritual Building to the Glory of God. A sermon preached at the consecration of the Southborough chapel by the Right Reverend George Lord Bishop of Rochester, on Wednesday, August 25, 1830* (London, 1830), p. 7.

18. John Plumptre, *A Sermon Preached at the Consecration of a Chapel at Cradley by the Right Reverend the Lord Bishop of Worcester on Wednesday the 12th of September 1798* (Kidderminster, 1798), p. 7.

19. Francis Storr, *All the Words of Their Life: a sermon preached at the consecration of the Church of St John, Woodbridge, on Thursday, the twenty-seventh of August 1846* (Ipswich, 1846), p. 19.

20. Isaac Williams, *A Sermon Preached at the Consecration of the Church of Llangorwen in the Diocese of St David's, December 16, MDCCCXLI* (Aberystwyth, 1841).

21. Jane Platt, *Subscribing to Faith? The Anglican parish magazine 1859–1929* (Basingstoke, 2015), p. 3.

22. C. A. H., 'Our Church Window', in *The Old Church Porch* 2 (1856–7), p. 272.

23. So, for instance, A. Hugh Fisher's *The Cathedral Church of Hereford: a description of its fabric and a brief history of the episcopal see* (London, 1898) copies whole sections from T. F. Havergill, *The Visitors' Hand-Guide to Hereford Cathedral* (Hereford, 1865).

24. Robert Needham Cust, 'Some Account of the Church of Cockayne-Hatley, Bedfordshire' (1851), reprinted in Andreas Edward Cockayne, *Cockayne Memoranda: collections towards a historical record of the family of Cockayne* (Congleton, 1873), pp. 22–37.

25. Vernon Musgrave, *Church of S. Peter Hascombe* (London, 1885), pp. v–vi.

26. <http://www.hascombe.com/> (accessed 20 January 2016).

27. M. H. Port, *600 New Churches: the Church Building Commission, 1818–1856* (2nd edn; Reading, 2006).

28. William Plomer, ed., *Kilvert's Diary, 1870–1879* (1944; Harmondsworth, 1984), pp. 363, 299–300.

29. J. Mordaunt Crook, *William Burges and the High Victorian Dream* (London, 2013), pp. 209–11.

30. Sarah Foot, 'Has Ecclesiastical History Lost the Plot?', *Studies in Church History* 49 (2013), pp. 1–25.

31. Thomas Leach, *A Short Sketch of the Tractarian Upheaval* (London, 1887), pp. 177–8.

32. A. J. B. Beresford Hope, *The English Cathedral of the Nineteenth Century* (London, 1861), pp. 279–80.

33. Jean Halgren Kilde, *When Church Became Theatre: the transformation of Evangelical architecture and worship in nineteenth-century America* (New York, 2002).

34. Both quoted in William Whyte, 'Building a Public School Community, 1860–1910', *History of Education* 32 (2003), pp. 601–26.

35. Colleen McDannell, *The Christian Home in Victorian America, 1840–1900* (Bloomington, IN, 1986), p. 31.

36. For earlier generations see Rosemary Hill, *God's Architect: Pugin and the building of Romantic Britain* (London, 2007), John Martin Robinson, *James Wyatt* (New Haven, CT and London, 2012), Christopher Webster, *R. D. Chantrell (1793–1872) and the Architecture of a Lost Generation* (Reading, 2007). Christopher Webster has also edited *Episodes in the Gothic Revival* (Reading, 2012), which includes essays on John Carter, Thomas Rickman, Thomas Taylor, R. C. Carpenter, G. E. Street, and J. T. Micklethwaite.

Key figures in the mid-nineteenth century include Paul Thompson, *William Butterfield* (London, 1971), J. Mordaunt Crook, *William Burges and the High Victorian Dream* (London, 2013), and P. S. Barnwell, Geoffrey Tyack, and William Whyte, eds, *George Gilbert Scott, 1811–1878* (Stamford, 2014). The first chapter of David B. Brownlee, *The Law Courts: the architecture of George Edmund Street* (Cambridge, MA, 1984) provides vital context and Geoff Brandwood's *The Architecture of Sharpe, Paley, and Austin* (Swindon, 2012) offers insights into a major provincial firm. Later generations are elucidated in Gavin Stamp, *An Architect of Promise: George Gilbert Scott Junior (1839–1897) and the Late Gothic Revival* (Stamford, 2002) and Michael Hall, *George Frederick Bodley and the Later Gothic Revival in Britain and America* (New Haven, CT and London, 2014).

37. William Whyte, 'Scott's Office and Its Impact', in P. R. Barnwell, Geoffrey Tyack, and William Whyte, eds, *George Gilbert Scott (1811–1878): an architect and his influence* (Donington, 2014), pp. 213–29.
38. Neil Levine, *Modern Architecture: representation and reality* (New Haven, CT and London, 2009), pp. 116, 118.
39. Rosemary Sweet, *Cities and the Grand Tour: the British in Italy, c.1690–1820* (Cambridge, 2012), p. 257.
40. Philip Aspin, 'Architecture and Identity in the English Gothic Revival, 1800–1850' (DPhil, Oxford University, 2013).
41. Rosemary Sweet, *Antiquaries: the discovery of the past in eighteenth-century Britain* (London, 2004), p. 260.
42. Chris Brooks, *The Gothic Revival* (London, 1999), pp. 135–7.
43. Nicholas Jackson, ed., *Recollections: the life and travels of a Victorian architect, Sir Thomas Graham Jackson* (London, 2003), p. 120.
44. Chris Miele, 'Real Antiquity and the Ancient Object: the science of Gothic architecture and the restoration of medieval buildings', in Vanessa Brand, ed., *The Study of the Past in the Victorian Age* (Oxford, 1998), pp. 103–24.
45. Helpfully, one is reproduced in Christopher Webster, ed., *'Temples . . . Worthy of His Presence': the early publications of the Cambridge Camden Society* (Reading, 2003) as well as an appendix in James F. White, *The Cambridge Movement: the Ecclesiologists and the Gothic Revival* (Cambridge, 1982).
46. Rhona Richman Kenneally, 'Empirical Underpinnings: ecclesiology, the excursion, and church schemes, 1830s–1850s', *Ecclesiology Today* 15 (January 1998), pp. 14–19, p. 17.
47. Aeneas Barkley Hutchison, *A Monograph on the History and Restoration of the Parish Church of St Mary Callington* (London, 1861), pp. 14–15.

48. M. R. Austin ed., *The Church in Derbyshire in 1823–4, the Parochial Visitation of the Rev Samuel Butler, Archdeacon of Derby* (Derby, 1970), pp. 28, 29.
49. N. S. Hardiung, ed., *Bonney's Church Notes: being notes on churches in the Archdeaconry of Lincoln, 1845–1848* (Lincoln, 1937), pp. 3, 97.
50. Nicholas Orme, *English Church Dedications, with a Survey of Cornwall and Devon* (Exeter, 1996), p. xiii.
51. Christopher Herbert, 'Permanent Easter Sepulchres: a Victorian re-creation?', *Church Archaeology* 7/8/9 for 2003–5 (2006), pp. 7–20, p. 17.
52. Eugène Viollet-le-Duc, *Dictionnaire raisonné de l'architecture française du XIe au XVe siècle* (9 vols; Paris, 1854–68), vol. viii, p. 14.
53. Quoted in Kirstie Blair, 'Church Going', in Matthew Bevis, ed., *The Oxford Handbook of Victorian Poetry* (Oxford, 2013), pp. 762–82, p. 774.
54. J. M. Neale and Benjamin Webb, *The Symbolism of Churches and Church Ornaments: a translation of the first book of the* Rationale Divinorum Officiorum, *written by William Durandus* (Leeds, 1843), p. vii. On the church, see Martin Wellings, 'The Building of Wesley Memorial Church, Oxford', in *Building the Church: the Chapels Society Journal* 2 (2016), pp. 21–35. I owe this observation to Nahum and Jacob Whyte, who noticed the weathercock one Saturday.
55. Graham Hague, *The Unitarian Heritage: an architectural survey of chapels and churches in the Unitarian tradition in the British Isles* (Sheffield, 1986), p. 85.
56. Ian Smith, *Tin Tabernacles: corrugated iron mission halls, churches, and chapels of Britain* (Salisbury, 2004).
57. John Baron, *Scudamore Organs, or practical hints respecting organs for village churches and small chancels on improved principles* (London, 1882), p. 17.
58. William Haslam Mills, *Grey Pastures* (London, 1924), p. 16.
59. J. M. Morris, *Religion and Urban Change: Croydon, 1840–1914* (Woodbridge, 1992), p. 85.
60. Bridget Cherry and Nikolaus Pevsner, *Buildings of England, London 2: south* (Harmondsworth, 1983), p. 212.
61. F. J. Jobson, *Chapel and Church Architecture as Appropriate to the Buildings of Non-Conformists, Particularly to Those of the Wesleyan Methodists* (London, 1850), pp. 15, 43, 40, 49–50.
62. J. Mordaunt Crook, *The Dilemma of Style: architectural ideas from the picturesque to the post-modern* (London, 1987).
63. Quoted in William Whyte, *Oxford Jackson: architecture, education, status, and style, 1835–1924* (Oxford, 2006), pp. 34–5.
64. Thomas Chamberlain, *The Chancel: an appeal for its proper use addressed to architects, church-restorers and the clergy generally* (London, 1856), pp. 21–2.

65. Quoted in Francis James Bettley, 'The Reverend Ernest Geldart (1848–1929) and late-nineteenth-century church decoration' (PhD, London, 1999), p. 124.
66. I am enormously grateful to Kate Giles for permission to quote her work.
67. Chris Miele, '"Their Interest and Their Habit": professionalism and the restoration of medieval churches, 1837–77', in Chris Brooks and Andrew Saint, eds, *The Victorian Church: architecture and society* (Manchester, 1995), pp. 151–72, p. 170.

Chapter 5

1. *Illustrated London News*, 30 August 1862, p. 246.
2. Arthur Thomas Bannister, *The Cathedral Church of Hereford* (London, 1924), p. 108.
3. See Ingrid Brown, 'The Hereford Screen', *Ecclesiology Today* 47–8 (July 2013), pp. 3–44.
4. R. P. Price in *The Times*, 26 August 1965.
5. *The Times*, 29 May 1862, quoted in A Hugh. Fisher, *The Cathedral Church of Hereford: a description of its fabric and a brief history of the episcopal see* (London, 1898), p. 40.
6. *The Times*, 29 March 1967.
7. <http://www.vam.ac.uk/content/articles/t/the-hereford-screen/> (accessed 9 November 2015).
8. Colin Fletcher, 'Foreword', in Becky Payne, *Churches for Communities: adapting Oxfordshire's churches for wider use* (Oxford, 2014), p. 9.
9. Christopher Costelloe, *The Victorian* 48 (March 2015), p. 3.
10. *General Synod Report of Proceedings* 46:2 (July 2015), p. 128.
11. <https://www.youtube.com/watch?v=IXcma9CDX3A> (accessed 20 November 2015).
12. Quoted in Simon Goldhill, *The Buried Life of Things: how objects made history in nineteenth-century Britain* (Cambridge, 2015), p. 56.
13. Martin Wellings, *Evangelicals Embattled: responses of Evangelicals in the Church of England to ritualism, Darwinism, and theological liberalism, 1890–1930* (Carlisle, 2003), pp. 12, 117.
14. *Congregational Yearbook*, quoted in Clyde Binfield, 'Art and Spirituality in Chapel Architecture: F. W. Lawrence (1882–1948) and his churches', in David M. Loades, ed., *The End of Strife* (Edinburgh, 1984), pp. 200–26, p. 215.

15. B. F. L. Clarke, 'Edwardian Ecclesiastical Architecture', in Alastair Service ed., *Edwardian Architecture and Its Origins* (London, 1975), pp. 290–300, p. 298.
16. Stephen Smalley, *Building for Worship: biblical principles in church design* (London, 1970), p. 13.
17. Gavin Stamp, 'The Architecture of Good Taste: Anglican churches in 1914', in Teresa Sladen and Andrew Saint, eds, *Churches 1870–1914* (London, 2011), pp. 145–65, p. 148.
18. Quoted in Joe Riley, *Today's Cathedral: the Cathedral Church of Christ, Liverpool* (London, 1978), pp. 33–4.
19. T. S. Eliot, *The Rock: a pageant play written for performance at Sadler's Wells Theatre 28 May–9 June 1934, on behalf of the Forty-Five Churches Fund of the Diocese of London* (London, 1934), p. 70.
20. Elain Harwood, 'Churches in England, 1915–1965', in Robert Gage, ed., *All Manner of Workmanship: papers from a symposium on Faith Craft* (Salisbury, 2015), pp. 11–38, p. 11.
21. N. P. Williams, *Too Much Stiffness: some considerations on extra-liturgical devotions to the Blessed Sacrament* (London, 1917), <http://anglicanhistory.org/sspp/stiffness.html> (accessed 23 November 2015).
22. Quoted in Kenneth Richardson, *The 'Twenty-Five' Churches of the Southwark Diocese: an inter-war campaign of church-building* (London, 2002), p. 9.
23. Rodney Warrener and Michael Yelton, *Martin Travers, 1886–1948: an appreciation* (London, 2003), p. 46.
24. Michael Bullen, 'Day, Nugent Francis Cachemaille (1896–1976)', *Oxford Dictionary of National Biography* (Oxford, 2004).
25. Bryan Little, *Catholic Churches since 1623* (London, 1966), pp. 211–12.
26. Edward D. Mills, *The Modern Church* (London, 1957), p. 19.
27. Peter Hammond, *Liturgy and Architecture* (London, 1960), p. 137.
28. Gilbert Cope, 'Clergy and Laity', in Gilbert Cope, ed., *Making the Building Serve the Liturgy: studies in the re-ordering of churches* (London, 1962), pp. 31–41, p. 41.
29. Elain Harwood, *Space, Hope and Brutalism: English architecture, 1945–1975* (New Haven, CT and London, 2015), p. 459.
30. Peter F. Anson, *Fashions in Church Furnishings 1840–1940* (London, 1960), pp. 361, 356.
31. Smalley, *Building for Worship*, pp. 50, 92.
32. Nigel Melhuish, 'Modern Architectural Theory and the Liturgy', in Peter Hammond, ed., *Towards a Church Architecture* (London, 1962), pp. 38–64.

33. Peter Hammond, 'A Radical Approach to Church Architecture', in Hammond, ed., *Towards a Church Architecture*, pp. 15–37, p. 34.

34. Nicolas Stacey, *Who Cares* (London, 1971), pp. 34, 45, 58, 72, 118, 120, 174, 27–81.

35. Hammond, 'A Radical Approach to Church Architecture', pp. 23–4, 18, 36.

36. Hammond, *Liturgy and Architecture*, p. 163.

37. Peter F. Smith, *Third Millennium Churches* (London, 1972), pp. 73, 66.

38. Mills, *Modern Church*, pp. 55, 112–13.

39. Alison and Peter Smithson, quoted in J. Mordaunt Crook, *The Dilemma of Style: architectural ideas from the picturesque to the post-modern* (London, 1987), p. 258.

40. A. C. Bridge, *Images of God: an essay on the life and death of symbols* (London, 1960), p. 11.

41. Keith Murray, 'Material Fabric and Symbolic Pattern', in Hammond, *Towards a New Church Architecture*, pp. 78–90, p. 90.

42. John A. T. Robinson, 'Foreword', in Cope, *Making the Building Serve the Liturgy*, pp. 5–6, p. 5.

43. Arthur Loundes Moir, *The Deans of Hereford* (Hereford, 1968), p. 61.

44. Quoted in Binfield, 'Art and Spirituality', p. 219.

45. Geoffrey Tyack, Simon Bradley, and Nikolas Pevsner, *The Buildings of England: Berkshire* (London, 2010), p. 447.

46. Anthony Symondson, '"Renovating Heaven and Adjusting the Stars"', in Damian Thompson, *Loose Canon: a portrait of Brian Brindley* (London, 2004), pp. 65–122, pp. 89–92.

47. Otto Saumarez Smith, 'From Cathedral Precincts to Pedestrian Precincts: the place of ecclesiastical architecture in post-war town plans' (unpublished paper).

48. Thomas Hardy, 'Memories of Church Restoration', in Thomas Hardy, *Life and Art* (New York, 1925), pp. 91–112, p. 92.

49. John Schofield, 'Repair Not Restoration', in Marcus Binney and Peter Burman, eds, *Change and Decay: the future of our churches* (London, 1977), pp. 153–4.

50. Chris Pickford, 'Our Parish Churches: some reflections on the passage of time', *Ecclesiology Today* 40 (July 2008), pp. 60–6, p. 62.

51. See, for instance, Richard Taylor, *How to Read a Church: a guide to images, symbols and meanings in churches and cathedrals* (London, 2003) or Denis R. McNamara, *How to Read Churches: a crash course in ecclesiastical architecture* (London, 2011).

52. Jane Garnett and Alana Harris, 'Church without Walls: mapping the sacred in east London', in Jane Garnett and Alana Harris, eds, *Rescripting Religion in the City: migration and religious identity in the modern metropolis* (Aldershot, 2013), pp. 115–30.
53. Carola Hicks, *Cambridgeshire Churches* (Stamford, 1997), p. 146.
54. Stephen Cottrell, 'Richard Giles, Tentmaker by Divine Appointment: a fellow traveller's appreciation of his ministry and influence', in Stephen Burns, ed., *The Art of Tent-Making: essays in hour of Richard Giles* (Norwich, 2012), pp. 28–40, p. 31.
55. Richard Giles, *Re-Pitching the Tent: re-ordering the church building for worship and mission* (Norwich, 1999), p. xiii.
56. Richard Giles, *Here I Am: reflections on the ordained life* (Norwich, 2006), p. 8.
57. Gilbert Cope, 'Introduction', in Cope, *Making the Building Serve the Liturgy*, pp. 11–16, p. 14.
58. Cottrell, 'Richard Giles, Tentmaker by Divine Appointment', p. 32.
59. David Brown, *God and Enchantment of Place: reclaiming human experience* (Oxford, 2004), p. 256.
60. George Carey, *The Church in the Market Place* (3rd edn; Eastbourne, 1995), pp. 55, 148.
61. Diocese of Norwich, *Church Buildings: a source of delight and a cause of anxiety* (Norwich, 2003).
62. Linda Monckton, '"An Age of Destruction?": Anglican church closure past and present', *Ecclesiology Today* 47–8 (2013), pp. 121–6.
63. William Whyte, 'The Ethics of the Empty Church: Anglicanism's need for a theology of architecture', *Journal of Anglican Studies* 13 (2015), pp. 172–88.
64. Michael Winter, *Mission or Mortar: a study in new pastoral structures* (London, 1973), p. 24.
65. Giles Fraser, *The Guardian*, 15 October 2015.
66. Sally Gaze, *Mission-Shaped and Rural: growing churches in the countryside* (2011; London, 2006), pp. 93–5. For a very different view, see Alan Smith, *God-Shaped Mission: theological and practical perspectives from the rural church* (Norwich, 2008), p. 22, which draws on Carol Roberts and Leslie Francis, 'Church Closure and Membership Statistics: trends in four rural dioceses', *Rural Theology* 4:1 (2006), pp. 37–56, to show that redundancy may *cause* falling attendance.
67. Giles, *Re-Pitching the Tent*, p. 238.
68. Church of England, *Report of the Church Buildings Review Group* (2015), <https://www.churchofengland.org/media/2383717/church_buildings_review_report_2015.pdf> (accessed 23 November 2015), p. 34.

69. English Heritage, *New Uses for Former Places of Worship* (London, 2012), <https://content.historicengland.org.uk/images-books/publications/new-uses-former-places-of-worship/New_Uses_for_Former_Places_of_Worship.pdf/> (accessed 22 May 2016).

70. Simon Jenkins, *The Guardian*, 22 October 2015.

71. Richard Halsey, https://www.youtube.com/watch?v=IXcma9CDX3A (accessed 20 November 2015).

72. Revd Toby Wright, quoted in *Oxford Times*, 10 October 2013, p. 8.

73. *Report of the Church Buildings Review Group*, paras 103, 104, 101.

74. Brown, *God and Enchantment of Place*, p. 22.

75. Giles, *Re-Pitching the Tent*, pp. 3–8.

76. This section draws on William Whyte, 'Not the Comfy Chair!', *Church Times*, 21 October 2016.

77. Jonathan Mackechnie-Jarvis, 'Pews: the view from a DAC secretary', in Trevor Cooper and Sarah Brown, eds, *Pews, Benches, and Chairs* (London, 2011), pp. 351–8, p. 351.

78. Payne, *Churches for Communities*, pp. 16–21.

79. Anthony Russell, 'Church Interiors for a Renewed Faith', *Church Building* 101 (September–October 2006), pp. 3–4.

80. *Church Building* 77 (September–October 2002), pp. 14–15.

81. In Christopher Webster, *The Rebuilding of Leeds Parish Church 1837–41 and Its Place in the Gothic Revival* (London, 1994), p. ii.

82. Simon Jenkins, *England's Thousand Best Churches* (London, 1999), pp. 545–6.

83. Howard Freeborn, *The Parish Church of St Mary Kidlington in the County of Oxford: the history and architecture* (Kidlington, n.d.).

84. M. Freeborn, *Thirty Years in an Oxfordshire Parish*, ed. John Amor (Kidlington, n.d.), p. 9.

Afterword

1. John Betjeman's 'A Lincolnshire Church' is © The Estate of John Betjeman 1955, 1958, 1960, 1962, 1964, 1966, 1968, 1970, 1979, 1981, 1982, 2001. Reproduced from John Murray Press, a division of Hodder and Stoughton Limited.

2. Nikolaus Pevsner, *The Buildings of England: Yorkshire, the North Riding* (Harmondsworth, 1966), p. 392.

3. Frank Morrall and Colin Davies, *A History of St Mary's Hampstead* (London, 1977), pp. 6–9.

4. C. E. B. Brett, *Buildings of Belfast, 1700–1914* (Belfast, 1985), p. 28.
5. Rosemary Hill, *God's Architect: Pugin and the building of Romantic Britain* (London, 2007), p. 360.
6. Nikolaus Pevsner, *The Buildings of England: Staffordshire* (Harmondsworth, 1974), p. 97.
7. *The Tablet*, 5 September 1846, p. 1.
8. Quoted in Michael Fisher, *'Gothic For Ever': A. W. N. Pugin, Lord Shrewsbury, and the rebuilding of Catholic England* (Reading, 2012), p. 199.
9. *Leeds Intelligencer*, quoted in Christopher Webster, *R. D. Chantrell (1793–1872) and the Architecture of a Lost Generation* (Reading, 2007), p. 279.
10. Henry Bowman, *Specimens of the Ecclesiastical Architecture of Great Britain from the Conquest to the Reformation* (London, 1846), p. 3.
11. Edward Royle, 'From Philistines to Goths: Non-Conformist chapel styles in Victorian England', in Christopher Dyer, Andrew Hopper, Evelyn Lord, and Nigel Tringham, eds, *New Directions in Local History since Hoskins* (Hatfield, 2011), pp. 186–215, p. 196.
12. Bridget Cherry and Nikolaus Pevsner, *The Buildings of England: London 3, north west* (London, 1991), p 598.
13. Michael Hall, 'What Do Victorian Churches Mean? Symbolism and sacramentalism in Anglican church architecture, 1850–1870', *Journal of the Society of Architectural Historians* 59 (2000), pp. 78–95.
14. Quoted in J. Mordaunt Crook, *The Architect's Secret: Victorian critics and the image of gravity* (London, 2003), pp. 49–51.
15. Cutting quoted in Francis James Bettley, 'The Reverend Ernest Geldart (1848–1929) and Late Nineteenth-Century Church Decoration' (PhD, London, 1999), p. 86.
16. Society for the Preservation of Ancient Buildings, *Appeal for the Preservation of Inglesham Church* (London, 1887), p. 5.
17. <http://medieval-church-art.blogspot.co.uk/2008/10/inglesham-church-wiltshire.html> (accessed 27 January 2016).

PICTURE ACKNOWLEDGEMENTS

1. The Bodleian Library, University of Oxford (Henry Jones Underwood *Elevations, sections, and details, of the church of St. Mary the virgin, at Littlemore* (Oxford, 1845), G.A. fol. A 325).
2. Reproduced by permission of the Historic England Archive
4. The Bodleian Library, University of Oxford (Henry Jones Underwood *Elevations, sections, and details, of the church of St. Mary the virgin, at Littlemore* (Oxford, 1845), G.A. fol. A 325).
6. Courtesy of Historic Environment Scotland. © John R. Hume.
7. The Bodleian Library, University of Oxford (Thomas Rawlins, *Familiar Architecture; or, original designs of homes for gentlemen and tradesmen, parsonages, summer retreats, banqueting-rooms, and churches* (London, 1795). 5 Δ 86).
8. From a collection of watercolours by Theodosia Hinckes and Rebecca Moore, courtesy of the Dean and Chapter of Lichfield Cathedral.
9. From a collection of watercolours by Theodosia Hinckes and Rebecca Moore, courtesy of the Dean and Chapter of Lichfield Cathedral.
11. The Bodleian Library, University of Oxford (Frances Paget, *Milford Malvoisin: or, Pews and pewholders* (London, 1842). 42.634).

12. The Bodleian Library, University of Oxford ('A Vicarage Home, in correspondence with the architecture of the neighbouring church', in J. B. Papworth, *Rural Residences* (London, 1818). Vet. A6 d.166).

13. The Bodleian Library, University of Oxford (John Sandford, *Parochialia; or Church, School, and Parish* (London, 1845). 45.1498).

18. Courtesy of the North Devon Athenaeum.

22. Courtesy of Jane Garnett.

23. Courtesy of the Manchester Climbing Centre.

26. © John Whitworth.

INDEX